SWANMORE SINCE 1

An illustrated history of a Hamps

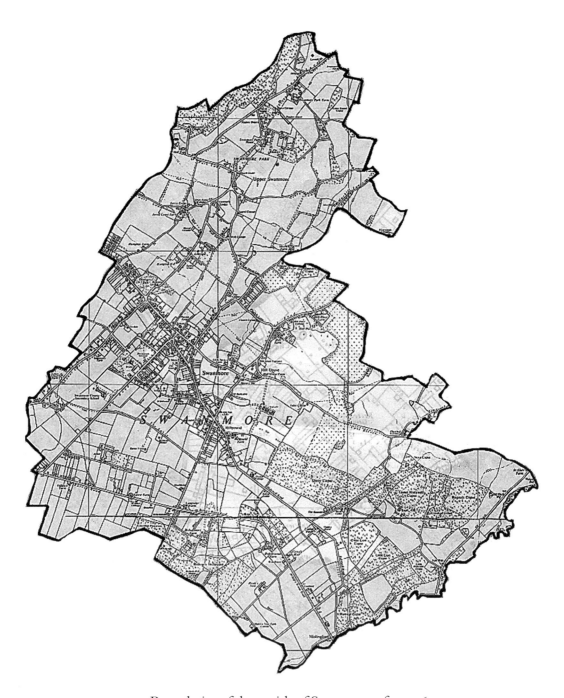

1. Boundaries of the parish of Swanmore after 1967

Reproduced by kind permission of Ordnance Survey

© Crown Copyright NC /01 /25274

SWANMORE
SINCE 1840

An illustrated history of a
Hampshire village

PETER R WATKINS

SWANMORE BOOKS

Published by Swanmore Books
7 Crofton Way
Swanmore
Southapton SO32 2RF

ISBN-0-9541566-0-9

The front cover includes the Swanmore Embriodery Panel
which was designed by Valerie Spendlove and stitched by
villagers of Swanmore led by Ann Wheeler, to celebrate
the 150th Anniversary of St Barnabas' church in 1995.

Designed, typeset and produced by
John Saunders design & Production, Reading
Printed in Great Britain by Biddles Ltd.
www.biddles.co.uk

Contents

Illustrations

To Jill, Anna and Kate
who lived for nearly twenty years in Swanmore
and to all Swanmorians past,
present and future

Preface

Local history is like an unfinished criminal investigation: there are always more clues to be found and solutions are tantalisingly difficult to reach. I started work on the history of Swanmore in the early 1980s, soon after we came to live in the village. I spent hours perusing old parish magazines and many wet days in the old Hampshire County Record Office studying maps, census returns and parish registers. I read the entire Minutes of the Parish Council from its beginning in 1894. It was absorbingly interesting but each day's research led not to conclusions but to further questions and new lines of enquiry. The more I learnt the more I realised what I did not know.

Then I went away to work, first in London then in York. I no longer had school holidays and research on Swanmore history was suspended. In the early 1990s, now semi-retired, I resolved to write rather than do further research. I managed to complete the history of the parish church of St Barnabas in time for its 150th anniversary in December 1995. The present book represents the second part of the resolution: to complete the history of the village, though only from about 1840. Before that it is impossible to disentangle it from the story of the mother parish of Droxford, writing a full history of which, though needed, would be a much larger undertaking.

There is inevitably some overlap with the earlier book, which is in any case now out of print The parish church has played an important part in the story of the village and to omit it would be to distort the picture. There is therefore some intentional repetition though I have here told the story of the church in less detail.

The first chapter on the ancient parish of Droxford is intended to set the recent history of Swanmore in context and is dependent on secondary sources, particularly Gordon Hope's brief but valuable *800 Years in Droxford*. Later chapters are based substantially on primary sources, most of which are deposited in the Hampshire County Record Office (HCRO) in Winchester. For the twentieth century I have made use of reminiscences of villagers, some of them collected for the Oral History project which formed part of the celebrations of the 150th anniversary of the parish church. Over the years I have collected photographs of bygone Swanmore, some given to me by the late Jack Hoar, a loyal and enthusiastic Old Swanmorian, though he had not lived in the village since 1918. Other photographs lent to me have been copied: I apologise if I have not been able to attribute their ownership correctly.

The writing of this history has been a labour of love. I am grateful to all who have helped in any way. I hope that past, present and future Swanmorians will derive pleasure from the story and the photographs.

Peter Watkins
Swanmore
October 2001

Acknowledgements

I wish to express my warm thanks to the following who have contributed in a variety of ways to this history of the village. The list is far from complete, so many people have expressed interest over the years and I have benefited from many conversations not I'm afraid all adequately recorded.

Former villagers with a keen interest in its history among them Kay Crawshaw 1913–1999, Doris Etheridge 1908–1993, Sheila Gadsby c. 1897–1990, Jack Hoar 1902–1992, Len Horner 1896–1994, Bob Reed 1909–1999.

Gordon Hope, historian of the old parish of Droxford and Brenda Austin for permission to use commissioned research on land ownership in upper Swanmore.

Barry Stokes for his exploration of the history of Swanmore House and for his invaluable help in the preparation and presentation of the photographs.

The Revd Bob Kitching for permission to use his work on the Droxford Primitive Methodist Circuit.

Pam Evans, Swanmore archivist, for the use of her Open University case study on the brickfields.

Keith Harrington for allowing me to use his study of Swanmorians who died in the two World Wars.

My younger daughter Kate who took the photographs of modern Swanmore.

My elder daughter Anna and her friend Hannah Young who advised on printing and publication.

The Revd Ron Paterson, who first fired my interest in Swanmore history and whose collection of parish magazines was an invaluable resource. They are now deposited in the Hampshire County Record Office, Winchester.

John Saunders who designed the cover and advised on and undertook all aspects of production speedily and with great good humour.

Hampshire County Record Office for permission to use part of the Milner map of Hampshire 1791, the Droxford tithe map and award 1841-42, the

Droxford enclosure map 1855, and the Ordnance survey maps, first edition 1810 and 6 inch edition 1910.

Weidenfeld & Nicholson for permission to use material from *Then and Now* by Philip Ziegler page 424.

Numerous people who provided written or oral reminiscences of life in the village including Arthur Blanche, June Clarkson, Ron Crook, Katharine Olding, Ron Paterson, Vera Tribbeck, Bill Woodley and contributors to the Oral History project whose names appear in the list of sources.

Introduction

*One of the many endearing characteristics of Swanmore
is that most people have not heard of it.*

Village Design Statement 2001

S WANMORE IS A VILLAGE IN HAMPSHIRE ABOUT EQUIDISTANT FROM Southampton, Winchester and Portsmouth, each of which contributes to its identity: it has a Southampton postal address, its local authority is Winchester City Council and since 1927 the parish has been in the Anglican diocese of Portsmouth. Unusually for a village of its size Swanmore is not on a main road. It lies in a rough triangle whose apex, to the south, is the village of Wickham where the A32 and B2177 join and whose base, to the north, is the B3035 running from Bishop's Waltham to Corhampton. Geologically the village is divided; upper Swanmore lies on chalk whilst lower Swanmore is on clay with the Bishop's Waltham road roughly marking the boundary. Historically upper Swanmore is medieval in origin; lower Swanmore is the creation of nineteenth century enclosure.

Swanmore is neither as architecturally distinguished nor as scenically beautiful, as its near neighbours, the villages of the Meon valley, Wickham or Botley. It is not named in Domesday, has no ancient parish church or manor house, no village green or village pond. There is no river flowing through it, though the river Meon forms part of its eastern boundary and a stream flows from east to west across the southern part of the parish to form a source of the river Hamble in the Moors Nature Reserve at Bishop's Waltham.

Yet beneath the surface there is much of interest. There are fields with ancient names, roads and tracks of medieval origin, farm sites occupied from time immemorial, a Quaker burial ground used in the seventeenth century, and a coaching road on the route from Gosport to London with an inn at which horses were changed. There are the remains of long disused brickfields and village wells needed until the advent of piped water after the first World War. In upper Swanmore is a large house rebuilt in the late 1870s which was the centre of a substantial landed estate until 1935.

The centre of the village is a T junction where the parish church and parish centre, primary school, War Memorial, small supermarket, and butcher's shop are to be found. The village is approached from the north and east through country lanes, some narrow and tree lined, which have no footpaths, kerbs, or street

lighting. The landscape of upper Swanmore is still entirely rural with lanes, scattered cottages, and a few larger houses screened from the road. In the centre of the
village are older houses predominantly Victorian and Edwardian but with substantial infilling of modern houses. Development since the second World War which
has doubled both the population and the number of houses has been chiefly in
small estates to the east and south of the village. All parts of the village are within
easy walking distance of the centre though relatively few people choose to walk,
preferring to drive even the short distance to post office, shop, school or church.
The schools – the primary school in the centre of the village and the secondary
school in New road- contribute to the vibrancy of the community even though
they also provide Swanmore's twice daily traffic jams.

For over a thousand years Swanmore formed part of the ancient parish of
Droxford. It was the 1830s and 1840s which began the evolution of Swanmore
into the village we know. A small school, built in 1833 where the War Memorial
now stands, and the church of St Barnabas', consecrated in 1845, were the first
institutions of the village. The tithe map and Census of 1841 provide tantalising
glimpses of the inhabitants – where they lived and how they earned a living. In
1855 Horders Wood or Waltham Chase was enclosed. New straight roads were
constructed and settlement took place in lower Swanmore. In the 1860s the
church was extended, the Primitive Methodist chapel built and the school was
rebuilt on the north side of the road. Personalities who were to dominate village
life down to the first World War came to the village in the 1870s. William Myers,
the Revd Walter Medlicott and Charles Martin – squire, parson and school master
– all had a strong sense of responsibility to the community, shared by many other
villagers, humble as well as exalted. When the Parish Council was formed in 1894
it was the same three men who were its acknowledged leaders.

   The village enjoyed a golden age in the last decades of the nineteenth century
with a variety of organisations and activities for young and old, many of them
sponsored by church and school. These were the years when the village supplied
its own welfare provision. The golden age ended abruptly in 1914: about 150
young men served in the first World War and 35 did not return.

   The post-war years saw the arrival of all but one of the amenities of twentieth
century life – the roads were surfaced, telephone, water, gas and electricity were
installed. Bus services began in the early 1920s increasing contacts with the outside
world. The village patriarchs of pre-war Swanmore were not replaced. When
William Myers died in 1933 the estate was broken up and Swanmore no longer
had a squire. During the second World War evacuees from Gosport arrived and
later refugees from the bombing of Portsmouth. Once more young men served in
the forces and some – though fewer than in the first World War – did not return.

   Since the 1960s change has been more rapid. The one service not installed earlier – mains sewerage – reached Swanmore in the 1960s. Village life became more

attractive to town dwellers and new estates sprang up to meet demand. In the second half of the twentieth century the population and the number of houses doubled, growing at a hitherto unprecedented pace. The secondary school serving a much larger area than the village was opened in 1961 and the primary school – as it then became – was rebuilt later in the 1960s. The new village hall replaced the British Legion hut in the 1980s and the Paterson Centre was completed by the church in the early 1990s. As the new century and millennium began Swanmore appeared to have achieved stability. Change now seems likely to be slower; there is less scope for the rapid increase which has marked the years since 1960.

I have told the story of Swanmore's development largely chronologically though there are chapters on the National School up to 1914, on the Primitive Methodists and on brickmaking which was until the second World War, after agriculture, Swanmore's main industry.

Those who live in Swanmore whether they are members of families whose roots in the village go back a century or more or who have moved here recently share an interest in and commitment to its history and heritage. Exhibitions of village life, oral history projects, reunions of those who attended the infant or junior school, displays to mark anniversaries of village institutions, all receive enthusiastic support. *Swanmore since 1840* is intended to inform and enhance this interest.

1

The Ancient Parish of Droxford

MANY OF THE INSTITUTIONS OF CENTRAL AND LOCAL government which characterise present day England were in existence over a thousand years ago. The monarchy, the shires and hundreds, dioceses and archdeaconries of the church, manors and parishes, first took shape well before the Norman Conquest. Village names, parish boundaries and the sites of churches all originated in Saxon times. After 1066 they were placed under new management but the institutions themselves survived.

The villages of the Meon valley – West Meon, East Meon, Warnford, Exton, Corhampton, Meonstoke and Droxford – all have names whose first use can be dated to the Saxon period. The name of the river appears first about 790 AD (*flumen quod appelatur Meonea* – the river which is called Meon) and was used to describe the area settled by the Meonware, dwellers beside the Meon.[1]

Documentary evidence for Droxford begins with a Saxon charter of Egbert (reigned 802-839) dated 826. He was crowned at Winchester and later buried there. In gratitude for his coronation as the first king of all England he gave to the prior and monks of St Swithun's priory at Winchester 28 hides of land at 'Drocenesforda'. The Charter describes in detail the boundaries of the parish of Droxford which included Shedfield and part of Swanmore.[2]

Two later Anglo-Saxon Charters, one of King Athelstan dated 939, and another of King Eadwig dated 956, also convey grants of land in Droxford but are confined to the southern part of present day Droxford and the later tithings of Hill and Swanmore.[3] The parish was a large one, though on a par with other local parishes, its southern extremities distant from the village and parish church, sparsely populated and largely uncultivated. In early Norman times Droxford ranked with Fareham, Alverstoke and Titchfield at a time when Portsea Island and Portsmouth had not developed. In Domesday it is recorded as a hundred on its own, belonging to the Bishop of Winchester for his monks. There were 51 households – 12 villeins, 13 bordars and six serfs, making it substantially larger than most other local settlements. It had a church and two mills and was worth £26.[4] It had already given its name to a Deanery which covered the whole Portsmouth area, in the large and important diocese of Winchester.

The name Swanmore appears in 1205, spelt Suanemere and in 1207 Swanemere.[5] It has always been assumed that the name referred to a pool (mere) on which swans belonging to the Bishop of Winchester were kept, in the area referred to down to the present day as the Lakes. This is not however entirely convincing. If this area was thinly populated and largely uncultivated why should it give its name to the tithing? The earliest settlement in what is now Swanmore was in upper Swanmore. The nexus of twisting lanes and footpaths, joining in the vicinity of Jervis Court and coming from Bishop's Waltham and Hoe, Dundridge, Droxford and the Heath or Horders Wood, all suggest a flourishing, if small, hamlet.

The older name for this hamlet was Polhampton, (meaning the farm of the village by the pool) suggested but not proved by the presence of this name in the Domesday entry for Droxford, and surviving perhaps in Hampton Hill. There is still in upper Swanmore a small pond or mere which may once have been larger. It appears in 1551 as Le Mere with the three acre Mere Croft lying to the north of it. It is at least possible that it was this pond at the centre of the small settlement which provided the second half of the name of the tithing. Nor is it certain that the other half of the name, *suane,* refers to swans. An alternative, appearing for example in Swanwick in the parish of Sarisbury, is *herdsman* (surviving in the word swain). If this is so then Swanmore derives its name from herdsmen who used the pond in upper Swanmore in the twelfth century.[6]

Gordon Hope the historian of Droxford suggests a further possible origin of the name Swanmore. In 1205 the Curia Regis rolls suddenly record the name of Geoffrey de Suanemere, whose family, Gordon Hope suggests, came from Worldham, near Selborne. Was there perhaps in that area a place named Suanemere from which the family took its name? If so Swanmore derives its name from a prominent land owning family which moved in the early thirteenth century and brought the name with it. Perhaps further documentary research will one day give us a conclusive answer one way or the other. References to the de Suanemere family occur frequently between 1205 and 1286, after which it disappears; perhaps the male line failed or possibly the family was wiped out by the plague.[7]

From the thirteenth century onwards there are sporadic references to the tithing of Swanmore in official documents but insufficient to provide a connected narrative or to differentiate life here from that on other medieval manors. National events only occasionally impinged on peasant life. Did the villagers notice when their Rector, John de Drokenesford was appointed Bishop of Bath and Wells in 1309 as well as being Chancellor of the Exchequer to Edward II ? It is unlikely that he spent much time in his parish though he continued to be Rector for a further year.[8]

One national event which did have a local impact was the Black Death of 1348-

49 which nationally killed somewhere about 40% of the population. There is no doubt that the fear of sudden death hung for many months if not years over people of all social classes. In the Droxford deanery which included the Portsmouth area almost half the clergy died whilst in the neighbouring manor of Bishop's Waltham 65% of all tenants died. Nor was the plague a one off; it continued to ravage the country in waves of varying severity for the rest of the century and beyond. Perhaps in Droxford, as in many other places, it began the move away from the open fields to enclosure, as well as towards money payments in place of services in kind.[9]

A tantalising glimpse of Tudor Swanmore is provided by a Manor Rental of Droxford, dated 1551. A conjectural map of the parish based on information in the rental shows that the present day pattern of lanes and tracks in upper Swanmore was well established in the sixteenth century. Names appearing in the rental, though usually differently spelt, include Damson Hill (Damsnege), Dodds Lane (Dod and Dodwell), Phrymph Copse (Frempthe), Hazelholt (Hasselholt), Ragnals Copse (Ragnelles Wood), Midlington (Mydlyngton) as well as many field names. Gervys Lane, later to become Jervis Lane and later still West Hoe Lane, appears. The name originated from the Gervey or Gerbey family. William Gervey held land at Hoe according to the Waltham rental of 1464.[10]

Longer lanes did not necessarily bear the same names throughout their length – after all there were no postmen. Sections might take the name of the tenant of the land they skirted. Some names appear to be attached to different stretches of road at different times. In the sixteenth century for example Dodwell Lane appears to have been the name of the lane leading to St Clair's farm which we now call Cott Street. The road from Droxford to Hill was named the Royal road or Warcombe Way at the Droxford end, then Hylstrete. When it entered Shirrell Heath it was once again referred to as the Royal road.[11]

There were two drove lanes which are so-called in the rental. They were used to drive animals to the water meadows by the Meon in the spring and to take them to market at Waltham in the autumn. One ran from Cott Street farm to join the Green Lane above the Meon valley and so down to Midlington. The other ran across upper Swanmore diagonally from Hoe to Droxford, following a route still marked by a well-worn right of way.

Upper Swanmore had by now been enclosed. About a quarter of the land was leased to tenants though a considerable amount, all however in the tithing of Droxford, was still demesne held directly from the lord. The holding of individuals had not yet been consolidated nor had money rents entirely replaced feudal services. John Spencer for example held about 45 acres of land in the tithing of Hyll [sic] but in five blocks varying from 20 acres to one and a half acres. For some of this he paid an annual rent of 6s.3d. He paid church scot in cocks and hens and customary services in the form of one day's labour shearing the lord's sheep, cutting his hay and making fences and hedges round his land in Frempth lane.[12]

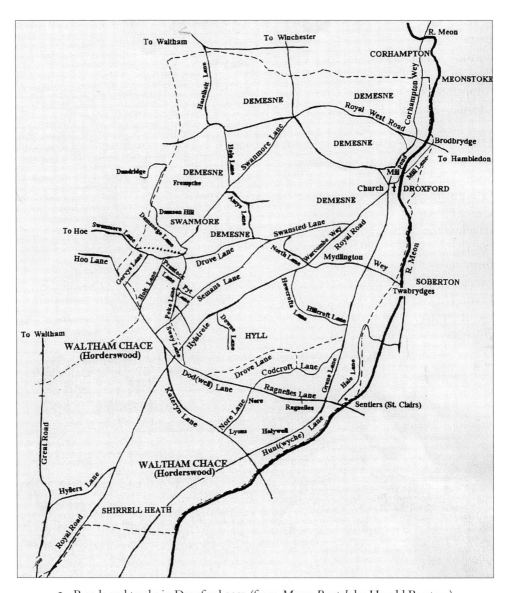

2. Roads and tracks in Droxford 1551 (from *Manor Rentals* by Harold Barstow)

In 1642, shortly after the beginning of the Civil war, Droxford parish church was seriously in need of renovation. Among the leading parishioners who petitioned for financial assistance to repair it were several from Hill and Swanmore – Edward Cluer, Richard Brewer and Thomas Clewer of Swanmore and Robert Barefoot (Hill Park), Edward Cleverly, John Knight and Henry Prowting of Hill. Clewer, Cleverly, Knight and Prowting are all names which appear in the 1551 rental and it seems that these families were of long standing in the parish.[13]

Robert Barefoot a yeoman farmer, was perhaps typical of these leading inhabitants. When he died in 1661 an Inventory of his property showed that his house
consisted of a hall, parlour, lodging chamber, closet, kitchen in which hung four
hogs of bacon, buttery, brewhouse, milkhouse, washhouse, cellar, barn, garners and
'topp loft'. He had three horses, two cows, two heifers and two calves as well as
'Beanes sett in the Garden.'[14]

Half way up Hampton Hill, about one hundred yards from the road, in a quiet field
on the left of the footpath leading to Jervis Court is an intriguing reminder of
Swanmore's seventeenth century past: the Quaker burial ground. The Society of
Friends (often referred to as Quakers) was founded as a result of the teaching of
George Fox (1624-91) and its beginning is usually dated to 1652, though Fox had
travelled the country almost from the beginning of the Civil War in 1642. Between
the return of Charles II in 1660 and the Revolution of 1689 all forms of dissent
from the established church were liable to persecution and the Quakers were no
exception. Quaker records show that meetings were held quarterly at Jervis Court
Farm. The land which is occupied by the burial ground belonged, in the middle of
the seventeenth century, to Richard Suet, a cordwainer, who lived in an adjoining
cottage. In 1661 he buried his small son Joseph in the orchard. Two years later he

3. Rededication of the Friends Burial ground by Canon John Vaughan,
Rector of Droxford 1908.

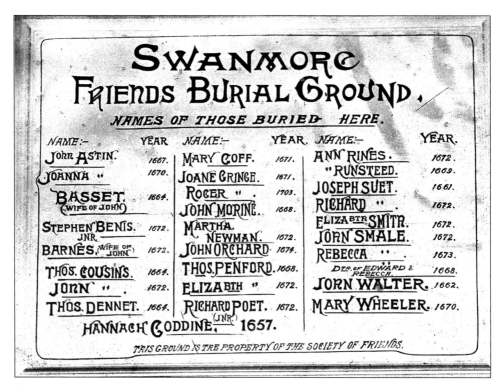

SWANMORE FRIENDS BURIAL GROUND.

NAMES OF THOSE BURIED HERE.

NAME:—	YEAR.	NAME:—	YEAR.	NAME:—	YEAR.
JOHN ASTIN.	1667.	MARY COFF.	1671.	ANN RINES.	1672.
JOANNA "	1670.	JOANE GRINGE.	1671.	" RUNSTEED.	1669.
BASSET. (WIFE OF JOHN)	1664.	ROGER "	1703.	JOSEPH SUET.	1661.
		JOHN MORINE.	1668.	RICHARD "	1672.
STEPHEN BENIS. JNR.	1672.	MARTHA. NEWMAN.	1672.	ELIZABTH SMITH.	1672.
BARNES. (WIFE OF JOHN)	1672.	JOHN ORCHARD.	1674.	JOHN SMALE.	1672.
THOS. COUSINS.	1664.	THOS. PENFORD.	1668.	REBECCA "	1673.
JOHN "	1672.	ELIZABTH "	1672.	DTR. of EDWARD & REBECCA.	1668.
THOS. DENNET.	1664.	RICHARD POET. (JNR.)	1672.	JOHN WALTER.	1662.
HANNACH GODDINE. 1657.				MARY WHEELER.	1670.

THIS GROUND IS THE PROPERTY OF THE SOCIETY OF FRIENDS.

4. Names of those buried in the Friends Burial Ground

sold the land, with right of access, for £1.8.0 to three trustees: Thomas Walter, a maltster, Thomas Penford, a blacksmith, both of Bishop's Waltham and Robert Ryves (or Reeves), yeoman, of Swanmore. The three were Quakers and were persecuted for their faith. Thomas Walter was excommunicated, had his cattle seized for non-payment of tithes and was imprisoned from 1667-73. Thomas Penford, who had a wife and three children was also excommunicated for refusing to pay 3d 'towards the Mass house' (presumably the parish church at Droxford). He was imprisoned in Winchester gaol in 1664, died there in 1667 and was buried in the Quaker field at Swanmore.

How the field came to be a burial ground is not however clear. In 1908 Canon John Vaughan, Rector of Droxford, speaking at a ceremony at the burial ground, told how its owner had buried his young son in the orchard among the apple trees and subsequently made over the field as a burial ground to the Society of Friends. Whatever the origin, twenty seven people who died between 1661 and 1703, though only one after 1679, were buried there, coming from as far afield as Portsmouth, Portchester, Alresford, Winchester and Titchfield. Richard Suet himself was buried in the field in 1672.

Not surprisingly the ground was subsequently neglected and it was not until early in the twentieth century that it was put in order through the initiative of Catherine and Florence Gladstone of Hampton Hill and Canon John Vaughan, Rector of Droxford.[15]

The Manor Court, the central institution of medieval Englsnd, continued at Droxford to meet until the enclosure of the village in 1855. Its function was to regulate the economic and social life of the village, to ensure that its customs were interpreted correctly and to deal with offenders against its practices. Its minutes record the perennial concerns of village life as surely as do those of the Parish Council two centuries later. A major preoccupation was the preservation of Horders Wood or Waltham Chase, the area between *The Rising Sun* and the Wickham border, from the depradations made on it for a variety of purposes. The Court attempted to stop illicit digging of clay for brickmaking, cutting bushes for fuel and burning of charcoal. It tried to control illegal encroachments. Some of the isolated cottages on the chase in Swanmore and Shedfield bear silent witness to its failure. The Pound (at Hill Pound) was a cause of regular complaint. It was used for cattle who had strayed into or been found grazing illegally on the Chase but was frequently in need of repair, perhaps sabotaged by those who preferred an excuse to allow their cattle to resume illicit grazing.[16]

The Parish Vestry, established in some places as early as the fourteenth century, took its place alongside the Manor Court, with functions which could, and sometimes did overlap. It was chaired by the Rector and often met in the church. At its annual meeting it appointed the churchwardens. At Droxford there were four, one for each of the tithings of Droxford, Hill, Shedfield and Swanmore. The other parish officers, the constable, way warden and overseers of the poor were also appointed by and answerable to the Vestry. At the first meeting of the Droxford Vestry of which records survive, held on 16th May 1763, vestrymen present included James Leekblade of upper Swanmore, George Grove, churchwarden for Droxford and overseer for Hill, George Pay and Edward Stone, farmers, both of Hill.[17]

The Vestry dealt with matters to do with church and village, a mixture of Parish Council and Parochial Church Council. None was more fraught than the relief of the poor, becoming increasingly costly at the end of the eighteenth century. Outdoor relief, a weekly payment to the various categories of poor, was the usual means of dealing with the problem. In 1785 the Vestry decided however to use capital from four parish charities to build its own poor house, five or if possible seven cottages on part of the waste in Horders Wood. Eight years later a similar resolution was passed so presumably no action had been taken. A poor house was however established at Shedfield. It was replaced in 1822 by another rented house near *The Hunters Inn* identified in the Tithe Award of 1842 as The Old Poor House. This in turn was superseded when the Poor Law Amendment Act of 1834 required parishes to unite to provide for the poor. The workhouse for the Droxford Union which

5. The Poor House c.1822-1837, now Hill Grove and Hill Grove Cottages.
Photo Kate Watkins

covered 11 parishes from Upham and Durley to Hambledon and West Meon with a combined population of almost 11,000, opened in 1837 in Park lane, Droxford with accommodation for 200 paupers [18]

In the last years of the eighteenth century the leading citizen of the parish appears to have been Peter Barfoot who bought the Midlington estate in 1770.[19] Landowner, lawyer, justice of the peace, Overseer of the Poor in the late 1780s, he died in 1814 at the age of 84 and is buried in the south-west corner of Droxford churchyard. Though the family remained at Midlington their leading place in parish affairs passed to Richard Goodlad of Hill Place, whose descendants were to live there until 1914. Goodlad was born in 1756, and was Sheriff of Hampshire in 1818. He and his second wife Frances Leonora died within a fortnight of each other in 1821. Richard Goodlad appears to have left behind something of reputation. When William Cobbett rode across Waltham Chase in1826, he passed 'a big white house upon a hill' (Hill Place) and commented that it had been occupied by

'one Goodlad, who was a cock justice of the peace and who had been a chap of some sort or another in India. There was a man named Singleton who lived in Waltham Chase and who was deemed to be a great poacher. This man, having been forcibly ousted by the order of this Goodlad, and some others, from an encroachment he had made in the forest, threatened

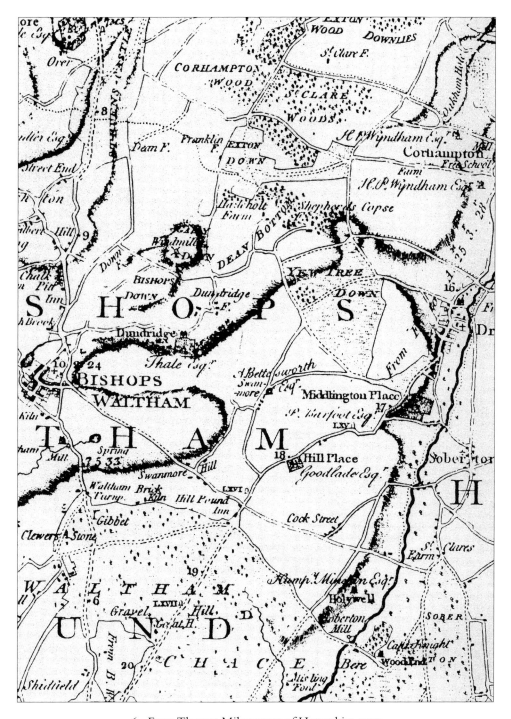

6. From Thomas Milner map of Hampshire 1791

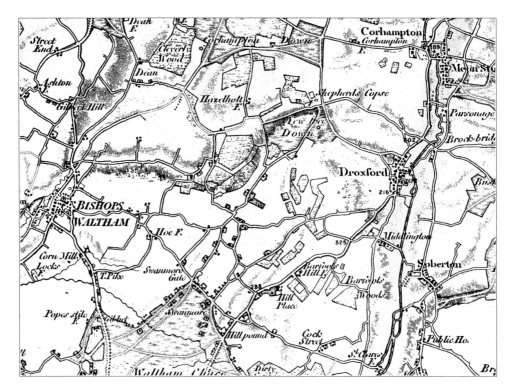

7. Ordnance Survey Map Hampshire first edition 1810

revenge. One night soon afterwards a horse was stabbed or shot in the night-time in a field and Singleton was taken, put on trial at Winchester convicted and transported. The people in that neighbour-hood were deeply impressed. Singleton was transported; but Goodlad and his wife were both dead and buried in less, I believe, than three months after the departure of poor Singleton'.[20]

By the 1820s the enclosure of the Chase, though not accomplished for another thirty years, was clearly under discussion. Cobbett disapproved: 'Never was so monstrous a proposition in this world . . . Here are a couple of hundred acres of land worth ten thousand acres of land in the New Forest.... Besides the sweeping away of two or three hundred cottages; besides plunging into ruin and misery all these numerous families, here is one of the finest pieces of timberland in the whole kingdom, going to be cut up into miserable clay fields, for no earthly purpose but of gratifying the stupid greediness of those who think that they must gain, if they add to the breadth of their private fields.'[21]

By the end of the eighteenth century the parish of Droxford was well served by transport between London and Gosport, which passed through Swanmore via *The*

Rising Sun. At the Droxford end the turnpike passed through the centre of the Midlington estate. At some time in the early nineteenth century it was diverted to follow its present route though the original course can still be followed on the ground. The Diligence from Gosport passed through at 11.30 on Monday, Wednesday, Thursday and Saturday and returned the same day between 5 and 6 o'clock in the evening. The stage coach arrived from London on Tuesday, Thursday and Saturday at 10am and returned on Tuesday, Thursday and Sunday at 10pm. Mr Padwick who owned the stage coach also possessed a wagon which made a weekly trip to London on Monday and returned on Saturday while Mr Knight's wagon arrived in Droxford from London at 1pm on Friday and returned from Gosport at 5pm.[22] Droxford was it seems by no means isolated from the wider world. The turnpike from London to Gosport of which the A32 was later to form part was authorised by Act of Parliament in 1759 but was built in sections and took a century to complete.

The population of Droxford grew slowly, until in the late eighteenth century it shared in the faster increase caused by better diet and improvements in health brought about by the lndustrial and Agricultural revolutions. Figures before the first census are conjectural. The population of the parish has been estimated at 346 in 1525, 497 in 1603, 612 in 1676 and 568 in 1725. In 1801 the first census gave a population of 1199. By 1871 the figure had doubled to 2325. By then however two new parishes had been carved out of Droxford and both were growing more quickly than the mother parish.[23]

2

Mid-Victorian Village
1840-1871

THE EARLY NINETEENTH CENTURY SAW A QUICKENING OF church life in town and village alike. It included disapproval of clerical pluralism and non-residence, an increase in the number and quality of church services and the provision of additional churches to enable all to worship, to have their babies baptised and their dead buried within reasonable distance of where they lived. This last meant the division of large parishes of which Droxford was one. In 1829 provision was made for the most remote part of the parish by the opening of a chapel of ease at Shidfield, though it did not become an ecclesiastical parish until 1843.[1]

At Swanmore provision for worship preceded the building of a church by almost a decade. In October 1836 the bishop of Winchester ,'granted his licence and authority for the performance of divine worship in a schoolroom situate in the Hamlet of Swanmore.'[2] The school built in 1833, stood on the site of the present war memorial and was enlarged for its new use. In appealing for funds to equip the school for worship the Revd James Adair Colpoys, Rector of Droxford wrote ' It is . . . proposed to enlarge the present School Room and fit it up suitably for Public Worship on Sunday Evening: for which purpose the Bishop has consented to grant his licence. The expense of the proposed enlargement is £180.'[3]

It was not until 1843 that the Rector of Droxford took a further initiative and appealed for money to build a church and a parsonage house.

The Hamlet of Swanmore, in the Parish of Droxford, Hants., contains a population of upwards of 500 souls, and is distant from the Parish Church between two and three miles. At this distance many of the Inhabitants cannot attend public worship at all, and none more than once a day. To remedy in some measure this evil, the Rector of the Parish has for several years provided, in addition to the two services at the Parish Church, one service on Sunday Evenings in the School-room licensed by the Bishop for that purpose. But this being an imperfect provision for the wants of the people , it is now proposed to build a Church and Parsonage House, and to make provision out of the Rent Charge of Droxford, which the Bishop of the diocese has promised to sanction.[4]

The bishop as lord of the manor provided land adjacent to the schoolroom and the foundation stone was laid on St Barnabas' day 1844. The architect was Benjamin Ferrey, a well known church architect then at the beginning of his career.[5] The builder was Charles Pink of Hambledon.[6]. The church was dedicated to St Barnabas and consecrated by the bishop of Winchester, Charles Richard Sumner, on 11th December 1845.[7] The patron of the living was the Rector of Droxford.[8]

Entrance was at the west end to a building which consisted of a nave with no aisles, chancel or tower, but with a small bell turret and bell to summon villagers to worship. The building was flint with stone dressings, neo-Norman in style with small round-headed windows and seated 300. It must have been dark and cramped. There was a west gallery and the church was heated with a coke stove with outlet through the roof. At the east end were reading desk, wooden pulpit and communion table (not in those days described as an altar). Slate tablets inscribed with the Ten Commandments were attached to the east wall. Swanmore had its own church but not one which could bear comparison with the medieval churches of parishes like Droxford, Meonstoke or Bishop's Waltham. It was utilitarian meant to meet the needs of the villagers rather than the gentry. Similar churches were being built during the same period for outlying parts of neighbouring parishes for example at Shedfield, Curdridge and Newtown.

Swanmore became a 'consolidated chapelry' under an Order in Council dated 21st April 1846. This meant that it was a parish carved out of two other parishes, mostly Droxford but it included a small part of Bishop's Waltham whose boundaries had hitherto come close to the site of St Barnabas'. The boundaries are described in detail in the order.[9]

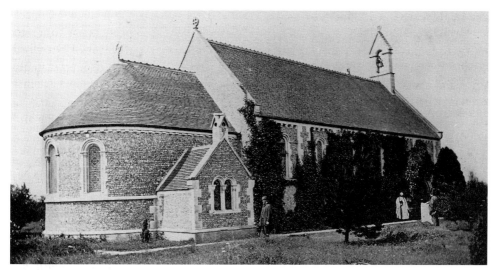

8. St Barnabas' church between 1863 and 1876 – after the building of the chancel and before the addition of the tower.

The new parish was crossed north-south by two roads. The coaching road from London to Gosport entered the parish from Droxford north of Hill Place and subsequently crossed The Chase to reach Shirrell Heath by what was then sometimes called Sheer Hill, now Gravel Hill. The second road, of which parts remain as a bridle way, was replaced about 1860 by a new direct road from Droxford to Wickham church down the Meon valley (now the A32). The old road can be walked from Midlington to Cott street, initially as a sunken lane, later on the brow of the hill with exhilerating views over the Meon valley. Its southern section from Mislingford to Wickham is marked by Frith Lane but the middle section through Holywell has disappeared.

The road running west to east from Bishop's Waltham to St Clair's farm is an ancient one. The remaining roads of the parish before the Enclosure of the Chase in 1855 were footpaths and tracks, including the footpath from the Bishop's Waltham road to Jervis Court and what later became Hampton Hill and Vicarage lane. Others led across the parish to the mother village of Droxford and its parish church. What is now known as Green lane, the track leading across the parish from Jervis Court, is named Mayhill lane on the tithe map, a name later transferred to the metalled road running in the same direction but further east. Ancient farm sites too are mostly in the north of the parish: Jervis Court, Mayhill Farm, Cot Street Farm, St Clair's Farm and, just outside the parish, Midlington Farm.[10]

In the 1840s Swanmore suddenly emerges into the light of day. Before that its history has to be reconstructed painstakingly from a variety of sources. Between 1840 and 1860 documentation becomes abundant. The Census of 1841 provides names and ages of inhabitants and for heads of households their trade or employment. The Tithe map of 1841 and accompanying terrier provide a wealth of information about land use, ownership and occupation. From its opening in 1845 the church was required to keep records of baptisms, marriages and burials in separate registers. Until about 1900 nearly all inhabitants used the established church for these rites of passage, so families can be traced in some detail. The registers are invaluable too for analysing age at death and can be used to estimate levels of literacy. Finally the Enclosure Award of 1855 establishes the topography of lower Swanmore as it emerged from Horders Wood.

The first national Census took place in 1801 but the 1841 census is the first to provide names, ages and, in the case of heads of households, trade or occupation. Ages up to 14 are recorded exactly, over that age they could be listed at five year intervals rounded downwards. This means that ages in the 1841 Census cannot be trusted, some are rounded downwards, others are given precisely.

Swanmore was above all a farming community. Surprisingly the 1841 Census names only seven farmers in the parish. George Penfold (40) one of Swanmore's first churchwardens occupied Hill Farm, George Cobbett senior (50) was at Hill Grove Farm whilst John Dollar (40) farmed at Mayhill and Edward Privett (40) at

Damson Hill Farm. Nancy Pufford (30) appears as a farmer at Cott Street and William Giles (45) is also a farmer in upper Swanmore. The great majority of those whose occupations appear in the Swanmore census were agricultural labourers usually abbreviated by the enumerator to 'Ag.Lab' – over 100 are so described. Mary Appleton (40) is described as 'Ag.Lab. Widow', with her five sons – Henry (23), Jacob (22), Charles (18), William (15), and George (12) all described as 'Ag.Lab'.

The second largest category comprised craftsmen whose skills were required by their neighbours or on the farms. The village appears for example to have been well supplied with shoe-makers: James Pink (61) and his son, another James (30) and Thomas Gardiner (60) all followed this craft whilst John Figgins (56) and Joseph Hendy (45) were cordwainers, another name for the same trade. There were at least four carpenters – John (25) and Richard Lloyd (65) and William Reeves (62) and James Earwaker(48). John Daysh (30) and James Catmore (50) were tailors and Richard Kent (35) and George Downe (30) wheelwrights. John (68) and David Hillyer (23) were chimney sweeps and Thomas Earwaker (60) and William Blackman (50) were blacksmiths. More unusual were the two parchment makers William Fridgell and James Hulbert both aged 25 and living in Cott street with wives and young families.

Relatively few women have occupations attributed to them. Harriet Smith aged 55 and her three daughters Lucy (25), Elizabeth (22) and Charity (15) who lived at Midlington were laundresses and so were Susanna Lee (50) and her daughter another Susanna (25). Susanna Bishop (25) was a governess at Hill Place where Charles (45) and Anne (25) Miller lived with their six children aged between six years and five months and a further eleven servants. Sarah (25), Marian and Jane Edney [? surname not legible] (both 15) were dressmakers.

The professions were not well represented in Swanmore; there were for example no doctors, lawyers or bankers. George Habin Appleby (39) was a land surveyor and William Terry (34) was a school master, perhaps at the village school though we cannot be certain. More unusual was James Grant, another young man, aged 29, who was minister of the Irvingite chapel. The Irvingites or Catholic Apostolic church were a sect which flourished briefly in the middle years of the century which combined an expectation of the Second Coming with a return to New Testament orders of ministry and catholic vestments and ceremonial.[11] The chapel of which James Grant was minister was on the north side of Church road near the site of the present primary school. It may have been a private house used for worship though the tithe map shows a building of some size. The owner according to the tithe award was Captain Robert Gambier who is described as Trustee of the Irvingite chapel. By the time of the next census it had disappeared and James Grant with it. Was its existence one of the reasons which impelled the Rector of Droxford to urge the building of an Anglican church in Swanmore? The Methodists were here too, worshipping in a private house though there is no evidence in the census or tithe map. (See chapter 7)

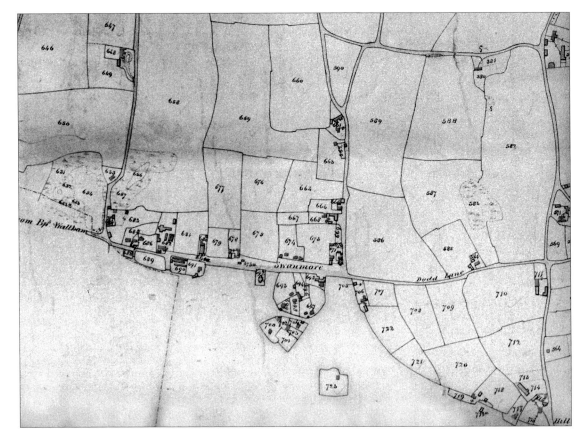

9 Part of Swanmore village in the Droxford tithe map and award 1841-42

Column 1 shows number on the tithe map, columns 2 and 3 indicate occupier (not owner) and land use. Column 4 shows occupation in Census of 1841 where this appears. The map and award are in HCRO 21M65/F7/63/1-2 and this extract is reproduced with permission.

1	2	3	4
664	Richard Souter	Arable	Potter
665	Joseph Hendy	Cottage & garden	Cordwainer
668	Richard Souter	Homestead	Potter
669	Richard Souter	Orchard	
670	John Figgins	Cottage & garden	Cordwainer
671	James Heath	Cottage, garden & shop	
672	John Davis	Cottage & garden	Carpenter
673	Richard Souter	Arable	Potter
674	James Gibson & others	Cottage & gardens	Ag.lab.
675	Richard Souter	Arable	
676	Richard Souter	Arable	
678	Mary Boswell	Cottage, garden and buildings	
678a	Mary Boswell	Sheds [in the road]	
679	Mary Boswell	Arable	
680	James Grant	Irvingite chapel	Minister
681	Edmund Reeves	Arable	
682	Ann Dollar	Public house [The Bricklayers Arms]	Victualler
683	William Edwards	Orchard	Brickmaker
684	William Edwards	Cottage & garden	
685	Harry Redman	Cottage & garden	Ag.lab.
686	James Earwaker	Cottage & garden	Carpenter
687	James Edwards	Cottage & garden	Ag.lab.
688	James Edwards	Garden	
689	Ann Dollar	Orchard	Victualler

Swanmore's main industry apart from agriculture was brickmaking. Peter Dollar(40), William Cresswell (31), William Edwards (45), George Reeves (30) and George Earwaker (25) are all described as bricklayers, brickmakers or brickburners. There was a pottery in an oblong building behind *The Rising Sun:* Thomas (40), Abraham (30) and William Harris (55), Richard Souter (35), Thomas Gibbs (60) and James Cobbett (15) are all described as potters. (See chapter 8)

If the Census of 1841 tells us for the first time the name of everybody who lived in the tithings of Hill and Swanmore and would shortly become the first parishioners of the new parish of Swanmore, then the tithe map of 1841 tells us where they lived. With painstaking use of the two the village of the early 1840s can be reconstructed in considerable detail.

From at least the eighth century tithe was paid by the laity for the upkeep of the church and its clergy, until the nineteenth century usually in kind. A series of tithe commutation acts in the 1830s substituted a money payment based on the average price of wheat, barley and oats during the previous seven years. In order to assess liability for this new method of paying tithe parishes were surveyed. Each field was named or described, measured precisely, and its owner and occupier were listed and its use — arable, meadow, wood, pasture or premise*s* — was recorded. Each piece of land was numbered and this has been used for identification ever since. The result is an invaluable picture of the Victorian countryside comparable in importance with the eleventh century Domesday Survey — and a good deal easier to interpret![12]

690	Ann Dollar	Brickyard & buildings	
691	Peter Dollar	House & garden	Bricklayer
691a	Peter Dollar		Sheds
692	——	School	
693	Henry Northeast	Cottage & garden	Ag.lab.
694	John Bone & another	Cottages & gardens	Ag.lab.
695	William Cresswell	Cottage, garden & shop	Brickmaker
696	Isaac Biddle	Cottage & garden	
697	John Daysh	Cottage & garden	Tailor
699	Thomas Gardiner	Cottage & garden	Shoemaker
700	John Titheridge	Cottage & garden	Ag.lab.
701	Mary Windsor	Cottage & garden	
702	Samuel Harding	Cottage & garden	Ag.lab.
703	Mary Windsor	Cottage & garden	
704	John Goldsmith	Cottage & garden	
705	George Cobbett jnr	Blacksmith's shop	Farmer
706	George Cobbett jnr	Cottage & garden	
707	George Cobbett jnr	Arable	
708	George Cobbett snr	Arable	
710	George Penfold	Coveys field	Farmer
711	George Penfold	Cottage, garden & buildings	Farmer
713	William Harris	Pasture	Potter
714	William Harris	Pottery & buildings	
715	William Harris	Cottage & garden	
716	Adam Watson	Hill Pound public house	Publican
717	Lydia Dollar	Cottage & garden	Grocer
718	Thomas Harris	Orchard	Potter
719	Thomas Harris	House & garden	
719a	Thomas Harris	Shed	
721	George Cobbett jnr	Pasture	
722	George Cobbett jnr	Pasture	

710 & 711 represent only a small part of George Penfold's 256 acres held from Richard Goodlad of Hill Place.

The tithe map and accompanying schedule written on large parchment sheets for the whole parish of Droxford were signed by the commissioners in August 1842. They needed to raise a gross rent charge in lieu of tithe of £1116-14-0 for the benefit of the Rector of Droxford. The parish of Droxford was according to the tithe map 6660 acres in extent of which 5355 acres were subject to tithe. Almost half the parish (3366 acres) was arable, there were 1135 acres of woodland (17% of the parish) and 548 acres of meadow or pasture. There were 206 acres of common land whilst 'common land in Horders Wood called Waltham Chase' was unenclosed and accounted for 1200 acres which was not subject to tithe. There were in addition 105 acres of homesteads and gardens each under 3/4 acre which were not subject to tithe either.

The tithe map shows no roads south of the Bishop's Waltham road. The line of what became in 1855 the road from Hill Pound to Swanmore road and later still part of Chapel road is marked by the curving boundary of properties but there is no road. South of the Bishop's Waltham road are clusters of cottages each surrounded by a garden or orchard, some probably the result of illegal encroachment on the Chase in the remote past. The entrance to the Chase is described as Hill Pound Gate and there are further clusters of cottages east of Hill Pound. In upper Swanmore cottages are more scattered though there are clusters of cottages round Jervis Court and in what was later named Hampton Hill. There are two named public houses. *The Bricklayers Arms* was kept by Ann Dollar (65), described as Victualler and *The Rising Sun* was kept by Adam Watson (30).

The roads were not of course surfaced, had no clear boundaries and tended to spread in wet weather. This was true of the main road through Swanmore. At two places near where the church was soon to be built the tithe map shows sheds standing in the middle of the road, one on property held by Peter Dollar and two more occupied by Mary Boswell who owned the land to the north. What we call Donigers Dell was, together with much land in Hampton Hill including 'the Burying Field', the property of Leonard Ledbitter (45) who lived at Jervis Court. It is described as Marls Dell. The triangle of land on which Walter Medlicott built the new Vicarage in the 1870s was owned by Richard Goodlad and is called the Lucern Paddock.

The largest landowners in Swanmore were Bettesworth Pitt Shearer of Swanmore Park and Richard Goodlad of Hill Place and both owned land across the whole of Droxford parish. Though Shearer farmed some of his own land 120 acres was let to Richard Hatch Stares and 160 acres to George Habin Appleby.

Amongst significant landowners or landholders were the Dollar family. John Dollar (40) lived at what is described as Mayhill Homestead and rented 76 acres of the surrounding fields, one called the Nine Acres (which measured seven acres according to the tithe map) and another the Seven Acres (which measured six acres on the tithe map!) as well as Weeches, a field with an ancient name on the north side of what was then called Mayhill Lane but which is now called Green Lane. In 1851 he was employing 9 labourers. At *The Bricklayers' Arms* lived Ann Dollar (65) who also rented an orchard and brickyard opposite. Peter Dollar who was the elder brother of John, had a house, garden and sheds opposite *The Bricklayers Arms*. In 1851 he is described as a bricklayer employing three labourers. In 1841 he was 'trustee of the late James Horner' and in that capacity held a cottage, garden and shop near the Old Still Room. Lydia Dollar (50) who may have been sister of John and Peter was a grocer and owned a cottage and garden near *The Rising Sun* where she lived with her daughter Charlotte (30). She also owned the Old Poor House which she let to William Edney. The relationships of the Dollar family are hard to unravel: in addition to those named above are Fanny and George aged 20 and 15 living at *The Bricklayers Arms* and Mary aged 17 who was a servant in the household of Leonard and Sophia Lidbetter who had five children under five.[13]

The enclosure of upper Swanmore from the open fields of medieval Droxford took place in the sixteenth century and resulted in the pattern of lanes and tracks, fields and hedges still evident today.[14] The Droxford enclosure of 1855 was of Waltham Chase or Horders Wood, as it was usually called, the area south of the Bishop's Waltham road. It concerned chiefly Swanmore and Shidfield. The land belonged to the lord of the manor, the Bishop of Winchester, and its use had hitherto been confined to those who owned property elsewhere in the parish. The procedure for enclosure was laid down in the General Enclosure Act of 1845

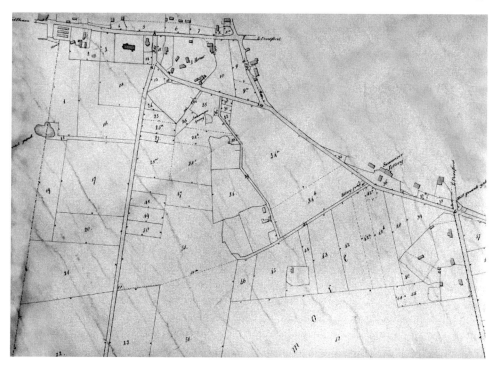

10. Part of the Enclosure map of Waltham Chase 1855 HCRO reproduced with permission

which specified, among other things, that in order to compensate for the gains
made by landowners, provision must be made for allotments, recreation and education for the labouring poor. There were two permanent commissioners who
appointed an assistant commissioner to survey the area and draw up the scheme
which had then to be approved by the landowners.[15]

Once the scheme was agreed in principle by the landowners a valuer was
appointed; in the case of the Droxford enclosure this was George Habin Appleby
of Swanmore Farm. His award was set out on a huge large scale map and accompanying parchment sheets engraved in copper plate handwriting in black ink
which has not faded and is as legible now as it was on the day in May 1855 when
he 'caused it to be engrossed'.[16]

The opening up of the Chase required the cutting of roads to enable field
boundaries to be specified and for the new owners to obtain access. The award
specifies the width of the new roads, 30 feet, 25 feet or 20 feet, and requires that
'good and sufficient fences' should be provided by the new owners within six
months. The present day field boundaries and some of the hedges in the area
enclosed in 1855 date from that time. The upper part of what is now New road as
far as what is now called Chapel road (outside the present day Post Office and
Mason's Stores) which the commissioners called Swanmore Church road was to
be 30 feet wide. The new road which ran from New road to Hill Pound, called by
the commissioners Hill Pound road was to be 25 feet wide while the branch of
Chapel road which runs from the main road, which the commissioners called
Upper Swanmore road was to be 20 feet wide.

The rest of New road is described as the Swanmore to Shedfield road and was
to be 25 feet wide. From being 'the new road', it soon became New road, or 'the
New road across the Chase'. At the T junction where it ended was a further new
road described as the Gravel Hill and Curdridge road which ran from the
Wickham to Bishop's Waltham turnpike to Gravel Hill (now Forest road). This
also was to be 25 feet wide. It was continued in a further road from Gravel Hill to
Mislingford (now Bishops wood road). A road running past the back entrance to
Holywell and described as the Holywell and Mislingford road was to be 20 feet
wide (now Mislingford road). To summarise: the enclosure of 1855 was of the
utmost importance to the future of Swanmore: all the roads south of the Bishop's
Waltham road originated then and it is here that almost all subsequent development has taken place.

Land was parcelled out into small plots allocated to landowners. Relatively few
obtained large amounts of land. The biggest were Peter Barfoot of Midlington
who was allocated 88 acres south of the Mislingford Road which was in turn
bought by Charles Pink. Thomas White of Clifton, Gloucestershire acquired 65
acres between Bishopstoke and Mislingford roads as a beneficiary of the will of
Richard Goodlad. Bettesworth Shearer of Swanmore Park was awarded 63 acres
to the east of New Road.

Six acres were reserved for public quarries to provide stone and gravel for the repair of the roads, one behind the church, a second east of the coach road south of Hill Pound and a third to the north of the road just short of Mislingford. Five acres were reserved as a place 'for exercise and recreation' and became the present recreation ground. Seven acres on the corner of Forest road and Gravel Hill were allocated for 'allotments for the labouring poor'. The ten acre field where the secondary school now stands was set aside as glebe to augment the living of Swanmore. Land was allocated 'for supplying a school at Swanmore', in three parcels, one behind the already existing school (now part of the churchyard, opposite the present post office), a second the four acre field on which the Village Hall and Scout headquarters stand and a third land where the infant school was subsequently built, now part of the Paterson Centre, and the adjoining graveyard.

There was provision for the maintenance of 'public pools' and 'water courses' including Broad Pond with its access road from New Road, Swanmore Spring, (shown on the map as a significant piece of water south of Chapel road), the Pottery Pond also on the south side of Chapel Road, Frith Pond, Mislingford (on the south side of the bridge between two branches of the river Meon) and the water course from Holywell road through the Lakes and across New road.

The Bishop of Winchester, whose manorial rights were extinguished, was allocated in compensation 130 acres in two parcels – one between Frith lane and the Meon south of Mislingford and the other which became known as Bishopswood, east of Gravel Hill and south of the new road from Gravel Hill to Mislingford.

Land was sold to defray the expenses of Enclosure. Charles Pink paid £65 for 4 acres of land at Mislingford. John Dollar who owned the brickyard behind and opposite the *The Bricklayers Arms*, bought 2 acres extending south to Broad Pond and then to the west of the new recreation ground. Peter Dollar bought 2 acres between Broad lane and the church as well as a further acre south of the recreation ground where the Cortursel factory stands and 5 acres on which Crofton Way now stands. Peter Dollar spent altogether about £134 (between £5000 and £6,000 in present day terms) on the purchase of over 8 acres presumably with an eye to later development of the brickfield. Lydia Dollar another member of the same family purchased land near the pottery at Hill Pound.

Used in conjunction with each other Registers of Baptisms, and Burials and to a less extent Marriages can be used to reconstruct families who lived in the village. What emerges puts flesh on the generalisations of historians. Families for example were large, births were spread over the whole child bearing years of the mother's life, artificial contraception was unknown, infant mortality was an ever present reality. The human story behind the statistics can be imagined: the fear and anguish of parents, brothers and sisters when illness struck, inevitably bringing the fear of death.

Our Victorian ancestors lived with death. Childhood and the early years of life were fraught with danger. In each of the years 1849, 1854 and 1858 there were no less than five infant deaths in the village (under the age of one year), representing between 20% and 25% of live births. The number of infant deaths fluctuated from year to year but showed no substantial improvement until 1910. In 1885 there were six infant deaths and in 1897, seven. The proportion of deaths of children under five to all deaths in the parish dropped from 34% in the late 1840s to 25% in the 1890s. By the 1930s it was 5.5% and in the 1950's only three out of 159 recorded deaths were of children under five.

Once an infection reached a family it was liable to spread to other children and a family which lost one child must face further anxiety and possible death. In 1854 the Vicar and his wife, Edward and Flora Creek, lost two daughters in ten days, one aged six and the other 17 months. A new baby might be named after a recently deceased brother or sister. John Dollar the younger, churchwarden of St Barnabas' from the mid 50s until 1873, and his wife Mary, had twelve children born between 1847 and 1865. Their second son John died when he was twelve months old in March 1850. Two months later their third child was born and named John. In 1859 their eldest daughter Maria died just short of her eighth birthday; two years later their ninth child, a girl was born and also named Maria. In the same year John II died aged eleven. Mary Dollar's last children born in 1865 were twins, boy and girl. The boy was named Douglas John. (see Table G2)

William Horn[e], a farm labourer and his wife Mary had twelve children born between 1830 when Mary was 16 and 1857 when she was 43. Three died in infancy or childhood in 1849, 1854 and 1858. A line of graves in the churchyard behind the chancel hints mutely at one family, the Burgesses, stricken repeatedly by fatal illness. Amelia died aged 23 in 1848, Kezia aged 27 in 1850, Ann aged 11 in 1852 and Stephen aged 31 in 1858. Stephen was married and his children Alfred and Ann died in infancy.

Not surprisingly the baptismal register records a number of illegitimate births, occasionally described bluntly as 'bastard child of ...' It was particularly frequent in the 1850s and 1860s when there were a total of 29 baptisms of illegitimate children, with several years in which there were three or even four. In some cases it appears that the girl left the parish to live with relations elsewhere; in others the child was brought up in the girl's home.

The ability of bride, groom and witnesses to sign their names in the marriage register is used by historians as an index of literacy. The first twenty marriages in the Swanmore register took place between 1846 and 1850; in only four cases did both bride and groom sign their name. In eleven marriages both partners made their mark, in a further four the bridegroom did and in one case the bride did. From the 1850s it became rare for neither partner to be able to sign but there are frequent cases of male illiteracy down to 1887. The last time anybody made a mark instead of signing was in 1909.

The mid-nineteenth century village was a closed community with limited horizons. Hours of work were long, particularly in summer, money was short and

II. First entries in the Marriage Register 1846. Both entries are signed by H. Hotham, Perpetual Curate. The names of partners and witnesses include prominent families – Horner, Reeves, Titheridge. Of the eight participants only two – both women, sign their names, the remainder make their mark.

holidays for working people lay far in the future. Not until the Bank Holidays Act of 1871 was there provision for paid holidays. It was natural therefore that most young people found their partners in Swanmore or neighbouring villages. Sixty four of the first hundred marriages recorded in the St Barnabas' register, between 1846 and 1869 were of couples from Swanmore and a further 23 from local villages. There were six from Bishop's Waltham, four from Fareham, three from Shedfield, and two from Droxford. Only eight came from outside Hampshire.

Frequent childbearing often caused the early death of women. There were fifteen marriages of widowers and eight of widows often in their 30s or 40s. By the end of the century the picture was different in relation both to local marriages and to the frequency of widowers and widows remarrying. Of one hundred marriages taking place between 1893 and 1907 only 47 of the partners were from Swanmore, a further 18 were local and 22 came from outside Hampshire There were eight widowers and three widows. Still a substantial number of marriages were local but mobility had increased with the arrival of the bicycle in the 1880s.

Many families were related to one another. The same surnames occur frequently in the census returns and parish registers: Burgess, Boswell, Earwaker, Horner, Pink, Linter, Singleton, Titheridge among them. Descendants of some of these families were to be found in Swanmore through much of the twentieth century.

12. Gravestone of Peter Dollar, first Churchwarden of St Barnabas', died 1884 and Mary Ann Dollar, his wife, died 1870. The date of Peter Dollar's death is incorrect on the gravestone.
Photo Kate Watkins

The marriage register requires both partners to declare their rank or profession. Between 1846 and 1869 seven men described themselves as farmers, 58 as labourers and most of the rest represented a variety of country crafts and trades; wheelwright, carpenter, bricklayer, potter, gamekeeper, basket maker, coppicer, shoemaker, veterinary surgeon, blacksmith, huntsman, hoop maker, builder and painter. A few are less expected: two soldiers, a surgeon, two seamen and three railway porters (from Bishop's Waltham, Bishopstoke and Fareham). Scarcely any brides in the early years had an occupation: there were three dressmakers, two servants and a farmer.[17]

The village grew slowly in the mid-Victorian years – from 674 in 1841 to 787 in 1871 with a comparable increase in the number of houses from 134 to 173. The increase was probably the result of a small excess of births over deaths rather than any significant inward migration. It was a young village: almost half (46%) of the

782 people recorded in the Census of 1871 under the two tithings of Hill and Swanmore were under 20, of these 24% were under ten years old. There is a significant fall in the number over 30 which is hard to account for though it was perhaps in part the result of deaths in childbirth. There were only 31 people over 70 (under 4%).

The character of the village changed little in these years. There were a few big houses, needing servants as part of their establishment. Next came the larger farms. Samuel Townshend (59 in 1871) at Hill Farm came from Somerset in the 1860s and in 1873 succeeded John Dollar as churchwarden. He farmed 400 acres and employed five men and five boys and had two living -in servants. William Townsend (31) who came from Sussex farmed 250 acres at Swanmore Farm. John and Mary Dollar at Jervis Court Farm now had 160 acres, employed four men and one boy and had two 16 year old governesses for the six children recorded in the Census of 1871.

The Census of 1871 records 29 farms, many of them consisting of a few acres and cultivated by the farmer himself perhaps assisted by his young son. The Census lists 111 agricultural labourers. The next largest category of employment was servant – 30 female and 13 male, followed by the 16 people employed in the brick making industry.

Many villagers practised a mixed economy growing much of their own food, keeping a few chickens, a pig and perhaps a cow. In addition the head of the family might work on one of the larger farms. Sons were likely to follow their father as a farm labourer or into his trade. Some had two occupations: Thomas Gardiner (64) who kept *The Hunters Inn* was also a shoemaker, George Earwaker was bricklayer and grocer, and Eliza Woodman grocer and draper.

A woman's place was in the home. Almost all the women with an occupation listed in the Census were either widowed or young and unmarried. They were usually servants and two are described as charwomen. Three were laundresses, one a needlewoman, another a dressmaker and one the postmistress.

For the old who had nobody to support them outdoor relief under the Poor Law might be granted. The 1871 Census lists at least seven people as pauper or living on 'parish allowance'. They were often living with unmarried relations. Mary Newland (85), Mary Layshley (59), Sarah Woodnutt (79) and Sarah Reeves (86) all lived with unmarried sons whilst Sarah Paice (84) lived on her own and Anne Bone (53) was a lodger at *The Hunters Inn*. Not all were women – Thomas Bigley (83) lived on his own and James Matthews (67) was a lodger.

The village was largely self contained: all necessities could be made or bought in Swanmore. For more ambitious purchases or the occasional outing there was Joseph Hillyer the carrier who according to the Post Office Directory of 1867 went to Southampton on Thursday, to Portsmouth on Friday and to Winchester on Saturday, returning in each case on the same day.

3

The Village School
1864-1914

N O NINETEENTH CENTURY PARISH WAS COMPLETE WITHOUT its school: education was the road not only to literacy but to morality and godliness and its provision was, it was assumed, the responsibility of the established church. The 1830s saw schools built at Bishop's Waltham, Curdridge, Droxford (1835) and Shedfield (1834) to add to those already erected at Upham in 1814 (one of the earliest) and Durley in 1823.[1] About the first Swanmore school we know very little. It was built in 1833 on the site now occupied by the war memorial, and extended in 1836 to enable evening services to be held there. The school received a grant from the National Society for the Education of the Poor in the Principles of the Established Church, founded in 1811. The 1841 Census lists William Terry (34) as schoolmaster and it seems likely that he served at the village school. In 1855 Mrs Elizabeth Singleton a Londoner born in Wandsworth was mistress of the National School and though now aged 71 she was still in post in 1861 assisted by her daughter Charlotte Gates.[2] In the meantime the Enclosure award endowed the school with three parcels of land. (See p. 25)

The primary school of today however dates its foundation from 1864, when a completely new building was erected opposite the church.[3] It contained a large room designed to accommodate 130 children, a classroom for 20 children, an infant room for 60 children and a teacher's house.[4] The sum of £750 was given by Mary Ann Booth (described as a Fundholder and born in 1799) and her sister Anna Maria Usborne (who died on 24th January 1878) of Swanmore Cottage and £100 by Richard Goodlad of Hill Place, towards the total cost of £1118. The remainder came from grants including one from the National Society. The school was opened by the Vicar, Edward Creek, on 11th September 1864 with 110 children present.[5]

In its early years the new school was plagued by staff instability. Between 1863 and 1871 no less than seven school masters and mistresses presided over its destinies, each regarded in turn and after brief acquaintance as unequal to the post.

The committee, determined to get the new school off to a good start, gave notice to Miss Willsdon that from May 1863 they proposed to obtain 'the services of a more experienced, certificated master or mistress'.[6] Mr Hellings appointed at a salary of £50 (£30 plus the school pence of £20), proved a disappointment. By early 1864 the Vicar was dissatisfied with his unpunctuality and his absence from Sunday School.'I shall expect to see you at your place always two or three minutes before the time, both at Sunday School and at the week day school and also . . . that the Sunday School shall be fostered by every means in your power. It is not what it ought to be or what it has been'.[7]

Mr Hellings' name does not appear again in the Minutes. He was followed by Miss Jones (1864), Sarah Coombs (1865), Miss Northeast (1867-68), Sophia Toller (1868) who' is not at present equal to her work' and Anna Smith (1869-72): the last a young woman of 24, born at Bradford-on-Avon, who lived in the School House with her sister, Mary an ex-pupil teacher aged 20.[8] They were expected to cope with over 100 children with the assistance of two monitors. The government grant was £35 and the annual salary bill totalled £72.[9]

The managers gave Anna Smith notice to leave at Christmas 1871 hoping to appoint an older and more experienced head preferably male, but they were obliged to ask her to stay and run the school with the help of two paid monitors since they had failed 'to obtain a schoolmaster to take the school after Christmas'.[10] In February 1872 they succeeded in their search and appointed Walter James Joseph Knight trained at Highbury College (1861-62) and his wife Mary Anne trained at Brighton College (1866-67) who began at the school on 5th April 1872.[11]

Staff were not however the only problem of the new school. Income came from four sources: government grant (£43 in 1872-73), private subscriptions (£46.4.6.) a small endowment in land (£9.15.0) and school pence (£22.18.0). In 1872-73 income just exceeded expenditure.[12] In April 1875 there was a deficit of £21 and it was urgent to increase the income. There was however now an alternative solution. Forster's Education Act of 1870 opened up the possibility of a School Board which would have the power to raise a rate and run the school. It was the solution widely adopted in the towns and indeed in neighbouring Bishop's Waltham but was regarded as a last resort, because the education provided in the Board school must be undenominational and the church would lose control.

The committee of Swanmore National School met its subscribers in April 1875 to discuss the situation. It was resolved 'to endeavour to raise the amount by voluntary subscription in preference to throwing the school on the Rates'. A list of suggested subscriptions was drawn up, and apportioned among the ratepayers of the parish, on whom a compulsory rate would fall in the case of there being a school board. A fortnight later a meeting of ratepayers ratified the scheme and Henry Woodman was appointed to collect annual subscriptions at a salary of 10/-.[13]

Swanmore National School.

Account of the Income and Expenditure for the year ending March 31st, 1880.

INCOME.	£	s.	d.
Grant from Education Department	95	10	0
Rents of School Land	9	15	0
Interest of Stock (Miss Usborne's Legacy) 1½ yrs.	4	1	0
Voluntary Contributions of Parishioners	54	7	6
Payments by children	49	13	5
Books sold	0	6	2½
Sale of work	0	12	6
Balance due to Treasurer March 31st, 1880	27	2	2½
	£241	7	10

W. H. Myers, *Auditor.*

EXPENDITURE.	£	s.	d.
Balance due to Treasurer April 1st, 1879	21	16	1½
Salaries : C. Martin, Master	87	11	8½
,, E. Martin, Mistress	50	0	0
,, A. Childs, Assistant Mistress	26	0	0
,, G. Threlfall, Pupil Teacher	9	0	0
,, A. Giles, Pupil Teacher	1	2	6
,, Monitors	3	12	0
Books, Apparatus, and Stationery	10	15	11
Fuel	5	18	3
Repairs and Furniture	14	15	6½
Insurance	0	12	6
Prizes	3	10	0
Materials for Needlework, &c.	5	16	10½
Trimming hedges, &c.	0	15	0
Sundries	0	1	5
	£241	7	10

Walter E. Medlicott, *Treasurer*

Number of Children on the books	-	181
Weekly average attendance	-	128

		£	s.	d.
Average Cost per child	-	£1	14	3½

The average cost per child in Board Schools throughout England is £2 2 0½

The average cost per child, in National Schools supported by Voluntary Subscription, is £1 14 7¾

Report of Her Majesty's School Inspector, for 1879.

" The School has passed a satisfactory examination in all subjects. The exercises done in needlework on the day of Inspection were for the most part very good."

Report of the Diocesan Inspector, as to Religious Instruction.

" Much earnest work has been done in the School, and the tone, and good demeanour of the children prove its good results. The knowledge of the Seniors is very satisfactory. With the infants the teaching is excellent in completeness and tone, a very fair number show at once a good understanding of their simple religious work, and all say admirably by heart."

List of Subscribers, year ending March 31st, 1880.

ANNUAL SUBSCRIPTIONS.

	£	s.	d.	£	s.	d.
The Ecclesiastical Commissioners	1	0	0			
Goodlad, the Misses	3	0	0			
Goodlad, R. R. Esq. (the late)	7	0	0			
Goodchild, Mr.	0	10	0			
Medlicott, Rev. W. E.	7	0	0			
Myers, Mrs. C.	5	0	0			
Myers, W. H., Esq.	5	0	0			
Rice, Admiral	7	0	0			
Shawyer, Mr.	0	5	0			
Tracy, C., Esq.	2	10	0			
Woodman, Mr.	0	10	0			
				38	15	0
Arrears from last year paid up				2	12	6

SPECIAL DONATIONS FOR THE YEAR.

	£	s.	d.	£	s.	d.
Goodlad, R. R. Esq. (the late)	3	0	0			
Medlicott, Rev. W. E.	3	0	0			
Myers, W. H., Esq.	3	0	0			
Rice, Admiral	3	0	0			
Tracy, C. Esq.	1	0	0			
				13	0	0
				£54	7	6

13. National School Accounts for the year ending 31st March 1880

Money however remained a problem. By 1880 the annual cost of a child's education at a Board school was £2-2-0 compared with £1.14.7 in a school supported by the National Society. The assumption seems to have been that church schools were run more economically than Board schools and were therefore better value for money. It seems more likely that the quality of Board school education was outstripping the resources of the church schools. The published accounts of Swanmore school for 1879-80 show income from government grant at £96, fees £50, parishioners' contributions at £54 and rent from school land £10, leaving a deficit on the year of £27. Expenditure on salaries for Charles and Emily Martin the new headmaster and his wife, an assistant mistress, two pupil teachers and monitors came to £177 leaving very little indeed for other items – books, stationery, fuel, furniture, repairs etc.

School fees were graduated according to ability to pay. There were three categories: children of labourers paid 3d per week, children of artisans, pensioners, servants, market gardeners etc paid 4d while the sons and daughters of farmers, shopkeepers and publicans paid 6d per week. The fees were however subject to deductions for regular attendance; 1d per week was returned at the end of the quarter to parents whose children had not been absent on average more than once a week. 'Irregular children are a hindrance to the work of the school and generally fail to obtain the government grant', wrote the managers. There was also a reduction for a third child and subsequent children in the school at the same time so for example a labourer would pay 3d per week for the first and second child but 2d for the third and subsequent children. In addition parents could qualify for regular attendance remission so a labourer with four children could send them to school for as little as 6d per week for the four. Finally under the Education Act of 1876 the Board of Guardians could pay the school fees of children whose parents could not pay on account of poverty.[14]

Until 1891 school attendance was neither compulsory nor free. Though the total number of children who attended in the year 1872-73 was 129 the average weekly attendance was only 62 (48%). This improved rapidly. In 1879 the number on roll had increased to 181 and the average attendance to 128 (70%).[15] The school and the head had every incentive to encourage regular attendance since only children who were present for 250 sessions (125 days) qualified for the annual government inspection on which the grant was based. Boys aged ten and above who were in work qualified if they attended on 75 days. The Vicar encouraged parents to send their older boys to school during the winter months and on wet days at other seasons in order to further their education (and of course the school's income). Parents may have thought that free education introduced in 1891 meant that the government now met all expenses of running the school. The Vicar was at pains to point out that this was not so: the school cost £240 per year but this left a short fall of £60 to be raised locally. The Vicar hoped that parents who no longer had fees to pay would contribute voluntarily.[16]

14. Charles and Emily Martin, schoolmaster and school mistress 1876–1913

Long term staff stability still eluded the school. After five years in the post Walter and Mary Knight resigned and in April 1876 Charles Martin and his wife Emily were appointed at a joint salary of £65 plus half the government grant and half the school pence (both means of encouraging him to promote regular attendance).[17] Born in Brighton, Charles Martin was 23 when he came to Swanmore, with his wife Emily, born in Hereford and aged 27; she was also a certificated teacher. They moved into the School House with Charles Martin's elder sister Agnes and here they raised a family of six children born between 1877 and 1889, (a further child died in infancy). They left the School House to live in their own house in 1890.[18] Before long the school became a family business. Emily Martin was on the staff, and became headmistress of the infant department in 1898, which was from then on regarded as a separate school.[19] Their eldest daughter, Agnes, became an assistant teacher before her 18th birthday in 1895 whilst Charles Martin's sister, also Agnes, is described in the 1891 Census as secretary to the headmaster.[20]

The contrast with the staff instability of the 1860s could scarcely have been greater. In the century following 1876 Swanmore school had only four heads. Assistants, usually young women still came and went, sometimes dismissed in favour of ' more experienced teachers'. Pupil teachers and paid monitors still supplemented 'certificated teachers'. George Threlfall, pupil teacher from 1879 to 1884, seems to have gained a special place in the affection of school and parish. When he left to enter the Diocesan Teacher Training College at Winchester (later King Alfred's College) he was presented with a silver watch and chain.[21] At the end of the century the staff consisted of two heads, two assistants and four monitors and the salary bill was £265.[22]

The school flourished in the last years of the century. By 1900 the average attendance had risen to 156. The building was uncomfortably crowded. In 1881 the infant room was enlarged at a cost of £77.[23] Less than two years later an entirely new Infants school was built on the other side of the road to the west of the church at a cost of £425. In both cases subscriptions came predominantly from the Goodlad-Daubeny, Myers and Medlicott families.[24] Annie Eliza Corney , a young woman of 22, was engaged as infant school mistress; she was a pupil teacher from 1875, when she was age 14, until 1880 and was to remain at the school until 1887.[25]

Other facilities were improved too. In 1885 a well 87 feet deep was provided for the School House.[26] In 1894 one quarter of an acre of land at the rear of the school was purchased and new 'school offices' (a Victorian euphemism for cess pit lavatories) were provided.[27] Meanwhile in 1892 the site of the original school with the land behind it was sold to the Vicar and churchwardens for £60 to enlarge the churchyard and the money was invested for the benefit of the school.[28]

Children walked to school along lanes and field paths from the outlying parts of the parish, summoned as they drew near by the school bell, a reminder of the virtue of punctuality. Once inside the day began with prayers and a Scripture lesson, (from which chapel children were excused), when the Catechism, Prayer Book collects and prayers, the Apostles' Creed and passages from the Bible were committed to memory. There was a strong emphasis on the three Rs with standards laid down in the Revised Code and inspected each year as a condition of government grant. Other subjects were not however neglected: geography and history qualified for grant as 'class subjects' whilst singing, drawing for boys and needlework for girls also attracted special grants. There was a capitation allowance for discipline and a grant in lieu of fees when these were abolished in 1891.

Parents were invited to the annual prize-giving. In 1872 William Horner won the attendance prize of a book and one shilling for 428 attendances.[29] Merit cards and money prizes were awarded for achievement in the three Rs and Bibles and Prayer Books for success in the Diocesan Examination in Religious Knowledge. Great store was set on needlework; there were work boxes, thimbles and 'housewives' given for the best shifts, bed gowns, shirts and pocket handkerchiefs and a

special prize for patching. In June 1877 the prize-giving was followed by a programme of songs, glees, recitations and readings.[30]

In the summer there was an annual treat. On Friday 3rd August 1883 165 pupils
assembled at school and, headed by banners, marched through the village to
Swanmore Park. Cricket was followed by tea. Then came prizegiving, further
games – sack races, hurdle and flat races, after which every child received a toy. The
day ended with more cake and ginger bread, fireworks and three cheers for their
teachers and the Vicar before they ' dispersed homewards well pleased and tired
over the glad things of the past day'[31]

Swanmore, it seems, scarcely needed legislation to achieve full attendance. In
1891 the year in which school became compulsory to the age of ten, all but eight
of the children between 5 and 12 were described in the census return as 'scholar'.
Only two families appear not to have sent their children of 8 and 6 and 11 and 13
respectively to school. Of children aged 13 eight were in school and seven were in
employment. At age 14 ten were in school and seven were not. Even at the age of
15 one boy and one girl were ' scholars' whilst eight were in employment. Those
who had left school at the age of 12 or 13 had in the case of boys become agricultural labourers or bricklayers' labourers and one was a grocer's assistant.. Girls who
were not in school were 'general servants' and one was a dressmaker. The children
of Charles Gunner who was a solicitor and banker, and Jessie his wife, who lived at
Swanmore Cottage, were not at school but educated at home, until the boys at
least went to board at a preparatory school and then to Marlborough College. At
Holywell House there was a governess and the Vicar's children did not attend the
village school either – though by 1891 they were in any case all above school age.[32]

Many families had two, three or even more children in school at the same time.
In 1891 there were five members of the Cresswell family on the roll, and Charles
and Emily Martin also provided five. The record however was shared by three
families. George and Maryann Brown of Forest road had six sons in school –
George, Frederick, Roderick, Ernest, Edwin and Alfred, aged between 13 and 4
with their younger sisters Alice and Bertha still to come. John and Ann Emery of
Bishop's Waltham road also had six boys at school – Horace, John, Raymond,
Cecil, Aubrey, and Archibald with twin sons Reginald and Vernon then aged three
yet to come. George and Blanche Horner of *The Bricklayers Arms* also had six children at school in 1891 – Walter, Percy, Albert, Ada, Evelyn and Herbert, whilst
Edwin, William and Helen were then aged two years, one year and five months
respectively. A further eight children were as yet unborn including Len born in
1896.[33]

The 1890s saw the beginning of evening classes in the countryside organised by
the County Council Committee for Technical Education to remedy deficiencies
in provision and to supplement what had been available in childhood. There were
classes each winter in the school. Charles Martin offered reading, writing, arithmetic, and principles of agriculture whilst Emily Martin taught domestic econo-

15. Swanmore National School 1899

my and needlework and the Vicar and his daughters vocal music. There were visit-
ing teachers for basket work, joinery and veterinary science. In October 1898 a
travelling dairy school took place for a fortnight in barns at Hill Farm teaching
butter making, soft cheese making and poultry trussing. Certificates were awarded
at the end of the course and could count towards gaining a scholarship to attend a
short course at Reading Agricultural Course.[34]

The Balfour Education Act of 1902 abolished the school boards and transferred
their schools and those of the voluntary bodies to local authorities. Controversy
was acute. To church schools it brought financial stability since county councils
would now be responsible for running costs including teachers' salaries. There was
however strong opposition from the nonconformist churches who had few
schools and did not see why a Church of England school should be paid for out of
the rates.[35]

For Swanmore School transfer to the county council brought relief from financial anxiety. The foundation managers – the Vicar, the Squire, Major Daubeny of
Hill Place and Murray Gladstone, recently moved to Hampton Hill – were joined
by two representative managers appointed respectively by the Parish Council and
the County Council.[36] If the school now enjoyed financial security it was at a
price. The managers were no longer free agents. In return for local authority
money they had to accept a degree of local authority control. The school was, they
were reminded, no longer Swanmore National School but Swanmore Church of
England School.[37] The managers could recommend the appointment of staff but

16. Staff with some pupils c.1900

they could not appoint; they could propose increases of salary for teachers but
they could not grant them,

Charles Martin, by now a bulky figure, well known for his range of coloured
waistcoats, continued as headmaster of the mixed school and Emily Martin as
headmistress of the infant school with a joint salary of £195. In the mixed school
there was a succession of assistants, usually young women, some hoping to go to
college to obtain the coveted qualification of certificated teacher. As late as 1905
the managers appointed a monitor at a salary of three shillings (15p) per week. In
the infant school Emily Martin was assisted by her daughter Madge.[38]

The school was full with 144 pupils in the mixed school and 50 in the infant
school. Additions to the building in 1913, at a cost of £350, increased capacity to
176. The school cleaner earned 4/6 per week in winter when presumably there
was more work to be done, only 2/9 in summer, and in addition 5/- per quarter
'for a special scrubbing'.[39]

Children often entered school at the age of three but began in Standard 1 at the
age of five and progressed by one standard each year to reach Standard 7 at the age
of 12.[40] Failure in the annual examination meant being held back to repeat the
year. The school bell rang from 8.45 to 8.50 and again from 8.55 to 9.00, heard by
children hastening along the lanes to school, after which the doors were closed

17. School pupils in Hampton Hill near Donigers Dell c.1910

18. Infant class with Emily Martin c.1910

19. Class 1 (top class) with Ernest Targett c.1912

and school began. The headmaster would call the register for the whole school in
the big school room. The daily scripture lesson then took place in classes, while
Methodists, whose parents had withdrawn them from denominational teaching,
went to the St John Ambulance hut next door. Teaching methods were traditional.
Slates were used, with slate pencils whose distinctive squeak could set the teeth on
edge. At the end of the day the slates were handed in with much clatter. On
Fridays ink wells were collected and washed out ready to be refilled with fresh ink
made from a brown coloured powder, and returned to the desks on Monday
morning by the ink monitor. There were nature walks, cricket fixtures with
Bishop's Waltham and more surprisingly swimming in the brick fields where
Crofton Way now stands.[41]

Punishment was frequent and usually with the cane. The leaving age was 14 but
there were plenty of exceptions. Pupils who reached Standard 7 and passed the
'Labour examination' could leave. When Len Horner reached Standard 7 in 1908
he was employed by the headmaster to do gardening jobs until he took the examination and left.[42] As part of their welfare provision the Liberal government which
took office in 1905 introduced school medicals and from 1908 all children were
medically examined three times in their school lives. Epidemics were a constant
hazard, likely to run through the entire school and therefore often necessitating

closure of the school. Swanmore school closed for scarlatina from 24th November 1892 to 9th January 1893 and for whooping cough in October 1908.[43]

Charles Martin's long reign as headmaster came to an end in August 1913. He remained in the village, active in the church as organist and lay reader as well as vice-chairman of the parish council, a post he relinquished a year before his death in February 1925. The new headmaster was Ernest Frank Whitaker, appointed at a salary of £135, whilst Mabel Wootton became headmistress of the infant school in October 1915. When the managers appointed Mrs Whitaker to the staff they received a letter from the Chief Education Officer 'deprecating the principle of appointing the wife of the headmaster'; they persisted nonetheless 'in default of other applicants'.[44]. Under Ernest Whitaker the older pupils were, for the first time, encouraged to take examinations to enter local secondary schools – usually Price's Grammar School at Fareham for boys or Winchester County High School for Girls.[45] To the young Jack Hoar he was an inspiration, instilling in him a life-long love of the English language and of the countryside, both of which he put to good use in adult life.[46]

4

Houses and People

THE OWNER OF SWANMORE PARK AT THE END OF THE EIGHTEENTH-century was William Augustus Bettesworth. It was he who began to consolidate the copyholds held by yeoman families since the middle ages and so to build up a substantial estate in upper Swanmore, a process continued by his nineteenth century successors. William Bettesworth died in 1805. The estate was inherited by his niece Augusta who was married to Alexander Shearer. In the late 1830s Swanmore Park passed to their son Bettesworth Pitt Shearer who was born in 1808 and baptised at St George's, Bloomsbury (see table G1).[1] Early in the century the public road which had run from South Lodge in front of the house to Dairy Cottage or Swanmore Park Farm was closed and a new road cut from the top of Damson Hill to North Lodge.[2]

20. Swanmore House before 1877. Photo Catalogue of sale 1877

Bettesworth Pitt Shearer lived at Swanmore House for over thirty years. Following the death of his first wife Elizabeth Mary in 1870 and of his second wife Elizabeth Cadogan Walker in 1875 at the age of 57 and 56 respectively, he sold the Swanmore Park estate and moved to East Molesey in Surrey where he died in 1903 at the great age of 94. He retained however strong affection for Swanmore, naming his house in Surrey after the village. He is buried in Swanmore churchyard alongside his wives. There is a memorial to him on the north wall of the nave of St Barnabas' church and a wheeled bier was given by his relations in his memory.[3]

The Swanmore Park estate was bought by Charles Myers in September 1877 for £21,000 (about £900,000 in present day terms). It then totalled 303 acres including park, pleasure gardens, entrance lodges, farmhouse and cottages as well as the right to four pews at the east end of the north aisle of Droxford church which still bear the inscription 'Faculty seats of Swanmore House Nos 9,10,11,12'[4] Charles Myers was a Liverpudlian by birth, a director of the White Star Shipping Line and now lived at Botley Grange. He bought the estate with the intention of demolishing the existing eighteenth century house and embarked at once on rebuilding it. He employed his fellow Liverpudlian, Alfred Waterhouse who was already the architect of the Natural History Museum in London, the Union Society, Cambridge, and Manchester Town Hall and was at work on Eaton Hall for the Duke of Westminster. The house cost a total of £36,250 excluding the land, and fees of 5%, over one and a half million pounds in present day terms. Myers was however rich even by nineteenth century standards. When he died suddenly in September 1879 at the age of 52, just two years after buying Swanmore Park and before the new house was complete, he left an estate worth £400,000, £16 million in present day terms — and death duties lay in the future. The funeral was held in St Barnabas' church and was conducted by the Vicar and the Revd J.P.Nash, Vicar of Hedge End. 'Mr Myers was about to take up residence at Swanmore House which has been entirely rebuilt.' reported the *Hampshire Chronicle*.

The Swanmore Park estate was left to his elder son William Henry Myers. Born at Aigburth in Lancashire, and educated at Eton and Balliol College, Oxford where he took his degree in 1877, William Myers was aged 24 when his father died and was reading for the bar at the Inner Temple, being called in 1881. Meanwhile his mother, Henrietta, widow of Charles Myers, moved into the newly completed house in November 1880, with her two daughters Henrietta, 14 and Evelyn, 9. Her staff was a substantial one. There was a governess for her daughters, a housekeeper, two ladies' maids, laundry maid, two housemaids, kitchen maid, scullery maid, footman and groom.[5]

Eight years later in July 1888, now a Hampshire JP, William Myers married Frances Mary Prideaux-Brune in an impressive society wedding held at St Paul's, Wilton Place, Knightsbridge. The officiating clergy were the bride's cousin, the Revd Edward Prideaux- Brune, Vicar of Rowner, the bridegroom's brother, the

Revd Charles Myers, Principal of St Stephen's House, Oxford, and the Vicar of Swanmore. The eight bridesmaids included William Myers' two younger sisters. On 21st August the couple returned to Swanmore. When their carriage reached the bottom of Swanmore Hill it was unharnessed from the horses, and with ropes attached it was pulled through the village and up Vicarage Lane, along a route decorated with flags and triumphal arches and preceded by the Bishop's Waltham Brass Band, to Swanmore Park.[6]

Four years later in July 1892 another triumphal procession took place: the squire was again drawn through the village to Swanmore House. This time it was to mark his election as Conservative MP for Winchester, a seat he occupied until 1906. William Myers was the archetypal country squire. Deputy Lieutenant of Hampshire, Justice of the Peace sitting on the Droxford Bench, he was elected to the County Council when it was formed in 1889 and was a member of the Roads and Bridges committee. He was not it appears a frequent contributor to debate; one brief profile of him commented. 'We never have to complain of undue loquacity in his public service'. In parliament he was in favour of reform at the War Office as well as a strong advocate of a powerful navy.[7]

In Swanmore he had become a churchwarden in 1880 and remained so for 50 years. When the Parish Council was first formed in 1894 it was natural that he should become its chairman; this post too he held for a record 36 years resigning in 1930. Universally recognised as the father of the village he is still remembered at the turn of the twenty first century by the oldest inhabitants as Squire Myers, the only squire the village ever had.

The newly built house was neo-Tudor in style, situated almost 400 feet above sea level and commanding a superb views in all directions, to the south over Portsdown Hill, the Solent and the Forest of Bere, with the village church then visible between the trees. It was described by *Country Life* in 1899 as 'charmingly quaint and Elizabethan in style with its creeper-clad red brick walls' and its owner as ' a thorough Englishman, loving sport, his gardens and farms'.[8] On the ground floor were drawing room (47 by 20 feet), dining room (30 by 24 feet), study, library and billiard room (48 feet in length) and a large central hall with skylight. On the first floor were nine principal bedrooms and dressing rooms, as well as a further seven guest bedrooms. On the top floor there were fourteen staff bedrooms. Domestic offices included housekeeper's room, servants' hall, kitchen, scullery and butler's pantry. In the basement were wine cellars, game larder, dairy and boot rooms while a separate block contained a model laundry with ironing room, drying chamber and a walled-in drying ground. The coach house was later turned into a garage which provided for five cars and included an inspection pit for their maintenance.

Just before the end of the century an additional wing was added. It included a new main entrance hall with toilets, library and billiard room with a two storey lantern roof.[9] In 1902 Swanmore House became the first residence in Swanmore

21. Swanmore House c.1885

22. Swanmore House 1899
Country Life 18th February 1899

to be lighted by electricity when a private generator was installed at the home farm.[10] Running water was pumped from wells to a storage tank on the roof.

The gardens were on a scale appropriate to the house. They may have been planted by Bettesworth Pitt Shearer; if not they were developed to maturity remarkably quickly. There are numerous accounts of the gardens in gardening magazines between 1884 and 1905.[11] There was an octagonal rose garden, walled kitchen garden approached through a pergola and water and rock gardens. Five greenhouses, six acres of orchard, growing every conceivable variety of fruit and five tennis courts completed the amenities. The house was approached through North Lodge gates via an avenue of lime trees and through the South Lodge gates from Swanmore village.

Myers' gardener and later farm bailiff was Edwin Molyneux, a Yorkshireman born at Sproxton near Helmsley in 1852, who lived at North Lodge. He acquired remarkably quickly an outstanding reputation as a gardener specialising, in his early years at Swanmore Park, in chrysanthemums. By 1884 there were already 200 varieties on display in the gardens and hothouses at Swanmore Park and Molyneux's exhibits swept the board at local and national flower shows. The annual Horticultural Show held at Swanmore Park from 1881 attracted exhibitors from far and near.[12] In 1896 the writer in the *Journal of Horticulture and Cottage Gardens* wrote that the name of Molyneux ' struck terror into the hearts of chrysanthemum growers, for so good were the blooms he exhibited that no one had a chance of taking a prize against him'. He was the author of the standard work on the subject: *Chrysanthemums and their culture* by Edwin Molyneux published in 1886.

On 13th September 1888 William and Frances Myers gave a Fete to celebrate their marriage. Nine hundred people were invited of whom between 500 and 600 were adults who sat down in a huge marquee to a meal of 'joints of beef, mutton, veal, ham and pies, tea, bread and butter and cake'. After dark the grounds were decorated with Chinese lanterns and there was a memorable fireworks display. [13]

The Myers had no children. Frances Myers was described by those who knew her in later life as ' mannish'; she wore thick tweeds, smoked a pipe and enjoyed the male sport of shooting.[14] The household was on a scale expected in those days of a landed family. By 1891 there were thirteen living-in servants. Eight were women: cook, ladies maid, two house maids, two laundry maids, a kitchen maid and a scullery maid. There were two footmen, a hall boy and two grooms. Only the last three were from Hampshire; the others came from Devon, London, Surrey and Essex, recruited presumably by advertisement. All were unmarried and apart from the cook who was 33 they ranged in age from 16 to 23.[15] They were expected to attend family prayers held in the drawing room each morning. There were houses in the grounds too for coachman and farm manager.

The Minutes of the Swanmore Park Cricket Club provide a fascinating cameo of aspects of upper crust life in Swanmore and beyond in the last decades of the nineteenth century. At a meeting held at Swanmore Park in October 1873 hosted by Bettesworth Pitt Shearer it was resolved that ' a Gentleman's Cricket Club be formed, with ground . . . in the Park at Swanmore'. Thomas Wilson of Hazelholt was elected its president, the Revd Walter Medlicott vice-president, Benjamin Hewitt of Bishop's Waltham secretary and Charles Gunner then of Brook House, Bishop's Waltham, treasurer. Its members, both playing and non-playing, were elected from the aristocracy of south Hampshire society. In 1882 its 93 members included the Earl of Northesk of Longwood, Owlesbury, four generals, three admirals, eleven army officers ranging in rank from captain to colonel, one member of parliament, J. Carpenter Garnier of Rookesbury Park, and several clergy. Its colours were dark and light blue, no doubt to reflect the Oxford or Cambridge provenance of many of its members. The annual subscription was one sovereign (£1 the equivalent of about £40 in present day terms). The ground was provided by B.P. Shearer who also supplied a shed to be used as a pavilion whilst the club bought tents to supplement the changing accommodation. The club bought ' a mowing machine' and engaged a groundsman, initially 'Moreton', later 'Judd', neither dignified with Mr, an initial or Christian name, even when they made up a team and appeared in the batting or bowling averages.

In the early days the club hired a professional coach:' Flanagan of Lord's Cricket Ground will attend at Swanmore for practices on Monday the 9th, the 16th and the 23rd April [1877] at Two o'Clock'.[16] Matches were played against clubs of comparable social standing, some military. In 1877 for example games were played against Portsmouth Garrison, Havant, Southampton, New Forest, Old Shirburnians, Winchester Garrison and the 21st Fusiliers. Fixtures were courteously declined with Botley and Horndean and the club never played Swanmore Village Cricket Club though on occasion the latter held some of its home matches at Swanmore Park. A caterer provided lunch on match days and a local licensee supplied beer whilst for festive occasions the club engaged the band of the 21st Fusiliers.

The future of the club was in the balance with the departure from Swanmore of its host, B.P. Shearer. Members met at the Crown Hotel, Bishop's Waltham in December 1877 to make a presentation to him of a silver inkstand fitted with bat, ball and wickets. The new owner of Swanmore Park, Charles Myers, had already written from Camp Hill, Woolton, Liverpool to T.H. Wilson indicating that the cricket pitch was too close to the house 'and too immediately in front of the new one, to be agreeable to me'. He would however make a new ground available further from the house. A year later the building of the new house was proceeding apace. In June 1879 Charles Myers had a further concern. The caterer was apparently selling liquor on match days not only to the teams and their guests but to all and sundry. 'This I cannot sanction,' wrote Myers, 'especially now while I have some 200 men working for me'. He called on the committee 'to abate this evil', which it agreed to do.

The club was dissolved in 1885, 'which is much to be deplored by all cricket lovers', apparently because 'no gentleman can be found to undertake the duties of secretary'. In fact the club in its last year had been less successful than hitherto, winning only six of its 18 matches, whilst three had been abandoned because 'so many members were unable to play at the last moment'. Although the club was solvent at the end, collecting subscriptions seems to have been a perennial problem – was this a sign of the agricultural depression which set in in the late 1870s? The mowing machine was sold to Hampshire County Cricket Club, some property was sold and the proceeds given to Shedfield Cottage Hospital whilst the remainder was divided between Bishop's Waltham, Corhampton, and Swanmore Village Clubs, the latter acquiring the sight screens. The pavilion which was near the South Lodge gradually fell into decay and collapsed about 1930.[16]

The second large estate in the parish was based on Hill Place and covered over 1000 acres when it was sold in 1916. The house, built in the early nineteenth century, was square, constructed of yellow brick and had a 'striking open balustraded parapet'.[17] Its owner at the end of the eighteenth century was Richard Goodlad who was born in 1756 and died in 1821 and served as Sheriff of Hampshire.[18] Throughout the century the Goodlad family lived at Hill Place. Richard Redfern Goodlad lived there until his death in 1880, with his first wife Emma who died in

23. Hill Place

1867 and his second wife Florence Harriet whom he married in 1872 and who outlived him (died 1888). His sisters Elizabeth (1806-90) and Leonora (1808-95) lived at Jervis Lodge after it ceased to be the Parsonage in 1873 but moved to Hill Place after the death of their brother.

Sometime after that their nephew Major Walter Augustus Daubeny came to live at Hill Place. Born in 1838 he served as a Major in the Buffs in the Second China War of 1860. He was a thin, aristocratic figure, with an ascetic appearance, slow moving and unsmiling and something of a martinet. He drove in his phaeton with the groom and was held in awe by his many employees. He was a meticulous timekeeper who would check his watch against the church clock as he arrived for Mattins: punctuality was a virtue he expected of his household and servants. It was his death on 30th April 1914 which led to the sale and break up of the estate. 'Major Daubeny died at Rookesbury aged 76' wrote George Titheridge. [19]

If William Myers owned most of upper Swanmore, the centre of the village formed part of the Hill Place estate. Attached to Hill Place itself were three coach houses, stabling and harness room, 'pleasure gardens and miniature park of 46 acres'. The estate included from west to east Jervis Court farm to Cott Street farm and from north to south Upper Hill farm on the Droxford boundary to Gravel Hill plantation on the Shedfield boundary (Hill farm 169 acres, Upper Hill farm 176 acres, Hill Pound farm 45 acres, Jervis Court farm 62 acres, Jervis Lodge, Hampton Hill cottage, Church cottage, Cott street farm 218 acres, Hill Park farm 45 acres)[20].

Swanmore's first Church of England minister, Henry Hotham, was probably not resident in the parish. He came to work in Swanmore in 1843 as a newly ordained deacon and seems to have stayed until 1847.[21] The provision of a Parsonage house was from the beginning part of the plan for the new parish. The search was already on in 1843, before the building of the church began. It was hoped initially to buy Swanmore Cottage (now Swanmore Lodge) which was on the market.[22]

The first Swanmore Parsonage (sic) was probably built in 1849 on the north side of the road near to Jervis Court Farm It cost £1100 and was mainly financed by two grants in 1846 and 1848 each of £220 from Queen Anne's Bounty and by a gift of £500 from the Rector of Droxford.[23] The first priest to live in Swanmore was Edward Basnett Creek. Born in County Down in 1816, he was curate of Kerswell in Devon for two years before coming to Swanmore in 1847, at the age of 31, with his wife Flora Ann, aged 27 and a young family, Edward born in Florence in 1843, Alice and Flora born in Devon in 1845 and 1846. There were to be five more children, all born in Swanmore. In 1851 his household included five living-in servants, a cook brought from Devon, house maid, man servant, nurse and schoolmistress.[24]

Edward Creek died suddenly at Southsea in March 1871, at the age of 55, leaving his wife and three children, Bertha, 16, Frances, 11 and Herbert, 9. Two other

24. Swanmore Parsonage 1849–1873 now Jervis Lodge
Photo Kate Watkins

children, Eliza and Emma, had died within ten days of each other at the ages of 6 and 17 months in 1854.[25]

Edward Creek's successor, Walter Edward Medlicott, was Vicar for 37 years, retiring at the age of 66 in 1907. He was educated at Harrow and Christ Church, Oxford, taking his degree in 1864. During his second curacy, at Buriton near Petersfield, he married his Rector's daughter. Edith Louisa Sumner was the grand-daughter of C.R.Sumner who had recently retired after over 40 years as Bishop of Winchester. She was also great niece of the former Archbishop of Canterbury, John B. Sumner, whose daughter was married to the Rector of Droxford, J.A.G.Colpoys. The Medlicotts had therefore impeccable ecclesiastical connec-tions. When they came to Swanmore they had two young children, Robert Sumner, later Vicar of St Thomas's, Portsmouth and Margaret. Two further chil-dren were born at Swanmore, Grace Katharine in September 1871 and Walter Barrington in November 1872.

Walter Medlicott's early years were marked by far- reaching changes in church life. His first project was a new Vicarage, closer to the church and more suited to its purpose than the existing Parsonage. He bought a triangle of land from Richard Goodlad of Hill Place. Building began in the autumn of 1872 and the Vicarage was

25. Swanmore Vicarage 1873–1985, in 1962.
Photo Revd Ron Paterson.

completed in a year.[26]. There were two wings with five bedrooms in one wing and a further four in the servants' wing. as well as spacious attics. There was a large cellar, coach house and stables and one and a half acres of garden. There was a superb view from the drawing room across to Church lane and beyond. It was an ideal house for a Victorian Vicar with a large family and the means to maintain it.

The Parsonage meanwhile was renamed Jervis Lodge and Elizabeth and Leonora Goodlad moved in. When they moved back to Hill Place probably in 1880 when their brother, Richard Goodlad died, Jervis Lodge was occupied in turn by Lieutenant-General Edmond Wodehouse and then by Reginald Freke Williams. About 1910 he was succeeded by the Revd George Maclean who lived at Jervis Lodge until the mid-1920s when it was bought by Rear Admiral Sir Edward Bradford.[27]

After less than three years living in the new Vicarage Edith Medlicott died at the age of 29 leaving the Vicar with four children under seven. He never remarried but relied on a staff of servants to help bring up the children and to assist with the great amount of entertaining which he undertook. In 1881 the Vicarage had five living- in servants, a governess and nurse for the children, cook, parlour maid and housemaid.[28]

Holywell House dates in its present form from about 1780. The estate was bought in about 1745 by Admiral Lord Anson, first Lord of the Admiralty during the

26. Holywell House
Country Life 18th February 1999

Seven Years War. He joined together two cottages to form a good sized farm house. When he died without issue in 1762 it was bought by Humphrey Minchin, who came from an Anglo-Irish family, and in 1793 was M.P. for Bossinney in Cornwall.[29] He remodelled the house to form a family seat adding the present kitchen, dining room and drawing room. Old materials were re-used including seventeenth century timbers and brickwork, which may have come from the Manor House at Soberton which was demolished at this time. Soon after 1775 the house was further remodelled. The large and distinctive semi-circular bows on the south and east, each with a tall central round-headed window and smaller flanking windows on the ground floor were added. The walled garden and barn also date from this period.[30]

During much of the nineteenth century the house was occupied by a succession of senior naval officers during appointments at Portsmouth though the Minchin family continued to own the estate. They included Captain Colemore, R N (1855), Captain W.J.Christie, R.N, (1859), Rear Admiral Cockburn (1867 and 1871). At the end of the century Tracy Courtney lived at Hill Place and at the beginning of the twentieth century Claude Brinckman.[31]

In 1917 the estate was sold by Major-General Faulkner Minchin to Maurice Portal. He carried out further alterations to the window lay out and added the Georgian-looking door case on the principal front. Holywell was sold again in

1960 to Nigel Birch, a member of Harold Macmillan's government who became a Life Peer as Lord Rhyl in 1970. On the death of his widow Esme, Lady Rhyl, it was bequeathed to her nephew the present owner, Laurence, 7th Earl of' Clarendon who has carried out further extensive alterations completed in 1994.

The Georgian south front is unaltered but the north part of the house has been reconstructed to make a new entrance with Tuscan porch and new arched staircase window. On either side of this new entrance the old farmhouse and the eighteenth century service wing have been reconstructed. The brickwork is an excellent match with the old. There has also been much sensitive internal reorganisation including substantial provision for the display of family portraits in the main rooms, some in their original seventeenth century frames. Swanmore has in effect acquired a new stately home though one which is not open to the public.[32]

At Swanmore Cottage lived in the 1860s Mary Ann Booth, a widow and her unmarried sister Anna Maria Usborn, major contributors to the building of the new school. The house was bought in 1887 by Charles R. Gunner, of Gunner's Bank, who then lived at Brook House, Bishop's Waltham and later returned there and built Ridgemede. Later owners of Swanmore Cottage, were Captain Richard Humpage (1904), Henry Thomas Gilson (1907 & 1911) and Judge Barnard Lailey (1927 & 1939). The house is now known as Swanmore Lodge.[33]

Hampton Hill House was owned according to the Tithe Award of 1842 by Leonard Lidbetter who had however left Swanmore by the time of the Census of 1851. Thereafter ownership changed hands several times. It was rebuilt in 1872 probably by Vice-Admiral Edward Bridges Rice who lived there from the early 1870s until he left Swanmore in 1883.[34]. It was then occupied by Colonel Skipwith and after his death in August 1886 by his widow.[35]. She was succeeded in October 1896 by Murray Gladstone who moved from Shedfield where he had lived at Shedfield Cottage and built Murray Cottages for his servants. His household at Hampton Hill included his wife Emily, daughter of Baron Newburgh, whom he had married in 1874, and his sisters Catharine and Florence, who ran a private lending library at Hampton Hill House as late as the 1920s. Books were covered in home made cretonne wrappers. In later years Murray and his wife were it seems estranged. When Emily died in 1927, a year before Murray, she was living in Southsea.[36] Villagers who remember the Hampton Hill family certainly believed that Murray Gladstone was unmarried. The Gladstones like the Myers and Goodlads had no children.

Murray Gladstone was a short, rotund man, who wore a wide-brimmed hat which accentuated his small stature and contributed to his nickname of 'Tubby'. He rode a bicycle as well as owning one of' Swanmore's earliest motor cars. His main claim to fame in the village was the founding of the Swanmore Scout troop in 1911.[37] The family were said to be early supporters of cremation. When

27. Leacock House, Church road.
Photo Kate Watkins.

Florence Gladstone died at the age of 82 in May 1935 George Titheridge records
not a funeral or that she was buried as was his usual practice but ' Memorial service for Miss Gladstone at Swanmore church', which seems to support the view
that she was cremated.[38]

Stephen Butler Leacock, the Canadian humourist, author of the once well-known
Literary Lapses, is sometimes described as the only famous person born in
Swanmore. It is a title however which he hardly deserves. In an autobiographical
volume published in 1939 he wrote 'I was born in Swanmore a suburb of Ryde,
Isle of Wight on 30th December 1869.' He subsequently discovered his error
through a solicitor in Ryde and wrote to the Rector of Bishop's Waltham who
sent the letter to the Vicar of Swanmore. He duly dispatched to the great man a
copy of the entry in the baptismal register of St Barnabas'. Leacock correctly
acknowledged the parish of his birth in a posthumously published autobiography
The Boy I Left Behind. The error is however reproduced in Frank Muir's *Oxford
Book of Humorous Prose.* The family moved continually until they set sail for
Montreal in 1876. In 1970 a plaque was placed on Leacock House, his birthplace
near to the church, unveiled by the Rt. Hon. James Auld on behalf of the
Canadian government.[39]

5

Church and Village
1871–1914

THE LATE VICTORIAN AND EDWARDIAN PERIOD WAS FOR SWANMORE a golden age. Though it was, for civil purposes, part of Droxford until 1894, the village nevertheless developed a social and community life of its own, centred on church, school and big house. Vicar, schoolmaster and squire, the three Ms – Medlicott, Martin and Myers – were acknowledged village leaders from the time of their arrival until well into the twentieth century. To the oldest inhabitants of today they are recalled as names and faces conjured up through folklore transmitted by parents and grandparents as patriarchs, men of mature years, wisdom and gravitas. It is therefore easy to forget that when they arrived in the village, within a few years of each other, in the 1870s, all three were under 30 and two of them were under 25. If it was a village hierarchy it was a young one. Walter Medlicott became Vicar in 1871 at the age of 29, Charles Martin was appointed headmaster of the village school in 1876 when he was 23 and William Myers inherited Swanmore Park on the early death of his father in 1879, at the age of 24.

The village was self-contained. Scarcely anybody worked outside the village, most were occupied in farming or rural crafts. Children went to the village school apart from the few who were taught at home or sent away to boarding school. The village provided shops and what entertainment there was. The occasional visit to Fareham, Gosport or even the Isle of Wight was an outing to be anticipated with pleasure and looked back on with nostalgia. The great majority attended church or chapel or were at least sympathetic to Christian belief and practice which provided a universally accepted philosophy and morality. All learnt the Lord's Prayer, catechism and creed at church, unless they were Methodists in which case chapel provided alternatives to creed and catechism but even more rigorous moral imperatives including total abstinence.

St Barnabas' church opened in 1845 provided for the basic needs of the parish. It could not be regarded as beautiful nor could it be easily adorned in its present

28. St Barnabas Church c.1895

form. Although theoretically capable of holding 300 it must have been uncomfortably full when many fewer than this were present. Attendance at both morning
and afternoon services often exceeded 200 and was apparently rising.[1] By the
early 1860s the Vicar concluded that an extension was necessary to provide
accommodation for the rising population of the village, 'the Enclosure of the
Forest having led to the erection of many new houses,' he wrote in his appeal for
money for the extension.[2] A chancel was built in 1863 with a vestry on the north
side in place of the existing one on the south side of the nave. Beneath the sanctuary lie the bodies of Julia and Ellen Frances, infant daughters of George and Louisa
Appleby, who died in 1848 and 1849. The inscriptions were presumably placed
there when the chancel was built over their graves and only recently uncovered.
There is a a window at the west end of the nave dedicated to their memory.

A decade later the new Vicar, Walter Medlicott, embarked on the alterations and
extensions which created the parish church we know today. In 1872 the coke
stove that had stood in the centre of the nave, and must have emitted noxious
fumes, was removed and a hot water system with pipes carried round the church
at floor level was installed. 'The west gallery' wrote the Vicar, 'an unsightly and
inconvenient structure, appropriated to the school children will be removed and
the seats in the Nave will be re-spaced so as to enable worshippers to kneel'
removed.[3] In 1876 a south aisle was built to provide additional seats to replace
those lost from the gallery. A three light window was inserted in the west wall and
a new vestry was built at the north end of the new south aisle, replacing the one

opening off the chancel. The chancel was fitted with clergy stalls and choir pews, and an additional window was inserted in place of the door leading to the demolished vestry. The long projected tower, with a peal of eight bells, was built in 1877, largely paid for by the Vicar as a memorial to his wife who had died in January. The 'old church bell' which had hung in the turret on the west gable before the tower was built was presented to the Universities Mission to Central Africa for use by a native church in Usambana district.[4] Finally the pipe organ planned since 1874 was installed in 1877.

St Barnabas' now became the recipient of gifts from leading parishioners. The lych gate on the north side of the church was given in memory of Emma Goodlad, the first wife of Richard Goodlad of Hill Place, who died in 1867. A brass eagle lectern, corona and reading desk lamp were presented as a memorial to Elizabeth Shearer, the first wife of Bettesworth Pitt Shearer of Swanmore Park, who died in 1870.[5] The original wooden pulpit was replaced by an alabaster and marble pulpit designed by Alfred Waterhouse the architect of Swanmore House, given in 1880 by the Myers family in memory of Charles Myers. Parishioners gave the stained glass windows in the new chancel in memory of Edward Creek (1871, probably the work of Clayton and Bell).[6] Those at the west end were in memory of Richard Goodlad (1880). In 1896 no less than 156 parishioners contributed over £82 (about £3,500 in present day terms) towards a memorial to Leonora Goodlad which took the form of a stained glass window over the pew on the north side of the nave which she had occupied for so long and silver gilt chalice and paten, cruet and alms dish.[7]

The new Vicar introduced changes in worship to conform with innovations becoming common in the Church of England in response to the Tractarian movement. He at once discontinued the wearing of a black preaching gown for the sermon. The singers who had sat in the west gallery were replaced by a male choir which took its place in the chancel for the first time in December 1871. From Easter 1873 canticles and psalms were chanted and on Easter Sunday 1882 the choir was robed for the first time, in black cassocks and white surplices presented by Mrs Henrietta Myers.[8]

In earlier years Holy Communion was celebrated only four times a year – at Easter, Whitsun, Michaelmas and Christmas. By the early 1880s there was a celebration fortnightly – at 8am on the first Sunday in the month and at 12 noon after Mattins on the third Sunday. From 1888 there was a celebration weekly but not until 1904 was there a service of Holy Communion at 8am every Sunday. The first Confirmation in St Barnabas' was held on 29th March 1873 by Bishop Samuel Wilberforce, shortly before his sudden death.

Until 1868 parishes were responsible through a compulsory church rate for the upkeep of the fabric of the church. Clergy stipend was provided from the endowment of the parish chiefly tithe and glebe. In 1851 the tithe of Swanmore was valued at £65 with a further endowment worth £10. In addition the Rector of Droxford contributed £50 and the Rector of Bishop's Waltham £15 making a gross income of £140. In 1879 when the episcopal estates belonging to Bishop Sumner who had recently died were sold by the Ecclesiastical Commissioners they gave £66 per year intending to raise the net value of the living to £300. By comparison the gross income of the Rector of Bishop's Waltham in 1851 was £1316 and of the Rector of Droxford £1103. Such inequalities in clergy income were however taken for granted far into the twentieth century.[9]

No compulsory church rate was levied in Swanmore. The parish relied instead on voluntary contributions from the better off parishioners collected annually by the churchwardens. Not until 1874 did this prove inadequate. From Easter 1874 there was a collection on the third Sunday of each month to meet expenses: 'It was resolved to give up the old plan of a collection once a year round the parish and to have a collection for the expenses of the church at both services on the third Sunday of every month'[10] Once introduced the temptation to increase the number of collections was irresistible: in the early 1880's the collection became fortnightly and in 1889 weekly, on the first and third Sunday for the sick and the poor and on the remaining Sundays for church expenses.[11] Rising income made possible additional expenditure. Soon organ blower (1878), organist and choir (1881), sexton, and verger all received remuneration, if on a modest scale.[12]

By the late nineteenth century parish Sunday Schools were almost universal. In 1872 St Barnabas' Sunday School had 102 on roll with average attendance of 63; the master of the National School was its superintendent and there were nine teachers including the Vicar's wife. The church choir had an identity endorsed by its annual celebrations whether Christmas party or summer outing. In July 1882 the outing was to the Crystal Palace. They travelled to and from Botley station night and morning by horse-drawn van provided by Miss Goodlad. From Botley the journey by special train 'afforded much pleasure especially to one or two who had never been in a train before, and whose faces showed a considerable amount of alarm as we emerged from the first tunnel'. The outing appears to have had an ulterior motive since much time was spent at the Church of England Temperance Society athletic contests, watching a Cricket XI of total abstainers and attending a temperance rally with a choir of 4000 voices.[13]

A Working Men's Reading and Recreation Room had been opened in 1872 to provide 'recreation during the long winter evenings for those who are otherwise

30. (left) William H. Myers, MP, early 20th century **31.** (right) Frances Mary Myers (*nee* Prideaux-Brune) c.1890. Portrait at Prideaux Place, Cornwall reproduced by kind permission of Mr Peter Prideaux-Brune.

32. Butler, footmen and hall boy at Swanmore House 1897. The butler is Francis Sandall
aged 27, the hall boy Albert Horner, aged 15, son of Blanche and George Horner.
Photo Kath Reed

tempted to seek it at the Public House' though it is not known where this was. It
was open three nights a week from 6pm to 9pm for men over 16. The subscription
was one penny a night, paid on entry, or 6d monthly. The rules stipulated that
there was to be 'no swearing or bad language,' on pain of a penny fine for each
offence, 'no intoxicating liquor or smoking nor games for any stake', 'no member
to keep a newspaper more than ten minutes if bespoke by another member' and
'that the senior member of the committee present preserve order and enforce the
rules'. Payments made from members' subscriptions included provision of games
and newspapers as well as lighting and fuel and payment to 'boy for lighting lamps
and fires.'

During the winter of 1872-73 a parish library was set up consisting of 400 books
presented by Leonora Goodlad. It was administered by Walter Knight at the
National School and books could be borrowed on Mondays at Noon and on
Saturday evenings, at a cost of $1/2$ d per volume or an annual subscription of one
shilling and sixpence. Periodicals included *Sunday at Home, Leisure Hour, Our Own
Fireside* and *The Quiver* all providing suitably serious and sober reading for Sundays.

The church was the organiser of welfare for the village, at a time when state provision was minimal. The Clothing Club operated a deposit account for members, enhanced by donations from comfortably off parishioners, and arranged for members to buy from tradesmen at a discount. There were 51 adult and 43 child members. It also operated a scheme for the loan of blankets in the winter and arranged for them to be washed and mended on return. In 1883–84 104 blankets were loaned to 72 families on the first Saturday in November.[14]

The Coal Club operated on a similar principle. Sixty four depositors paid an annual subscription of four shillings each (£12.16.0) but received coal to the value of £24 thanks to the donations of well off parishioners. In 1873 special donations were collected for a distribution of coal in February because the winter had been particularly severe.

The church encouraged the Victorian virtue of thrift. There was a Penny Bank of which the Vicar was treasurer, 'intended for the Working Classes only, and no person can become a Depositor without the permission of the Vicar'. One penny was added to every shilling invested up to 50 shillings; after that two and a half per cent per year was paid. The money was invested in the government savings bank.

Medical treatment too was in part available through the parish. Tickets for Hampshire County Hospital could be obtained on application to the Vicar and for Shidfield [sic] Cottage Hospital from Admiral Rice and the Vicar. Child birth, almost invariably at home, needed specialist equipment and the Maternity Charity existed to provide it on loan.[15]

A further innovation of Walter Medlicott's early years was the *Parish Magazine* Viable once printing and paper had become cheaper and literacy general, magazines spread rapidly in both town and country parishes from the late 1870's.[16] Swanmore's first parish magazine was published in June 1882. The first number recorded the ringing of ' a joyous peal' at 5.30 in the morning on 24th May to mark the 63rd birthday of Queen Victoria. From the beginning the magazine provides information about church and village life invaluable for the local historian. Each year parishioners were encouraged to have copies bound and these often surface when lofts are turned out. Early numbers of the Swanmore magazine provide details of the fixtures of the Swanmore Village Cricket Club, the accounts of the Churchwardens and the school, the choir outing to Crystal Palace, a monthly calendar of village events as well as church services, baptisms, marriages and funerals.

The magazine contains a full account of the village's celebration of ' the Jubilee of her Majesty, Queen Victoria who on the 20th of that month [June 1887] happily completed 50 years of an honourable and prosperous reign'. There was a service in church at 10.30 am with the National Anthem and a special verse added referring to the Jubilee. Swanmore Park was the scene of the afternoon's festivities. 'The children were collected in some shady glades near the house, and were supplied with abundance of tea and cake'. Meanwhile 'nearly 500 adults sat down in a long marquee to a substantial meal of prime joints, pies, and hams, accompanied with plenty of bread and butter and cake'. Games and sideshows followed. In the evening 'many came from neighbouring villages ...attracted by the prospect of a good display of fireworks, supplied by Messrs Brock, of the Crystal Palace'. When it was dark enough a fire balloon 'rose majestically into the air, sailing away towards Botley with a brilliant magnesium light suspended from it'. Then for nearly an hour rockets, shells 'bursting into lovely coloured stars, or waterfalls of golden drops', Bengal lights, and Catherine wheels, kept the sky continually alive 'with all sorts of fiery messengers.'

Ten years later the Diamond Jubilee was marked by special services on 20th June 1897. Two days later, the actual anniversary of the Queen's accession in 1837, there was once more a Fete at Swanmore Park.. 'Tea was served for 250 children and 400 adults, 'selected from the poorer parishioners of Swanmore'. The Bishop's Waltham brass band ' marched through the village playing lively tunes' on its way to Swanmore Park. 'This is ' wrote the Vicar, ' a most memorable day, the like of which may never occur again in the history of our country'.[17]

When Queen Victoria died at Osborne House in the Isle of Wight on 22nd January 1901 an era was felt to have ended. On two successive Sundays services were devoted to the only topic on everybody's mind. On the Sunday following her death the Vicar preached in the morning on *The Queen's Death* and at night on *The Queen's Character*, whilst a week later Mattins was supplemented by the Burial Service and was a memorial service for the Queen. In the afternoon there was a memorial service for children with an address on, *Some lessons from the Queen's life* and at Evensong the Vicar preached on *Running the race well*.

When the Boer War ended in June 1902 a weeknight service was held at which *Te Deum* was sung and on the Sunday following sermons were on, *All events ordained by God*, and, *The blessing of peace*. The Coronation of Edward VII took place belatedly in 1st August 1902 and the Vicar marked the occasion with sermons on *The gift of wisdom* and *The Coronation*.[18]

The Mothers' Union was the inspiration of Mary Sumner, wife of the Revd George Sumner, Vicar of Old Alresford, and aunt by marriage of Walter Medlicott. She began meetings for 'cottage mothers and lady mothers' in her husband's parish in 1876.[19] The Swanmore branch of the Mothers' Union was founded in March 1887 with a visit from the founder herself.[20] In 1898 the branch had 60 members and associates.[21] There was also a Mothers' Meeting for mothers and young children held in the Church Room by Margaret Medlicott, the Vicar's daughter.

The Girls' Friendly Society was another national organisation with local roots. It was founded by Mrs Townsend of Shedfield Lodge and its first general meeting was held in Swanmore Vicarage in January 1875. The Swanmore branch for girls over 14 met weekly to encourage growth in the Christian life.

In most parishes in the late nineteenth century drink was rightly regarded as a major social evil. Great efforts were made to keep young people out of the pubs and to persuade them of the virtue of total abstinence. At Swanmore there was an active branch of the Church of England Temperance Society. In February 1883, at a meeting held in the school room, there were songs led by the Temperance Glee club followed by an address by the Rector of North Walsham, described as 'deeply interesting and thrilling'. He spoke for 'upwards of an hour', and concluded with 'an earnest appeal to all present to assist the great temperance movement which is now doing so much good in our land, by giving their names as members of the Swanmore branch'. The meeting resulted in twenty new members of the society. In the following month the Swanmore Temperance Society held a tea for 82 people followed by a magic lantern slide show. Early in April there was a public meeting to advocate Sunday closing of public houses and in August the society enjoyed a day's visit to Portchester castle.[22] The temperance message was communicated to youth through the weekly meetings of the Band of Hope, held for boys on Mondays at 6 pm and for girls on Wednesdays at 4 pm, dedicated to informing them of the evils of alcohol and encouraging total abstinence.

Every organisation had its special events summer and winter. The school treat was held in August usually at Swanmore House or the Vicarage when upwards of 170 children enjoyed 'tea and cakes, bread and honey on the lawn', played games and were each given a present by Mrs Myers. In 1900 the 205 children present included some from the Droxford Union workhouse. Before tea there was 'scrambling for sweets and coker-nuts' [sic] whilst the Bishop's Waltham Brass Band played. Each child received a a bun and before they dispersed there were fireworks and *God save the Queen* accompanied by the Brass Band.[23]

The choir summer outing was usually to Hillhead for paddling and sightseeing, always accompanied by the Vicar. For a year or two around 1900 there was a Mothers and Lads outing. In 1899 they 'inspected the new line of railway and saw some of the navvies at their work'. In 1900 two brake loads and a waggonette left Church Cottage for Portsmouth and Ryde returning late that night tired but happy. In August 1911 the hot summer took its toll. Choir, ringers and Sunday School teachers left Swanmore at 8.40 to catch the 11.10 boat from Portsmouth to Ryde but 'intense heat affected the horses to such an extent that they failed to catch it'.[24]

The Vicar held an annual Christmas party for church workers. In January 1905 choirmen, ringers, Sunday school teachers and parish helpers totalling 60 'sat down to an excellent supper'.[25]

There were summer fetes too. In October 1902 at a Coronation fete at Swanmore House the children received toys and a Coronation mug from Mrs Myers. In August 1906 a thousand people were estimated to have attended a fete at Hampton Hill House when Donigers Dell was illuminated with Chinese lanterns and fairy lights and the tennis court was arranged as a concert room with platform and seats for 400. There were self-help concerts with solos, duets, dialogues, humorous sketches and comic songs as well as lectures with the magic lantern.[26] Harvest Home was another annual celebration; the church was decorated for the services and there was a supper at Swanmore House hosted by William and Frances Myers.[27]

Christmas was marked by parties for all under the auspices of church and school, financed by the same group of benefactors. On New Year's day 1883 the choir and ringers enjoyed a beef and plum pudding supper at the Vicarage followed by hand bell ringing, music and dancing.[28] In 1891 the school gave ' a capital entertainment' of songs, recitations and musical drills carried out with great spirit'. A week later Leonora Goodlad gave her treat to the Sunday school when the annual prizes were presented to 33 children and Mr George Heyes gave 'a conjuring and ventriloquial entertainment'. That same evening, 150 people filled the schoolroom. Choir, Sunday school teachers, Temperance Society, Mothers' Union, Girls' Friendly Society, boys' and girls' Bible classes and missionary collectors all gathered 'to see and hear Mr Heyes' amazing performance.' The Christmas season was rounded off with the Vicar's party for all church workers at the Vicarage, when upwards of 60 people sat down to supper.[29]

Walter Medlicott's long reign as Vicar ended in November 1907. In 1896 the parish had marked his silver jubilee by presenting to him a pair of silver bowls, a silver loving cup and an illuminated address.[30] At the beginning of the new century he engaged a curate for whom he provided salary and accommodation, successively Charles Graham, 1901-4 and John Godefroy, 1904-8. On 3rd November 1907 he took services for the last time as Vicar, writing in *The Preacher's Book* ' The Revd W.E. Medlicott resigned the living this day, having been incumbent since June 1871'. He retired to Whingarth, Shedfield, where he became a manager of the school and took a keen interest in the Cottage Hospital and in village activities. He dedicated the Lych gate on the east side of the churchyard in April 1911 and in March 1919 conducted the funeral in Swanmore churchyard of Henrietta Myers, mother of William Myers. One of his last acts was to open the Parish Room which was added to the Recreation Room in 1922.[31]

In the nineteenth century clergy came and stayed; from the 1890s, for reasons not wholly understood, they came and went. In its first sixty years as a parish Swanmore had two Vicars. In the next 90 years it had ten, who stayed an average of nine years each. Only one, Revd Ronald Paterson, Vicar for 23 years from 1962-1985 had an impact on the village comparable with the nineteenth century incumbents. When John Henry Hodgson, Vicar from 1907-1917, came to Swanmore in his early fifties he had already held three livings in the Winchester diocese. Within two months of his arrival in December 1907 he had visited all the 280 homes in the parish. Like his predecessor the new Vicar was a widower but in 1911 he married Edith, daughter of Sir Frederick Fison. Almost the whole parish contributed to a wedding present which took the form of a bicycle. There was further rejoicing in February 1912 when the Vicar's wife gave birth to a son, Paul Francis.[32]

Church life continued its even tenor with the round of activities begun in the late Victorian years well established. It was still in these pre-war years at the centre of village life. Congregations were not perhaps what they had been in Victorian times. In May 1911 the Vicar arranged for a Church Army Mission fortnight, 'Earnestly hoping that it may be a means of bringing many back to regular attendance in God's house'.[33] It led to the introduction of a short-lived Men Only service, an indication that this was the constituency missing from church.

For those who did attend church the routine was familiar. The front seats on the north side of the nave were occupied by the gentry with William Myers in the front pew whence he could easily reach the lectern to read the lesson and Walter

33. Major Walter Augustus Daubeny 1838–1914. Photo Jack Hoar

Augustus Daubeny in the second pew. On the south side sat the house servants of the big houses. There was a choir of men and boys; the latter paid one penny for each attendance at service, practice or wedding. A new choir boy was by tradition 'bumped' – taken by the ears and his head knocked on a surplice peg in the vestry.[34]

Sunday was a day of rest for all: 'no one knocked a nail that day', wrote Jack Hoar. Children attended Sunday School at 10 a.m. in the schoolroom and then marched across the road and occupied the pews in the south aisle for Mattins, leaving before the sermon. In the afternoon there was a children's service with series of addresses on for example the Ten Commandments, the Creed or Old Testament characters.[35]

There were few changes to the fabric of the church in these years. The new churchyard, bought from the school was dedicated by the Suffragen Bishop of Guildford, George Sumner in 1893, and first used for burial in March 1900.[36] The Lych Gate on the east of the church was given by the Myers' family in memory of Evelyn Myers, sister of Squire Myers, who died at Sandleford Priory Newbury in

1909 at the age of 37. It was designed by C.F.Ponting a distinguished architect, influenced by the Arts and Crafts movement.

Confirmation classes were held each Spring separately for boys and girls, who were confirmed at about the age of 16.[37] Candidates were presented in turn at Shedfield, Droxford, Swanmore or Bishop's Waltham with perhaps as many as 150 candidates altogether. They subsequently received their first communion in their home parish. Ninety two candidates (41 boys and 51 girls) from St Barnabas' were confirmed between 1908 and 1914 twenty five in 1911 and twenty one in 1914. Following church on Good Friday children would walk to Droxford Downs via Mayhill equipped with sandwiches and bottles of water. Here they tobogganed on pieces of fence, played games and rested.[38]

In the first week of May a race meeting was held at Hambledon. Many race goers returned through Swanmore in horse-drawn vehicles. Children would hear the post horn of the four-in-hands and the trotting of the horses and line the route in the hope of catching coins thrown by the race goers.[39] The Hambledon Hunt met each yeaar at Hampton Hill and bread and cheese were served to the followers and beer to the grow ups.[40]

There is evidence in the Parish Magazine of the martial spirit which gripped the country in the early years of the century and was to surface dramatically on the outbreak of war in 1914. In 1907 at a smoking concert there was an appeal to young men to join the First Hampshire Volunteers. In the same year it was decided to start a Rifle Club. Headquarters were provided in a shed in New road equipped as a range with rifles and targets. The subscription list was headed by Claude Brinkman of Holywell and Walter Daubeny of Hill Place. Admiral Humpage of the Dell was its president and Walter Medlicott treasurer. Initially accommodation was spartan: the Magazine commented with heavy humour, 'The room is to be warmed with a stove as it is not intended to be a practice ground for shooting bears in the polar regions'! When in September 1912 a flag was presented to the school William Myers delivered an address on Patriotism and the National Anthem and Rule Britannia were sung. Finally in 1913 a recruiting campaign for the Hampshire Royal Garrison was held and 12 young men responded.[41]

There was one new welfare initiative in the years before the war – the Nursing Association. In 1909 the Vicar announced that a parish nurse would shortly start and invited contributions towards expenses. Nurse Chambers, Nurse Hall and Nurse Trowsdale followed each other with bewildering speed. They lived at Sunnyside, New Road and were supported by donations from the well to do and annual subscriptions from potential users at three levels according to financial circumstances. The scheme attracted 140 members but lasted only two years. Nurses changed rapidly and some perhaps lacked the skills or personal qualities needed to establish and keep the confidence of villagers.[42]

6

The Parish Council and pre-war village life

1891–1914

ETWEEN 1891 AND 1911 THE POPULATION OF SWANMORE INCREASED
faster than at any previous period, by about one third in twenty years
compared with 10% in the previous twenty years. It is not clear quite why.
After 1875 the death rate began to decline nationally but the infant mortality rate
remained high until the twentieth century. Visible evidence of Swanmore's rise in
population is to be found in the number of late Victorian and Edwardian houses
to be found in the centre of the village.

The Census of 1891 is the last one to be taken before Swanmore became a civil
parish and also the last one at present available for study. It is the first one in which
many of the road names of the village are to be found though we do not know
whether this is because the names were newly adopted or had not been used in
earlier censuses. Vicarage road (*sic*), Hampton Hill road (*sic*), Spring lane, Mayhill,
Cott street, Gravel hill are there but so are Broad road and Hatch road, names no
longer in use. The age distribution had changed little since 1871 and was close to
national norms. Over a third of the population (35.8%) were 14 or under. Rather
more than the national average were over 65 – about 8% compared with 4.8%
nationally. The median age of Swanmore's population was 23. Families were still
large – the average number of children per family nationally was still between 5
and 6 but this takes account of those who did not have children and women who
died before the end of their child bearing years. Public discussion of artificial
means of birth control was stimulated by the prosecution of Charles Bradlaugh
and Annie Besant in 1877 and spread slowly from town to country and from higher to lower social groups. There is no evidence in Swanmore of any differentiation
by social class: Charles and Jessie Gunner, one of the very few professional families
in Swanmore to have children, for example had nine children as did some agricultural labourers.[1]

Swanmore remained a farming village. There were fifteen farmers, one farm
manager and seven farmers' sons as well as seven market gardeners. Agricultural

labourers outnumbered all other categories of worker: there were over one hundred named in the Census including cow keepers and shepherds. Amongst craftsmen there were 11 carpenters and wheelwrights, 8 shoemakers, 6 gamekeepers, and 3 thatchers, a blacksmith, a sawyer, a woodman and two chimney sweeps. The professions were sparsely represented : Vicar, solicitor and banker, certificated teacher, and a Prudential insurance agent. William Myers is described as ' barrister at law and Justice of the Peace' though he did not practise as a barrister. There were 8 shop or inn keepers. Brickmakers and bricklayers' labourers accounted for 11 men and potters a further 2. Amongst the others were a licensed hawker, an Inspector of Nuisances, a retired coastguard and no less than 5 naval pensioners. There were a total of 16 male servants including – butler (3), footman (2), groom (3), coachman (7) and one hall boy.

More women now had a 'profession or occupation' but the range was still very limited. The largest category, not surprisingly, is 'servant'. Most girls on leaving school became living-in servants in one of the big houses or in that of a substantial farmer or stayed at home to help bring up the younger children. There were 31 domestic servants with a further 34 who claimed some form of specialism: cook (6), housekeeper (4), laundress (10), housemaid (3), charwoman (2) ladies maid (3), kitchen maid, scullery maid, laundry maid, nurse/general servant – one each. A few worked in shops, three were described as 'farmer's daughter'. A second category contained 15 women, described as dressmaker, needlewoman or seamstress.

The only professions represented had to do with education: certificated teacher, secretary to the headmaster, governess, 'monitoress' (sic) and pupil teacher.

Finally there were two categories of both men and women who had no profession or occupation. There were four men and no less than 18 women, mostly elderly, described as 'living on his / her own means'. These it appears were people who had saved for a rainy day, practising the Victorian virtue of thrift and supporting themselves in old age, often living with relations. A few years later they would be amongst those opposed to the introduction of the Old Age Pension by the pre-war Liberal government, because it discouraged the provident and rewarded the improvident who were happy to rely on the state. The second category was those living on poor relief, now very few, one man and three women.

With a growing population the amenities of the village were increasing. The post office is one example. The introduction of Penny Post in 1840 together with the spread of literacy later in the century enhanced the importance of postal services. Swanmore post office, like many others, was at mid-century no more than the place where letters were received and from which they were dispatched. The first post office appears to have been at *The Bricklayers Arms*. Hunt's *Directory of Hampshire* 1852 lists 'Dollar, John, Bricklayer's Arms, brickmaker and post office' whilst Kelly's *Directory* 1855 names Mary Dollar, the widow of John Dollar as 'receiver'. In 1859 the post office is 'at Mr Dollar's, Swanmore'. This was Peter Dollar who lived next door to *The Bricklayers Arms* at what is now Rose Cottage.

In 1867 Richard Carpenter who by then lived next door to *The Bricklayers Arms* is described as 'receiver' and in the Census of 1871 his widow Eliza is described as postmistress.[2] It appears then that from the late 1850s until the early 1870s the post office was at Rose Cottage.

Meanwhile the Woodman family had come to Swanmore in the early 1850s from Bishop's Waltham. Eliza Woodman, the daughter of Peter and Ann Dollar, set up as a grocer in a new house where Mason's Stores now stands, and lived there with her three small children Mary Ann, Elizabeth and Henry. (see Table G11) Her husband Henry was 'in the lunatic asylum', presumably the newly built Knowle Hospital, and died there in 1868. By 1875 her son Henry, now aged 25, is described as 'sub-postmaster' and the post office was run in conjunction with the grocer's shop. After Eliza's death in 1882 Henry took on the grocery and drapery business while his sister Mary Ann became sub-postmistress. Henry was it appears an entrepreneur. According to George Titheridge the store was enlarged in 1882, new stables were begun in February 1883 and in September 1891 'Finished Woodmans Shop'. Henry is described in *Kelly's Directory 1895* as 'grocer, draper, baker, and assistant overseer'. He was enumerator of the Censuses of 1881 and 1891 and in 1882 at the age of 32 became churchwarden alongside William Myers.

After the early death of Henry Woodman in 1898 his sister Mary Ann, who never married, ran the shop and the post office. Jack Hoar describes her as 'serving haberdashery and transacting postal business . . . with quick movements and an abrupt manner of speaking'. She advertised 'Good dairy butter, home made bread, Huntly and Palmer's biscuits and home cured pork and ham'.[3].

Meanwhile the scope of the post office expanded. The Census of 1891 is the first to list a Swanmore postman. He was Henry Houghton aged 30 born in Botley who lived in a house next door to Woodman's stores and post office. By 1895 you no longer had to go to Droxford or Bishop's Waltham to obtain or cash a postal or money order. The post office also offered the facilities of a Savings bank, insurance and annuity office. In 1902 after a request from the Parish Coucil the post office became also a telegraph office: 'Telegraph Wires Put up to Swan. (*sic*) Post Office' wrote George Titheridge on Christmas Eve 1902.[4] Letters could be posted at the post office but by 1895 also in a wall letter box at Swanmore Cottage and in a pillar box at Mislingford. All three were emptied twice daily.

No invention of the late nineteenth century had a greater impact on the lives of ordinary people in the countryside than the bicycle. It was far more significant than the motor car which came rather later but remained the preserve of the affluent until at least the 1920s. From the beginning the bicycle was within the means of all ages and social classes and both sexes. As writers of a history of technology state quaintly if politically incorrectly:' the bicycle which brought new life to the roads, romance to the young and emancipation to the weaker sex . . . did much to transform the leisure hours of civilised man'. The so called 'safety bicycle' (with geared up chain and drive to the rear wheel) became a commercial proposition from 1885. The free wheel and better steering were further improvements by the end of the century.[5]

We have already noted the effect of the bicycle in increasing the choice of partner for Swanmore's young men and women (see p. 27). It also created a new trade. George Linter (b.1833) had been a shoemaker in Swanmore since the 1850s and remained so. In 1895 his sons William (34) and Edward (15) described themselves as 'cycle agent' as well as continuing the family shoemaking business. For William the cycle business became his speciality. In 1899 he is described as 'Cycle maker and agent, all kinds of repairs executed on the premises. Swanmore Cycle depot'.[6]

The growth of bicycling was not without its problems. The new Droxford Rural District Council clearly had reservations. As early as 1896 it expressed the view that cyclists should hold a yearly licence costing 2/6 and that 'all cycle machines should have upon them clearly marked the owner's name'.[7] Bicycling soon began to have an impact on churchgoing. The church's reply was to organise Cyclists services and to invite the Sunday Cycle Club to stop for a specially organised afternoon service at one of the churches on their route and so maintain the habit of churchgoing.

Swanmore had five public houses: the licensees of *The Bricklayers Arms* and *The Rising Sun* are named in Kelly's Directory, the occupiers of the others are described as 'beer retailer' or 'beer house' though the pub they ran can be deduced from other evidence. David Hillyer had been at *The Blackboy Inn* since the 1860s and it appears to have been so named because he was also a chimney sweep. By 1895 his widow Caroline is described as 'beer retailer' and by 1899 it had a new landlord. William Boswell was the longstanding landlord of *The New Inn* (1870s – c 1912). William Parrington had recently taken on *The Rising Sun*. David Gough succeeded William Bevis at *The Bricklayers Arms* and Joshua Cooper kept *The Hunters Inn*.

Swanmore now supported a widening range of shops. In addition to Woodman's stores and post office, Phillis Rose, the widow of James Warren kept a grocery store in Bishop's Waltham road, assisted by her son James Warren (23) and daughters Phillis (21) and Barberina (13). Thomas Staite kept a shop at Hill for 30 years from the 1870s. James Tribbeck, landlord of *The White Swan* in Bishop's Waltham and married to Jane Pink a member of the Hambledon family, one of whom built St Barnabas church, moved in 1895 into Wassall Hall Farm in Bishop's Wood road and set up business as dairyman and baker.

Early in the twentieth century more shops were opened. George Stone opened a grocery store opposite the recreation ground in New road, run for many years by his son Fred and his wife Lottie where Jack Hoar recalled buying toys and sweets. By 1907 Frank Turton was running a baker's shop in Forest Farm road where by 1911 Alfred Marsh had a dairy. Opposite *The Bricklayers Arms* Irene Florence 'Polly' Fletcher had a milliner's shop where she also sold sweets. She had, according to Jack Hoar, a 'clipped manner of speech and flashing pince nez'. She advertised 'Alterations and trimmed millinery will receive careful attention.

34. Swanmore Post Office 1908

Costume buttons a speciality'.[8] Finally in 1910 Charles Martin's son, Bernard 'Bim', built and opened a sweet shop at the junction of New road and Chapel road. He was a well known village character, a gifted comedian who could be relied on to fill the school hall when he contributed items to village entertainments.[9]

As a result of the Local Government Act of 1894 the ancient parish of Droxford, over one thousand years old, was split into three civil parishes of more or less equal area though not equal population. – Droxford, Shedfield and Swanmore. Swanmore had petitioned the County Council earlier in 1894 to become a civil parish. It now became fully independent for the first time from the mother parish of Droxford, with its own parish council and separate representation on the new Droxford Rural District Council (RDC). Any parish with a population of over 300 was entitled to an elected council with between five and 15 members which would take over the powers previously exercised by the Vestry and the churchwardens, except those to do with the church and ecclesiastical charities. The Vicar contributed an article to the Parish Magazine explaining the new act.[10]

The meeting to elect the first Swanmore Parish Council was held in the village school on 4th December 1894 (the date specified in the Act). Reginald Freke Williams of Jervis Lodge took the chair. According to the Minutes about 55 people (predominantly men) were present though the Parish Magazine claimed an attendance of 90-100.[11] Only one woman is known to have been present – Mary Ann Woodman, the sister of Henry Woodman, a churchwarden, who jointly proposed

March 4th 1907.

The Parish Meeting was held in the
Schoolroom on Monday evening
March 4th 1907. Mr. W.H. Myers J.P. in the
chair.

Fifteen nomination papers were handed
to the Chairman; & the show of hands
resulted as follows.

Allen D.H. Baker. - - - - - 43 votes
Bedford A. Cycle Agent. - - - - 28 "
Clark. H. Primitive Methodist minister 32 "
Cresswell. S. J. Builder - - - - 8 "
Flowers. F. Certificated Teacher. - 34 "
Gladstone. M. Gentleman. - - 73 "
Houghton. H. Fly proprietor - - - 31 "
Martin. C. Certificated Teacher. 79 "
Medlicott W.E. Clerk in Holy Orders. 70 "
Molyneux E. Farm Bailiff - - 70 "
Pace. W. Cooper - - - - - 31 "
Silvester. J. Farmer - - - - 57 "
Staite. J.A.H.W. Insurance Agent. - 43 "
Tomlinson. G. Gentleman - - - 20 "
Westbrook H.R. Retired Farmer - 53 "

No poll being demanded the Chairman
declared Messrs Martin. Gladstone, Medlicott
Molyneux, Silvester, & Staite duly elected
/ as Messrs Allen & Staite had tied for the
seventh place, the Chairman gave his

35. Parish Council elections 1907, from *Parish Meeting Minute book*.

the Vicar for membership of the Council. The chairman was required to allow 15 minutes for nominations to be received. They were placed in alphabetical order and a vote was taken by show of hands. A further ten minutes had to elapse during which a poll could be demanded: it was, by George Horner who had come bottom of the twelve candidates and James Lipscombe who had come bottom but one. Horner subsequently withdrew his request; Lipscombe did not.

The meeting adjourned abruptly and with ill-humour without having elected a parish council and the parish was obliged to undergo the expense and inconvenience of a ballot. At the election which was held on Monday 17th December from Noon to 8pm, there were 12 candidates for the seven places and 121 out of the 189 qualified electors cast their votes.[12] When the result of the poll was declared all those elected at the parish meeting were elected to the parish council with the exception of George Apps who was replaced by Charles Martin who had not previously been nominated .

The first meeting of the newly elected council was held on 31st December 1894. Its first duty was the election of officers. The triumvirate of village patriarchs, squire, parson and schoolmaster, were elected respectively chairman, vice-chairman and treasurer and honorary clerk. The three Ms – Myers, Medlicott and Martin – were to dominate the Parish Council as they dominated every other aspect of village life. There is a certain irony about the outcome of the election since one of the objects of elective local government in the villages was to break the stranglehold of squire and parson on the countryside. Swanmore was not however unusual in voting to power those who had previously held it as of right. The other members of the first council were Francis Flowers, described as 'dealer', Charles Ricketts, market gardener, James Warren butcher and farmer and Thomas Staite, at 28 the youngest member of the council. An insurance agent and a Methodist, born at Fratton and in 1891 lodging with William and Ada Horner he was an unusual candidate in a number of ways.[13] Though eligible for membership from the beginning it was not until 1925 that a woman was elected to the Swanmore Parish Council.(see below p. 112)

Until 1899 elections were held annually in March each year, from 1901 to 1913 and again from 1919 to 1937 triennially, usually by show of hands at the annual meeting, but occasionally a ballot was demanded. This was resented since it involved the expense of hiring a polling station and paying a returning officer. After the first election William Myers did not stand for the council but was each year elected chairman from outside as was permissible. In 1904 two members had the temerity to propose that the council should elect a chairman from within the council. Their rebellion was defeated by 5 votes to 2 and Myers continued to be re-elected annually until in 1930 he stood down at the age of 75 after serving as chairman for 36 years.[14]

Attendance at the annual parish meeting varied from about 25 (1901) to over 100 (1913) though in years when there was no election interest faltered. In 1902 attendance was 'small' and in 1905 'very poor'. The Parish Council met quarterly and like most such bodies did much of its work through committees. The earliest to be set up were Allotments and Footpaths and Recreation Ground committees and by 1904 Finance and Spring Wells committees had been added. The Council elected annually two or three Overseers of the Poor with an Assistant Overseer who was paid and who collected the Poor Rate (Henry Woodman until his death in 1898, then James Warren).[15] Additional parish meetings were called from time to time. In April 1902 and again in April 1911 consideration was given to celebrations to mark the coronations of Edward VII and George V. On the latter occasion a committee of 17 was set up including women, mostly wives or relations of Council members. In February 1903 a parish meeting was called to consider improvements to the recreation ground and agreed to the erection of 'a building for the cricketers and footballers and others'.

In March 1895 the Council requested a polling station for Swanmore: hitherto electors had been obliged to register their vote at Bishop's Waltham.[16] Although there had for a long time been a post office at Swanmore, there was no telegraph office until the council wrote to the Post Master General requesting one. By 1900 the Meon Valley railway was under construction and the parishes of Shedfield, Soberton and Swanmore jointly petitioned the railway company to provide a halt at Mislingford to serve the three parishes. The request was unsuccessful and so was a later one made in the early 1920s.[17]

Complaints about the state of the parish roads appear with monotonous regularity. The problem was insoluble until properly surfaced roads began to appear in the parish just before the First World War. There were no footpaths, no road drains or kerb stones and the surface consisted of layers of stones embedded with the newly introduced steam roller. Roads were often dusty in summer and water-logged in winter. Until the arrival of the motor car in about 1904 roads were the preserve of farm carts, horse drawn traps, bicycles and pedestrians.

As early as 1895 the Council expressed concern about 'the state of the road leading from upper Swanmore to lower Swanmore by the Vicarage' and 'the New road across the Chase, where the ditch in many places wants thoroughly cleaning out'.[18] They asked at the same time for 'ashes, sand, gravel or other suitable matter [to be] scattered over the steep parts of the road [at Swanmore hill] during slippery weather.' In January 1900 the council was of the opinion that 'the state of the roads in the Parish required the immediate attention of the road surveyor. They wish especially to complain of the long interval elapsing between the laying of the stones and the arrival of the steam roller'.[19] In 1903 the council drew the attention of the RDC 'to the utterly impassable state of the Cott Street Road' and 'to the generally unsatisfactory state of the roads especially Forest Road, and the road to Mislingford.'. Overflowing ditches and water courses as well as overhanging and overgrown hedges were frequent causes of complaint. In the same year the clerk 'was instructed to write to the RDC about the overflow of the pond near *The Bricklayers Arms* and to call attention to the want of rolling in the stones at Cot Streeet, Forest Road and the bottom of Gravel Hill'[20]

The advent first of the bicycle in the 1880s, and then of the motor car at the turn of the century, brought roads into a prominence they had not enjoyed since the end of the coaching era half a century earlier. The first motor car we know of in Swanmore was an attrraction at the Swanmore Show held on 24th July 1901. It inspired a humorous piece in the September edition of the Parish magazine.

Walk hup, walk hup, ladies and genelmen, and see the wonderful new Show. The carridge what goes wi'out a hoss. P'raps you've seen afore now, a hoss what goes wi'out a carridge, but this 'ere carridge w'at goes wi'out a hoss! Walk hup, walk hup, and look for yourselves, ladies and gentlemen, here's a arf-a-crownto anyone who can find his 'ead or 'is tail, 'is heels or 'is 'ocks! The trewth is the only part of 'im we keep is 'is hinside, and that's wery much out of the common -its for all the world like the 'inside of a watch, only you mustn't go for to think it would be a werry convenient size to carry in your weskit pocket. This 'ere hoss is werry heconomical, 'e don't want no corn, nor wittels, nor sich like -yhou've only got to pour three penn'orth of oil into him, and set fire to it with a leucifer, and in 'arf a crack he'll be off at a busting pace all over the world! Walk hup, walk hup, ladies and gentlmen, trial trip just a going to commence! Only two-pence, worth five times the money. Oh, don't be afraid, 'e don't kick or bite, 'es warranted agin all haccidents. Should hany hunfornutate littl ewent occur, afive -pun note will be distributed among the widows an' orphans, and all arms an' legs will be allowed for at a waluation. Now's your chance, ladies and gentlmen, step up and take your seats for the Trial Trip. I'm just a going to strike the leucifer!

The first motor cars in Swanmore were those of Murray Gladstone who owned a Humber and William Myers who bought a Daimler but soon possessed more than one motor. He exchanged coachman for chauffeur and coachhouse for garage about 1904. In October 1906 George Titheridge thought it noteworthy when a wedding party 'rode to church by motor'.[21] For the bulk of ordinary people bicycles remained the universal means of transport. Better roads were needed. In 1897 the RDC decided on further trials before buying a steam roller and thought it ought to have ' a sleeping van' for the driver. They were not in favour of 'margins' (kerbstones) which they regarded as dangerous to 'vehicular traffic' and asked the County Council to reconsider the need for them.[22]

Motor cars passing through the village were a rarity until well into the new century. The Parish Council had its attention drawn to the Motor Car Act of 1903 and traffic warning signs were placed at the junction of Lower Chase Road, Hampton Hill and Swanmore Road and at the Hill cross roads.[23] By 1910 there was further concern about traffic at the Hill cross roads and the council asked for a finger post at Hill Pound.[24] In 1913 another one was placed at Gravel Hill whilst a school warning sign was erected by the Hampshire Automobile Club. Gradually the roads were surfaced – covered with tarred flints overlaid with gravel and rolled in by a hissing steamroller. In 1910 George Titheridge records ' Stoned the Road in front of our house after forty years', whilst in 1912 he noted 'Laying Granit with Tar' and in June 1913 'Finished Tarring Swanmore Hill'.[25]

Maintenance of footpaths was a further responsibility of the Parish Council. They were walked regularly not as now by parishioners seeking recreation but of necessity – by men on their way to work, women shopping and children on their way to school. The path appearing most frequently on the council's agenda was the one from Hill Pound to Ledville's corner via New road, following the watercourse called the Lakes. The council regularly urged those whose property it skirted to keep the watercourse free from obstruction as they were obliged to do under the Enclosure Award of 1855. The footpath opposite the church was a route for those living in upper Swanmore and was frequently obstructed. There was controversy too over the path through the grounds of Holywell House to the river Meon and Soberton Mill.

The administration of allotments at Gravel Hill was handed over by the Charity Commissioners in 1895 to the new parish council. The Allotments Committee was responsible for the allocation of allotments – usually in 1/4 acre plots at the rate of 30 shillings per acre per year – for collecting the rent and for taking action when allotments were neglected, by terminating the lease and reletting the overgrown plot at a temporarily reduced rent. If all else failed defaulters were 'county courted' (sic). In 1905 the clerk was reimbursed 2 shillings for hiring a trap to attend court at Winchester in a case of obdurate non-payment.[26]

Responsibility for the recreation ground was also handed over by the Charity Commissioners to the Parish Council. The Commissioners had made a complex scheme for managing the recreation ground in 1891. They set up a body of 16 managers who were to meet at least twice a year and were to include the churchwardens and overseers of the poor for the parish of Droxford who were to be known as official managers. The non-official managers were to be appointed for seven years by the Vestry of the ecclesiastical parish of Swanmore It is perhaps as well that such a cumbrous body did not exist for long. Under the scheme the only game specifically permitted on the recreation ground was cricket and the managers had the right to prohibit all other sports. The rules also excluded from the ground 'persons of known profligate character, intoxicated persons and beggars'.[27]

The recreation ground has throughout its history given rise to endless petty problems. Lost keys, blocked toilets, broken locks, swearing and rowdyism (particularly on Sundays), screws missing from seats, all caused conflict over the years. In the early years of the century there were two cricket clubs each using the recreation ground: Swanmore Cricket Club captained by John Godefroy, Walter Medlicott's curate, and the Workmans' Cricket Club (sic). The first proposal to erect a pavilion made in 1897 was rejected.[28] One was provided in 1903 on the initiative and at the expense of Catherine and Florence Gladstone of Hampton Hill House.

36. The recreation ground c.1910

In 1907 smoke and fumes from Churchers' brickyard were regarded as a danger and the Council wrote to William Churcher.[29] Edwardian boys were no more likely than their Elizabethan successors to behave in an exemplary fashion. In 1903 the clerk was instructed to write to Aubrey Emery, then aged 19, warning him about his behaviour in the future and at the same time the Council decided to print and circulate notices forbidding cricket, football and other games on the recreation ground on Sundays.[30]

Like many rural communities Swanmore had no piped water until after the First World War. Almost every house had its own well or pump. In addition there were small ponds at the roadside and in fields to meet the needs of cattle while spring wells provided public sources of drinking water. The three parish wells (in Lower Chase Road, Spring Lane and Forest Road) needed constant vigilance if they were to be kept clean and safe. After a site meeting in January 1899, for example, it was agreed to raise the well in Spring Lane, cement the stone curb and place a lid on it at a cost of £5. In October 1905 a new galvanised lid and fixed bucket were supplied. Five years later the Council decided to place a pump on both wells and to re-gravel the surrounds.[31]

In 1903 the Gosport Water Company built a reservoir on Gravel Hill and was keen to supply piped water to nearby parishes.[32] At first Swanmore residents seemed enthusiastic. In July 1908 the Parish Council received a petition asking for

piped water .The company was requested to prepare a scheme to supply all acces-
sible parts of the parish including Hampton Hill and the Vicarage and the Assistant
Overseer of the Poor was asked to canvas owners of property along the route. In
March 1909 James Warren presented his report on what was now referred to as
'the water question'.[33] The Secretary of the Water Company met the Council in
May 1910. Doubts about cost began to surface and opponents adopted delaying
tactics: the Water Company was asked if it would bear the cost of bringing the
water to the parish boundary, the opinion of Dr Edgar Pern, the Medical Officer
of Health was sought on the purity of the existing wells and the views of the
RDC were canvassed![34]

By the end of 1910 the Council decided 'to get the price of a small scheme' and
adopted it; in effect to provide piped water to lower Swanmore but not to upper
Swanmore where houses were scattered and unit costs therefore higher.[35] The
scheme was put to a Parish Meeting called for the purpose in March 1911 but
rejected by 56 votes to 29. Three years after the original petition, controversy over
'the water question' still divided the village. The Council asked Edwin Molyneux
and Thomas Staite to undertake a further canvas of 97 houses on the proposed
route: 22 householders said yes, 42 said no and 33 did not reply. Staite expressed his
disappointment 'that the very people who had agitated for the water had now
failed to support it and he should not bring the matter forward again'.[36] It was not
until July 1921, almost ten years later that 'the water question' appeared again on
Council business.[37]

Piped water was not the only amenity which many villages lacked at the beginning of the twentieth century. When 'Dink' Harvey moved with his parents from
Portsmouth to Swanmore in 1912 'it seemed like going back to medieval times'[38].
There was no gas, electricity, street lighting or mains sewerage, no pavements,
trams or trains. In the towns the roads were surfaced with wood or granite blocks
or cobblestones; in the country there was no durable surface at all. In winter open
ditches often overflowed, in summer the traveller, whether walking, cycling or
driving a pony and trap raised clouds of dust. The countryside was dependent on
wells, oil lamps and privies and for heating and cooking the open range. There was
as yet no radio and no telephone. News was passed by word of mouth. That was
how Jack Hoar heard of the death of Edward VII and of the sinking of the *Titanic*.
It was as he was returning from a Sunday evening walk with his parents on 4th
August 1914 that they were told by a passer-by that war had been declared on
Germany.[39]. Yet despite narrow horizons and limited opportunities, the period
before the war was looked upon, by those who lived through it, though from a
later vantage point, as a golden era savoured with poignant nostalgia.

'Almost the scarcest commodity in Swanmore' wrote Jack Hoar, reminiscing
about his pre-war childhood in the village, 'was money'. The families of farmers or
those with their own businesses were better off than the majority who worked on

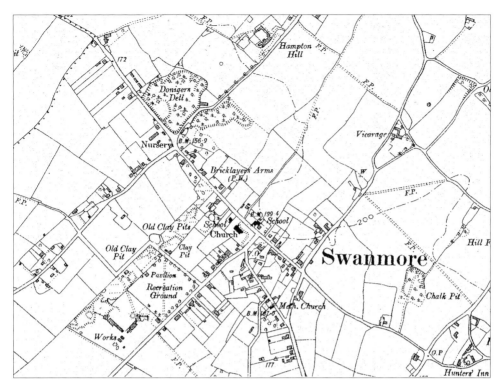

37. Ordnance Survey map 6″ series 1910

the estates or as farm labourers. Some children paid weekly to a 'penny bank' run at school. During school holidays in particular children could keep themselves in pocket money by casual employment: leading horses at haymaking at 1/- per day or picking strawberries at 1d a basket which took three quarters of an hour to fill. The money earned would be spent on sweets (11 raspberry drops for a farthing) at Woodman's stores, Lottie Stone's, 'Bim's' or 'Polly' Fletcher's, or toys – tops, marbles, masks, fireworks, spring guns or pocket torches – whilst cigarette cards could be cadged from smokers.

Swedes and turnips could provide a banquet for a hungry child – you bit off and spat out the dirt and skin to reach the sweet bit near the end and then happily munched the remainder. Children above the age of five wore boots, buttoned for girls, laced for boys whilst mothers made clothes for both sexes. Clothes were passed down from elder to younger patched and repaired repeatedly. It was by no means unknown for children to be kept away from school because they had no boots.[40]

Almost everybody who lived in the village worked there too; on farms, smallholdings and shops or as village craftsmen or at Shorts or Churcher's brickyards. The big estates, Swanmore Park and Hill Place employed gamekeepers, carpenters

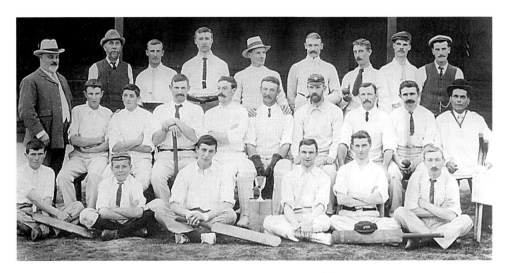

38. Swanmore Cricket Club, Winners of the Bishop's Waltham & District League 1907
*C. Martin W. Churcher G. Savage F. Sandall J. Colmer J. Hewett E. Downs F. Stone F. Merritt
F. Kerton W. Ainslie L. Pragnell A. Watson J.E. Warren Revd J. Godefroy W.J. Horner W. Stroud G. Titheridge
H. Ainslie J.E. Warren jnr W. Crook B.J. Martin A. Carpenter W. Allen*

39. Swanmore Football Club. Winners of the Meon Valley league and
the Gladstone cup 1907-1908
*W. Palmer B. Martin F. Kerton J. Terry (Captain) A. Watson H. Thorne B. Woods W. Ashby
W. Allen F. Lilleywhite W. Terry F. Thorne W. Ainslie (Vice-captain) A. Carpenter A. Flowers
H. Tilling J. Hazzard A. White F. Knight W. Holford*

and estate workers, often providing tied cottages for their employees at subsidised rent, acquiring thereby a hold over them which meshed with the deference due to those of higher rank in society. Jack Hoar's father came to Swanmore from Beauworth as carpenter to Major Walter Augustus Daubeny of Hill Place. He earned 21/- per week out of which he paid 2/- rent for the house opposite the church built for the estate in 1899, of which he was the first occupant[41]

William Horner was builder, wheelwright and undertaker and advertised ' good seasoned timber kept in stock'. When there was a death in the village the church bell would sound the knell – six times for a man, five for a woman and three times for a child. There was no chapel of rest so the coffin would be made the same day and the body would lie in it in a darkened room in the house until the funeral. There was no hearse: the coffin would be carried or wheeled to church, children often acting as bearers, and it would remain on the bier during the funeral service. The village would pay its respects by drawn curtains on the day of the funeral.[42]

A variety of dairymen with anything between two and ten cows delivered milk round the village ladling it into jugs from a metal measure which hung over the churn. Those farmers with surplus milk would take it daily to the stations at Bishop's Waltham or Droxford for sale in the towns. The village was visited by a variety of peddlers and hucksters, offering goods and services not normally available in the village – sharpening scissors and shears, selling saucepans, kettles, clothes pegs and baskets.[43]

There was no doctor in Swanmore but for a small commission medicines would be brought by the postman from the doctor in Droxford and could be collected from the Post Office. At 7.20 each night the horse-drawn mail van passed through the village collecting the post on its way to Droxford station. From 1896 Swanmore had its own policemen living in the police house at the corner of Vicarage Lane and Swanmore Road but changed frequently to prevent him becoming too identified with the village and its characters. The first one PC Newsam stayed only six months before being replaced by PC Harefield.[44]

Children may have had little money but there was no shortage of home made amusements. Fishing for minnows or sticklebacks in Broad Pond was popular. Birds, bees, butterflies and wild flowers flourished in an abundance which is now scarcely believable and gave to the countryside, scents, sights and sounds which are acutely evocative to anybody who experienced them. Birds nesting was a universal hobby for boys, not frowned on at a time when every ten yards of hedgerow contained a nest. Tops, marbles, hoops, hop scotch and kite flying succeeded each other in popularity in unpredictable rotation.

The years before the war brought new activities to add to those already available. Baden Powell held his first Boy Scout camp on Brownsea Island in 1907 but Scouting did not reach Swanmore until 1911 when a troop was started by Murray Gladstone of Hampton Hill House, a somewhat mature recruit, assisted by Ernest Targett, master at the village school and Geoffrey Mack who lived at Donigers

40. Scouts at Peak Farm camp 1913
Photo Jack Hoar

(both killed in the first World War). Before long there was a troop of 30 boys in four patrols, with a bugle band, later augmented with fifes and piccolos taught by the Bishop's Waltham bandmaster, Edgar Evans. Activities included tracking and night operations in Donigers Dell which was owned by Murray Gladstone as well as weekend and summer camps at Peak Farm and Bursledon. [45] A St John's Ambulance brigade unit was started using a hut next to the school. There was a Lads' club too meeting on one night a week.

The village abounded in characters who often lived up to the caricature created for them. Some were shopkeepers, school teachers or village craftsmen; others were village aristocrats. Some had nicknames, 'Primmer' Pink, 'Polly Hopscotch'(Miss Fletcher), 'Tubby' Gladstone, 'Dustman' Titheridge, 'Bim' Martin, the origin of which was often obscure. Alf Gibson was deformed from birth and frequently sat in his chair at the bottom of Swanmore Hill with his tiny legs folded underneath him. He had long slender hands and a deep resonant voice. [46]

One village character of the early years of the century gained his fame in village folklore by longevity, another added to his, posthumously, through the record of local and national events which he kept for over sixty years whilst a third belonged to the largest family recorded in Swanmore's history – he was one of 18 children.

On the north side of the church is a gravestone erected by public subscription by the people of Swanmore to the memory of William Horne who died on 15th April 1907, allegedly a fortnight before his 104th birthday. The memorial is to commemorate somebody who was believed to be Swanmore's only centenarian. "Granfer' Horne, as he was known, claimed to have been born in Fareham on 30th April 1803 and to have remembered when news arrived of the victory of Waterloo. He was a farm labourer who earned 10/- a week and with his wife Mary had twelve children, three of whom died in infancy. After Mary Horne died in November 1896 he lived at Myrtle cottage, Hill Pound with his daughter Mrs Stratton.[47] He was a pipe smoker who took a keen interest in events, reading a newspaper to within a year of his death. It seems unlikely however that he was a centenarian. He was born well before the registration of births, marriages and deaths was introduced in 1837. When the first census in which names and ages were recorded was taken in 1841 his age was entered as 28 and that of his wife as 26. Between the censuses of 1871 and 1881 however his age advanced from 57 to 75 and by 1891 he was apparently 85 whilst his wife Mary was 76. Even if his age in

41. William Horne, Swanmore Centenarian, 1803–1907 (?), 42.Memorial to William and Mary Horne, in Swanmore churchyard, erected by public subscription. Photo Kate Watkins

1891 was entered correctly he would have been born in 1806 not 1803 as he claimed. It seems likely that he registered his age correctly in 1841 and that he was born in 1813 and died at the age of 94.[48]

George Titheridge was a member of a family whose name appears at least seventy times in the Swanmore church registers before the end of the nineteenth century. He was the youngest of the eight children of Richard and Maryann Titheridge and was born in April 1853. He was a cripple from birth, known by all as 'Stumps' Titheridge, never able to work and living on poor relief. 'My Parish Pay Raised to 6/- Per week', he wrote in September 1913. He nonetheless spent as active a life as his disability allowed. As an adult he lived in a small cottage at the bottom of Hampton Hill opposite Doniger's Dell, now demolished. 'A New Brick Floor Put down in our Kitchen' he records in September 1873.

Gwen Woods whose husband was George's nephew, recalls that he loved having visitors and kept the door of his cottage always open. 'You went down two steps from the door' she writes 'and just inside was a parrot whose favourite remark was

43. George ('Stumps') Titheridge, Swanmore diarist, 1853–1937

1885 Jan	24	Dustmans Horse Droped dead
	—	Explosion in London at the Towers
		& House of Commons
Mon	26	Khartoum Taken & Gordon Killed
Sat	31	Tom Tier Died Waltham Cross
Feb Mon	2	Old James Stonage Died Bp Waltham
Sat	14	Wm Bachelor Burried Swan
Mon	23	Lee Hung 3 Times Then Respited
Sat	28	The Brick Kilns Pulled down
Mar Thurs	12	Mr Myers set at Droxford Bench The first Time
	—	The Old Tilehouse & stable Pulled
	—	Down in The Old Brickyard
Sund	22	A Great Snow Storm
Tues	24	A Pigeon Shooting Match Black Horse
Sat	28	The University Boat Race
April Sat	4	Mrs Godchilds Died
Sun	5	Geo Titheridges Birth day. Aged 32 yrs
Tues	14	Mrs Myers Birthday age 18 yrs
	—	Ford Blackman & Apps Released from Prison
Thur	23	Soberton Races Held &
		Confirmation Held, Swanmore
Wed	29	Fossetts Circus Came to Bp Waltham
May Mond	4	G. Apps Bought a Piece of Land &
Tued	—	Put up a New House
Wed	6	Dick Downs Died in Hospital
	—	Winter found Drowned in Cell
		The Landlord of the Crickiters

44. A page from the diary of George Titheridge 1885 recording his 32nd birthday

Give us a grape'. George was a great friend of the Revd Edgar Mack, a near neighbour at Donigers, who gave him a Bible which he had read many times. George was short and dark, with intense blue eyes and bushy eyebrows. He wore a peasant smock, by then long outmoded, perhaps to conceal his deformity, rocked along on his crutches and smoked a briar pipe. He was scorer for the cricket club and took a keen interest in all aspects of village life.[49]

His claim to fame is the diary he kept. It is a modest document whose interest for Swanmorians is out of all proportion to its length or eloquence. It consists of a single quarto hard-backed exercise book. The first entry is dated April 1860, the second January 1869 and the first page covers events to 1878, not all in chronological order. There are no entries between March 1880 and January 1881. The consistency of lay-out and handwriting suggests that he may have written up later entries from a rough draft. The last entry is for February 1937 shortly before he died at the age of 84. Most entries consist of a single line recording an event, personal, family, local or national which happens to have caught the diarist's eye, with an occasional brief comment. It is nonetheless a fascinating and invaluable document for anybody interested in the history of the village. It is a means of establishing or confirming the dates of events, significant in the life of an individual or the village. More important it provides the perspective of an ordinary villager but an alert observer of events. It is not easy to determine the origin of his information but village gossip and newspapers must have been his chief sources.

George Titheridge shows an acute awareness of national and international events. He records the death of Lord Beaconsfield (1881) and the final resignation of William Gladstone (1893), the opening of the Forth railway bridge, the death of W.G.Grace as well as that of the Duke of Clarence (14th January 1892 'Prince Albert Victor of Wales Died'), the election of Lady Astor to the House of Commons and the appearance of the first ten shilling note (October 1919). The 14th April 1912 was a date he could not overlook:'The Loss of the Biggest Liner in the World the Titanic with 1635 lives. The Biggest Disaster Known'.

Births, marriages and deaths in the village and beyond are meticulously recorded, including suicides and murders. Landmarks in village history, for example the first football match played on the recreation ground at Swanmore on 27th December 1902. (Hitherto the recreation ground had been reserved for cricket.) He recorded events in the law courts both national and local noting the execution of prominent criminals as well as justice meted out to local malefactors. In February 1885 'Lee Hung 3 Times Then respited'. On 16 October 1902 he records '3 poachers sentenced to 3 months, 6 months and one month Respectfully [sic] for knocking J.Weeks keeper about at Corhampton'.

He was a keen observer of the weather. The winter of 1880-81 was particularly severe; on 18th January there was 'A Fearful Snow Storm. Drifts 15 feet', 'Second addition on the 20th', 'Roads Cleared from Droxford to Bishop's Waltham' (22nd January). On 29th April 1882 'A Great Hurrican [sic] of Wind and Rain'. On 26th

45. Swanmore Hill early twentieth century

December 1886 'A Fearful storm Raged over England. Snow and Rain doing a great deal of Damage. Botley Bridge washed away'. The winter of 1890-91 was also severe and we can follow its progress from the diary. The first fall of snow was on 12th December, on 18th December another heavy fall of snow and 'Waltham Pond froze'. On 30th December ' a very sharp Frost. Froze in our Teapot'. On 12th January 'Tea on Alresford pond', whilst a week later ' Waltham Pond still froze over'. After this there was a general thaw but winter was not yet over. On Monday 9th March 'A Heavy fall of snow, Lasting to Wednesday Blocking the Roads'. The winter of 1894-95 also made the record books: 12th January ' A fearful snow storm blocking the roads', 6th February '28 degrees of frost', 10th February ' Still Frost and Snow very sharp', 2nd March ' Frost still continues a Heavy Fall of Snow', 5th March ' A General Thaw'. There are similar entries for later years in the 90s confirming that the weather during this decade was particularly harsh.

Not all weather was bad: the autumn of 1897 was 'Finest Autumn Known for Years'. In 1898 he noted 'wonderful hay and straw crops'; by early September he reported 'water very short' and by 18th September 'our well dry, never known before'. 1882 was 'a wonderful nut year' and 1907 ' a wonderful plum year'. There are full references to the weather in the hot, dry summer of 1911 when the village wells dried up and water had to be carted from Mislingford. For Wickham Fair on

20th May it was hot and dry. On 12th June it was still 'Hot and Dry'. 'Fine and hot throughout July', whilst Wednesday 9th August was 'The Hottest Day. Registered 97 degrees'. By 13th September 'Springs very Low'. Not until 21st October did he record 'A Nice Rain'.

To the Horner family falls the distinction of running through the whole length of Swanmore's history as a separate parish as well as the record for family size and remarkable evidence of longevity in successive generations. The Swanmore Census of 2001 is the first since 1841 which does not include the name Horner. Len Horner the last representative of the male line to live in the village died in June 1994 at the age of 97, though his niece Kath Reed still lives in Broad lane.

The Hampshire Directory of 1792 includes the name of Richard Horner who was a maltster. It is however the Census of 1841 together with the will of James Horner dated 1838 which provide details of the family in the early Victorian years. James Horner died in 1838 and his second wife Ann in 1840. James had ten children by his first wife and one by his second wife. The Census of 1841 lists four boys – Henry (19), Charles (17), George (14) and Ann's son William (6). They lived with their elder sister Maria (26) and her husband William Cresswell (31), a brick layer and business partner of Peter Dollar. James Horner left his house, where the Meon Valley Printers in Church road now is, in trust to Peter Dollar

46. New road early twentieth century

47. The Bricklayers Arms before 1920

for his sons. The Cresswells had their own family of four children aged between six years and six months.

Of the four boys it was Charles born in 1823 who was Len Horner's grandfather. Charles was married in 1847 to Mary Ann Dowse and they had ten children before she died in 1870. By this time Charles had become blind and his daughters Eliza (24 in 1871) and later Alice (19 in 1881) kept house for him. Some time before 1891 he remarried, Phoebe, who however died in 1900. Len had keen memories of his grandfather, a wheelwright and carpenter, and of the cottage he built for himself. He recalled the open range over which he cooked, the hob and the tap from which he obtained hot water, the well in the garden, and the paraffin lamp and the candles needed for lighting. In old age he was looked after by the couple to whom he let the cottage next door which he had also built. His daughter Kate married Edward Ainslie and settled in the village as did his four sons, George who was Len's father born 1854, Henry born in 1856, William James in 1864 and Albert in 1866. Charles Horner died in his own cottage at the age of 84 in 1908.

Charles Horner's children were prominent citizens of Swanmore, active in village life and members of the last generation of country craftsmen. William 'Uncle Bill' carried on his father's business, was a member of the church choir for 50 years retiring in 1925, and churchwarden from 1922 to 1935. He marrried Ada Scammell in June 1888, living at Northdene, where they brought up three daughters and a son. They celebrated their golden wedding in 1938 and William died at the age of 93 in 1951.

George Horner, the eldest son of Charles was Len's father. He was a carpenter working on a number of the large estates in the Meon valley, amongst them Swanmore Park, Hill Place, Corhampton House and Rookesbury Park, all of which he reached by bicycle. He married a Portsmouth girl, Blanche Humby in 1876 and over the next 25 years they had 18 children of whom two girls, died in infancy. Childbirth was then a hazardous undertaking, yet for several years Blanche Horner bore a child each year to add to the growing family. The record is so remarkable that it should be recorded. Horner children were born in October 1876, September 1878, September 1880, June 1882, September 1883, July 1884, February 1886, March 1887, August 1888, August 1889, October 1890, November 1891, January 1893, August 1895, November 1896, December 1897 and May 1901. (I can only find 17 entries in the Register of Baptisms: it seems likely that the 18th was still born and not baptised) It should also be recorded that Blanche Horner lived to be 89!

Len was the 15th child and was born in November 1896 at Ada Cottage, where Spring Vale now stands, though the family moved to Mislingford shortly afterwards. In old age he used to like to recall that he was a frail baby who had been baptised privately at home in case he did not live long enough to be brought to church! He went to the infant school when he was three in 1899 and graduated to 'the big school' when he was five. He claimed to be the only Horner brother who did not join the church choir – instead he was organ blower at one penny per service. At the age of 12 he reached Standard VII and school had no more to teach him so he was employed by the headmaster Charles Martin to weed the garden of his house, Highfield, and to empty the school's earth closets, until he could take 'the labour exam.' at Droxford which qualified him to leave school.

Len's first job in 1908 was with the Revd George Maclean at Jervis Lodge where his work included the twice daily chore of pumping water from the well and where he earned 2/6 per week. With an eye to the main chance he moved after a few months to work for another Anglican clergyman, the Revd Edgar Mack at Donigers where he cleaned the boots, shoes and knives as well as gardening and was paid 5/- per week. From there he moved to Hampton Hill House where Murray Gladstone paid even better – 7/6 per week.

When war came Len Horner was just short of 18; he joined up under age, the 9th Artillery Gun Battery at Hilsea was sent to France and fought at Arras and the Somme. He was gassed, invalided home, recovered, returned to France and was in the army of occupation in Germany until August 1919. From the 1960s to the 1980s Len used to read the names of the fallen at the annual Remembrance service in church. He could recall every one of those who had died in the First World War. They had been his school friends, people with whom he played football or knew from village activities.

After the war Len went to work for an elder brother who had a coach building business in Lewisham and it was there that he met and married Mary Pope in 1923. He returned to Swanmore in 1943 and was the village postman living at the Post Office, working from 5 am to 5 pm initially for £11 per week. On his retirement in February 1964 he and Mary went to live in a bungalow in Spring Vale. He remained active in the village almost to the end of his long life. [see Table G7]

7

The Primitive Methodists

BETWEEN THE LATE SEVENTEENTH CENTURY AND THE 1830S WE have no record of the existence in the parish of dissent from the established church, whether Roman Catholic or Protestant. There may of course have been individual households who were prepared to travel a distance to worship according to their conscience but if so evidence has not survived. In the 1830s the Primitive Methodists arrived in the district and before long groups of converts were meeting in private houses for preaching, worship and fellowship. It was not however until the 1860s that they could afford to build their own chapels.[1]

48. The Primitive Methodist chapel before 1909. Photo Alma Parsons

Primitive Methodism originated in North Staffordshire where the first Camp Meeting (an outdoor evangelistic service) was held in 1807. It was a revivalist movement, reverting it believed to the emphases of early or primitive Methodism, lost sight of by the increasingly respectable Wesleyans. It made substantial use of local (lay) preachers, held camp meetings and based its beliefs and practices closely on scripture. The movement reached Hampshire in the early 1830s, and often encountered hostility from the Church of England. It was missionaries from Micheldever whose evangelistic work led to the creation of a society (the Methodist word for a church) in Swanmore. The earliest reference to Methodists in Swanmore is in Minutes of the Micheldever Circuit in September 1842: it was resolved that 'we try to establish a Sabbath school in Swanmore'. In March 1843 it was decided that the minister William Harvey should 'go to Swanmore and make enquiries about land for a chapel' and in September 1843 'that salvation meetings be held at Swanmore'.

In 1843 there were 13 members in the Primitive Methodist Society at Swanmore including John and Hannah Barfoot, Joseph, Ann and Matilda Hendy, John Butcher and members of the Millard and Reeves families. Those who were not yet members but attended services were referred to as 'hearers'. Services were held in a private house. The Religious Census of 1851 lists Henry Giles, a young man of 25, as 'Manager and class leader' and records the attendance at services on Sunday 30th March as 12 in the morning and 59 in the evening, and makes the unlikely claim that the house could hold 90 people.[2]

The only other Primitive Methodist society in the district recorded in the census was at Meonstoke. It too met in a private house. The Rector, Charles John Hume, however was obviously nettled by its claims. It could not, he wrote, in a note appended to the census return, possibly accommodate 60 people sitting, with standing room for a further 20, as was claimed. What is more the attendance of 183 spread over three services did not represent the strength of dissent in the village: 'A meeting room being opened they came from surrounding places', he wrote, 'and on the day of the census extraordinary pains were taken to get up large numbers'. The Methodists themselves admitted that they did not normally hold a morning service but did so on census Sunday.[3]

The Swanmore society was part of the Bishop's Waltham mission formed to carry out evangelistic work in the villages of the Meon valley under the auspices of the Micheldever Circuit. In 1853 Swanmore became part of the Winchester Circuit, consisting of a large number of small, scattered village chapels. The 1860s saw a spate of chapel building: Swanmore was opened in 1863 and was followed by Shirrell Heath, Hambledon and Meonstoke in 1864, Waltham Chase in 1869 and Warnford in 1870. Though remaining part of the Winchester Circuit these new chapels were described from 1885 as constituting the Hambledon Branch, in effect a separate circuit. Seven years later this was renamed the Droxford Circuit, as it remained until 2000 when it was renamed the Meon Valley Circuit. (see Table C)

Non-conformists, as they were usually termed, were acutely aware of their inferior status in relation to the established church. In 1888 the Circuit Quarterly meeting passed a resolution reminding chapel members of their recently acquired right to be buried in the parish churchyard by their own minister and listed local preachers prepared to officiate in each parish. It was not until 1903 that a dissenting minister conducted a funeral in Swanmore churchyard, an event which merited an entry in George Titheridge's diary: 'Mrs Apps died . . . Buried by a Chapple Minister. Taken to Chapple and from there to the Church Yard. First burriel Like it in Swanmore'[4]

A far more serious and longstanding example of what nonconformists felt to be discrimination against them arose at the beginning of the twentieth century. The Balfour Education Act of 1902 provided rate support for church schools, of which by far the greatest number were Anglican. The Droxford Circuit Quarterly Meeting voiced its opposition while the bill was passing through parliament and its minister Walter Barnsley later went to prison at Winchester for refusing to pay the rate. Nationally the leader of opposition to the bill was the veteran Baptist Dr John Clifford and the slogan which encapsulated – and exaggerated – the case was 'Rome on the Rates'. In rural areas there was usually no choice of school, and children of free church parents had no option but to attend the Anglican school, where religious education was sectarian and where the head and often staff were required to be confirmed members of the Church of England. Parents could withdraw their children from worship and denominational religious instruction which, for this reason, invariably took place at the beginning of the day but this did not remove the resentment.

The Revd John Leach, who arrived as Circuit Superintendent in 1908, was a man of strong and uncompromising convictions, chiefly remembered because he spent a fortnight in Winchester gaol through refusal to pay that part of the rates which were earmarked for education. He wrote in the Circuit News Letter for June 1910 a passionate piece headed Passsive Resistance'.

We are within eight hours of leaving home for Winchester gaol as we write this . . . It is awful to contemplate, that there are 16,000 schools in this land where no man or woman can become Head Teacher if they are Primitive Methodists. It is therefore to secure the rights and liberties of your children that your minister goes to gaol. Justice has been superseded by persecution and a scarcely veiled attempt to terrorise into submission to a diabolical law.[5]

The sole minister of the Droxford circuit was responsible for nine chapels stretching from Hambledon to Bishop's Waltham and from Shirrell Heath to Warnford. He was described as a Travelling Preacher, because he was stationed (another Methodist word) in a new circuit usually every three years. Continuity in chapel and circuit life was provided by Local Preachers who took most of the Sunday and weekday services alongside their daily work in secular life. Though the minister normally conducted the sacrament of the Lords's Supper (the usual Primitive

49. The Revd John Leach, Primitive Methodist minister at Bishop's Waltham
station leaving to serve his prison sentence in Winchester gaol for refusing
to pay education rate. The caption reads 'Revd J.Leach, P-resister
Going to goal (*sic*) B.Waltham, 1909'
Photo John Bosworth.

Methodist name for Holy Communion) held in most chapels monthly following
either the morning or evening service, local preachers were also authorised to do
so. Local preachers were expected to be men of probity – there were no women
preachers in the Droxford circuit until 1932. The circuit insisted that all who

desired to become local preachers 'must be Total Abstainers and Non-smokers'
whilst Leaders were 'to urge upon the members the necessity of entire consecration to the service of God'. In addition to two services on a Sunday each chapel
held a weeknight preaching service. At Swanmore it was described on the circuit
plan as 'Wednesday Preaching 7 p.m'. In September 1910 the minister John Leach
preached at a total of 13 weeknight services in the circuit as well as two services
every Sunday.[6]

The Droxford Circuit went through a lean period at the end of the nineteenth
century; in 1898 its total membership dropped to 110, the lowest recorded. By
1914 it had recovered to 165. In 1906 when the membership was 17, Swanmore
chapel attributed its decrease in income to 'our people who are chiefly market
gardeners having had a bad season for crops and so less money has been raised and
spent'. In 1910 there were 161 members in the circuit; Shirrell Heath had 44,
Bishop's Waltham 27, Waltham Chase 24 and Swanmore had risen to 25, though
attendance at Sunday services usually exceeded membership. Members came from
a group of loyal and inter-related families: Butcher, Edney, Staite and Richards
among them. The baptism records show parents of baptised children who are
described as labourer, coachman, house decorator, gardener and carter.[7]

Primitive Methodist ministers came from a very different social stratum from
Anglican clergy. Their life style was simple, their manse unpretentious and their
stipend small – at the beginning of the century about £100 per year. The minister's house was rented. From 1859 one of the ministers of the Winchester Circuit
lived at Swanmore but later moved to Droxford. In 1905 the minister moved back
to Swanmnore but in 1914 moved again, this time to Shirrell Heath. Ministers stationed in a Circuit for three years found it impossible to relate to the parish as
could the Anglican Vicar. The Revd Fred Clark, a man of 27, when he arrived in
the circuit in 1905, stood for the Parish Council in 1907; unsurprisingly he was not
elected.[8]

The pre-war years saw the Primitive Methodist circuit flourishing. During the
ministry of John Leach, 1908-11 the new St Paul's church in Basingwell street
Bishop's Waltham was opened, replacing the old Mission Hall in Free street. At
Swanmore a school room was added to the church, at a cost of £272 and opened
in August 1909. Thomas Staite, also a Swanmore Parish Councillor was secretary
of the Circuit Quarterly Meeting, and his wife, the daughter of William Richards,
was organist and caretaker. William Richards was an active Liberal, at a time when
Anglicans were likely to be Conservative and free churchmen Liberals. His death
in 1910 after 50 years as a local preacher was a great loss to the chapel and was the
occasion of eloquent testimonies both at his funeral at Shedfield parish church
and at a memorial service held at Swanmore chapel. The Revd John Leach
preached at the memorial service on a text from the first book of Samuel :*And
thou shalt be missed because the seat will be empty*. He wrote in the next Handbook of
Services: 'This great warrior against the world, the flesh and the devil, this friend

of the poor and afflicted, this servant of the churches of this Circuit, passed to the great Homeland on May 15th 1910'. On the next circuit plan his name appeared inside mourning lines and against the address was written 'Heaven'.[9]

The first World War had a serious effect on all the churches not least the smaller ones where the departure of young men for the front left gaps which could not easily be filled. In December 1914 the Circuit Quarterly Meeting expressed its deepest sympathy for Mr and Mrs Spencer on the death of their son. Two years later one of its young local preachers on trial Henry Gamblin (22) from Shirrell Heath was killed in action and shortly afterwards the meeting resolved to print a Roll of Honour on the circuit plan.

Inveterate opposition to alcoholic drink became, at the end of the nineteenth century, a characteristic of all branches of Methodism and of many Anglicans too. In 1915 the circuit reluctantly removed the name of one of its local preachers from the plan on grounds of his 'insobriety'. In March 1917 the meeting, moved by the shortage of food nationally, passed a resolution urging the prohibition of the manufacture of intoxicating liquor ...' because it involves the destruction of food ... its consumption involves dangerous delays in vital industries and is a prolific source of violence and crime and is a most potent means of undermining the morals of the nations'. The meeting wanted 'a complete prohibition of this pernicious traffic'.[10]

During the first World War all branches of Methodism relaxed the rule that ministers normally spent only three years in a circuit before moving on. Longer ministries became and remained more common. Between 1924 and 1939 the Droxford Circuit had three ministers including Percy Hassam who stayed in the Circuit for six years, 1924-1930, and James Ridge for seven, 1932-1939. The inter-war years were a period of unprecedented growth in the circuit. Membership which had stood at about 160 from 1917-23 rose to 317 on the outbreak of war, a figure never again reached. (In 1994 the circuit membership was 270, in 2000 it was 280).

Percy Hassam was a popular and effective minister. Born in Kent in 1889, he was converted in 1909 and entered the Primitive Methodist ministry in 1915. A brief stay in Nigeria caused a breakdown in his health and he returned to work in south Yorkshire. He came to the Droxford Circuit in 1924 at the age of 35 with his wife and four children. 'From the coal miners of south Humberside to the strawberry fields of south Hampshire', he wrote, 'was a big change but the need for a direct gospel message was just as real in the rural south as in the industrial north'. He practised what he preached reporting that ' Camp meetings have been held in all the places in the Circuit with splendid results'. When he left in 1930 three new churches had been opened, Sunday schools had grown, new local preachers had been recruited and membership had increased. Nor had Percy Hassam's energies been wholly absorbed by the church; he served in addition as a Parish Councillor for Shedfield.

When James Ridge arrived in 1932 the circuit was obliged to overcome its doubts about the propriety of women in the pulpit. The Primitive Methodists

appointed women as local preachers from the earliest years and in the early nineteenth century also had women travelling preachers (ministers). The new minister's wife was already a local preacher and so was the first woman to preach in the
churches of the Droxford circuit. The year 1932 also saw Methodist union when
the Primitive Methodist church joined with the Wesleyan and United Methodist
churches to form the Methodist Church. The Droxford Circuit, however, was
unaffected. It did not join with the churches of other Methodist traditions as it
might have done. It continued its Primitive Methodist customs and remained
evangelical and biblical in its emphasis. For over 20 years after Methodist union all
its ministers were former ministers of the Primitive Methodist church. To this day
it is a circuit whose churchmanship and theology bear the marks of its origin and
history.

8

Brickyards and brickmaking

BRICKMAKING FLOURISHED WHEREVER SUITABLE CLAY WAS TO be found: Bursledon, Funtley, Fareham, Durley, Upham and Bishop's Waltham are local examples. Until the twentieth century it was a small scale industry dominated by family firms making bricks, tiles and pipes largely for a local market. From at least the late eighteenth century until the late 1930s Swanmore's only significant industries were brickmaking and and the related craft of pottery.[1] The terms brickburner, brickmaker and bricklayer are used inter-changeably in the nineteenth century. The trade was seasonal with more to do and

50. The brickfield c.1930 – site of Crofton Way
Photo Bob Reed

greater demand in the summer than the winter. Some of those engaged in the brickmaking trade were also builders hence bricklayer.

We do not know when brickmaking began in Swanmore. *The Hampshire Directory 1792* describes Peter Dollar as 'bricklayer' and John Lacy as 'brickburner'. By the time of the Census of 1841 and the Tithe Award of 1842 the Dollar family was amongst the leading families of Swanmore – soon Peter Dollar would become one of the first churchwardens of the new parish – and the most prominent in the brick making industry. Ann Dollar, the widow of the recently deceased Peter Dollar, owned *The Bricklayers Arms* behind which there were brick kilns and associated buildings. On the opposite side of the road Ann Dollar owned an orchard, and further east a second brickyard and buildings whilst her son Peter Dollar owned the adjacent house, garden and sheds also on the south side of the road. Ann Dollar possessed other property in the village – a cottage south of Hill Pound occupied by Eli Underwood, the cottage and garden next to *The Bricklayers Arms* (now called Rose Cottage) where James Earwaker, a carpenter lived, and a further cottage and garden behind what is now Mason's Stores occupied by Henry Northeast, another agricultural labourer.

At least two other families were involved in the brick making industry in 1841. George Reeves (30) lived at Hill and his premises are described as 'brickyard' whilst William Cresswell (31) born at Upham rented a cottage, garden and shop owned by Peter Dollar as trustee of the late William Horner in Church road, where Meon Valley Printers now is. He is described as brickburner. By 1861 he had been joined by his sons George (24 in 1861) and Henry (18), the latter described as 'bricklayer's labourer'[2]

John Dollar, the brother of Peter, moved from Jervis Court Farm by 1851 into *The Bricklayer's Arms*. He described himself as 'victualler, brickburner and farmer of 80 acres, employing 9 labourers'. We may wonder which of these demanding activities occupied most of his time? (His nephew John (29) who by now had a growing family, moved into Jervis Court Farm). Peter Dollar remained active described as bricklayer according to the censuses of 1851 and 1861. By 1871, now aged 70 he was described as ' retired builder'. His grandson 'Young' Peter, the son of John Dollar the younger, lived with his grandfather until he went to London to become an architect in the early 1870s. 'Old' Peter Dollar died in December 1884 and was buried in Swanmore churchyard. (See Table G2).

Although the Dollar family was no longer active by 1871 there were still nine men whose occupation is described as brick maker or brick layer including William Cresswell and his son Samuel (17), George Apps (26), John Stone (54) and his three boys Henry (21), Alfred (18) and William (16), all born in Bishop's Waltham, Walter Boswell (25) and Emmanuel Earwaker (39).

The original brickfield was behind *The Bricklayers Arms*. By the 1880s the clay there was exhausted and in 1885 the tilehouse, stables and kilns were demolished.[3] It seems likely that the scale of work may have declined at the same time. The

Census of 1881 contains the names of only five bricklayers: George Apps, now 36, Walter Boswell (35) who was also licensee of *The New Inn* , Emmanuel Earwaker (50) and his son James (17) who lived in Gravel Hill and Thomas Pink now aged 69. The site opposite the original brickfield, now occupied by bungalows, was already in use for clay and the pits were gradually extended south towards Broad Pond, through what are now woods which bear clear evidence of clay workings. Pits were as much as 25 – 30 feet deep. Older villagers can remember playing in 'the puggies' (pug pits) on the way to school in the 1930s.

The brickyard appears to have been bought by Freemantles who according to George Titheridge started burning in May 1886.[4] The family does not appear to have lived in the village since their name is not in the census and in any case they sold the brickyard in 1894.[5] In the last years of the century the main brick making family was Stones. In 1894 George Stone, bought the brickyard and his sons George (22 in 1891) and Alfred (13) joined him in the business though George Stone the younger appears to have gone to live in Sydney, New South Wales.[6] Walter Boswell was still licensee of *The New Inn* as well as a bricklayer and there are four other men whose trade is bricklayer in the 1891 Census.

By now the brickfield extended down behind the recreation ground to include the land on which Crofton Way stands. George Stone built himself a house in New Road, just below the recreation ground named York House. His wife is said not to have liked the house and he therefore built another one, diagonally across the recreation ground, opposite Broad Pond, named Victoria House whose garden still contains a pond which originated as a clay pit.

In 1902 the brickyard changed hands yet again and was bought by William Churcher. It was from the Churcher family that Frederick Reed bought the brick-works in 1924. The Reed family had been brickmakers at least since 1812, latterly at Southall in Middlesex. By now the brickyard was confined to land bounded by the recreation ground, New Road and what is now the secondary school field. It covered land later occupied by the Cortursel factory and Crofton Way. Two sheds remain on the site from the brickworks, one by the road housed brick-making machinery, the other was where land drains, pipes and tiles were made.

In the 1920s there were five permanent employees with up to a dozen men brought in during the summer. Bricks had to be dried in the open before firing and this could only take place in the summer when there were unlikely to be frosts. In winter clay was dug and the bricks made in the summer were burnt.

Swanmore clay was dense, deep red in colour and good quality, requiring no additives. (Chalk, coal dust, iron oxide or salt, were used in some places to change the colour or enhance the quality of the bricks.) Firing took three days and three nights and required watching throughout. There were three kilns, each taking a load of 40,000 bricks. Tiles and land drain pipes were stacked in the centre among the bricks. The kilns were coal fired and coal was delivered in truck loads from Bishop's Waltham station.

Some 750,000 bricks were made each year. They were sold at £3 per 1,000, mostly to local builders. Many houses in New road for example were built of Swanmore brick. No advertising was necessary since local builders knew where to buy their bricks. William Horner, one of the leading builders of Swanmore, lived at the top of New road in what is now Brook's Garage. He used the wall of the house next door as a good example of Swanmore bricks as well as of his own workmanship.

In 1927, only three years after coming to Swanmore, Frederick Reed collapsed in his office at the brickworks and died.[7] His seventeen year old son Bob Reed found he could not carry on the business and it was sold. In the late 1930s the brickyard was closed and brickmaking came to an end in Swanmore after close on two centuries, unable to compete with larger and more mechanised firms.

There was a second brickyard in Swanmore, about which however much less is known. It was located between New road and Forest road and in 1911 is called Forest Farm Brickyard. Its proprietor according to Kelly's Directory was Silas Short and Sons. In the 1930s S.A.Evans is listed as its proprietor and it was apparently still in business in 1939.[8]

The pottery behind *The Rising Sun* was also a going concern for much of the nineteenth century. At least four heads of families are described as potters and lived near the pottery. In 1851 James Cobbett aged 29, is described as 'master potter, employs 5', Whilst two nephews, William (16) and Absolem Harris (13) lived in and are described as apprentices. Twenty years later James Cobbett was still Swanmore's potter assisted by his 16 year old son. By 1881 the pottery has been taken over by Henry Hammond (48) and his son Thomas (24). Henry Hammond had by 1891 retired and the pottery was in the hands of George Aburrow whose residence is described as 'pottery, Hill Pound.' Soon after the beginning of the twentieth century the clay was exhausted and the pottery door closed. Fragments are however often unearthed in the garden of the bungalow which now occupies the site.[9]

9

Institutions and amenities
1914-1939

WHEN WAR BROKE OUT IN 1914 THERE WERE TWO ASSUMPTIONS about its nature: it would be short, 'over by Christmas', was the opinion of the Vicar of Swanmore amongst many others, and it would have little effect on the civilian population.[1] Britain had, after all, not been involved in a major European War for a century. Both propositions were rapidly proved wrong. Men flocked to join the forces in response to popular pressure as well as to Kitchener's famous recruiting poster, sometimes on impulse – 'D.Knight came home a soldier', reported George Titheridge (26th September 1914), 'Alf Light left his Wife and Joined the Army Ambulance' (14th October 1914). Later in the war: 'Fred Linter joined the Hants. Regt.'(22nd October 1915), 'Bert Wood joined up' (18thMarch 1916). In the first four months of war 100 men from Swanmore joined the army or the navy, a high proportion of all men of eligible age.[2]

The reality of war was brought home to the village almost at once. Of the 35 people whose names appear on the War Memorial the first to die was Lieutenant Arthur Maclean of the Argyll and Sutherland Highlanders on 26th August 1914. He was not by then living in Swanmore but in Crowborough, Sussex but he was the son of the Revd George Maclean of Jervis Lodge. The sinking of *HMS Bulwark* torpedoed off Sheerness on 25th October had a much greater impact in the village. All but twelve of its crew of 800 were drowned, among them Able Seamen Sidney Barnes (19) and Reginald Flower from Swanmore and Sub-Lieutenant Edward Gunner (20) son of Charles and Jessie Gunner of Ridgemede, Bishop's Waltham whose family had previously lived at Swanmore Cottage.[3]

On 6th November Andrew Blanch, a Sergeant in the Royal Engineers died in the retreat through Flanders. He was a career soldier who had joined up under age in 1897 and served in the Boer War. He was married in St Barnabas in 1904. His young widow returned to Swanmore with her three orphaned children, to live with her mother Mrs Gray, a daily reminder of the horrors of war. She subsequently became the village postmistress.[4] Soon afterwards a family of Belgian

refugees came to live in Swanmore, with tales of the horror of the German invasion of their country.[5]

In January 1915 the Vicar wrote 'The year that has closed has been marked by a
calamity such as the world has never known before'. A Roll of Honour of those
who had joined the forces was made by Archie Ainsley and placed in the church
porch. The Vicar urged 'every able-bodied man to come to the rescue of his country at this crisis. On 3rd January there was a Day of Intercession and Humble
Supplication to Almighty God in connection with the war, in which all Christian
bodies shared.[6] By December 1915 the number on the Roll of Honour was 155
and nine men had died. Meanwhile a drill class had been started for those unable
to join up.[7]

The village was reminded of war in other ways. Soldiers passed through on
their way to embark from Portsmouth to join Kitchener's army in France. In
September 1914 they camped in Swamore Park. In February 1915 the Sixth
Hampshire Territorials were billeted at Hill Place, leaving for Scotland a month
later.[8] The London Volunteers were billeted throughout the village and in
November 1915 the South Wales Borderers passed through.[9] Jack Hoar records the
excitement he felt on seeing the Northuberland Fusiliers and the Durham Light
Infantry march through the village 'with fat, shining horses, jingling steel harness
and the stern expressions of the men in peaked hats'. Later wounded soldiers in
hospital blue were to be seen and German prisoners came to work on local
farms.[10] George Titheridge noted on the outbreak of war the sale of horses at
Corhampton Park 'for government use'.[11]

Ernest Targett who had been a teacher at the school since 1908, married in 1912
and had a young son born in November 1914, joined the Ninth Hampshire Cycle
Corps in France in March 1916. Eighteen months later he was killed near Ypres at
the age of 31. He had been at the heart of village life; Scout master, leader of the
St. John's Ambulance Brigade unit, a gifted musician who player the piano, violin
and mandolin, bandmaster at Knowle hospital and organist and choirmaster at the
church since 1913. To the young Jack Hoar, now 14, his death was a loss he remembered and recalled poignantly throughout his life. Ernest Targett had lodged with
Jack's family at Church Cottage until his marriage. The Scout parade in memory
of him on 14th October 1917 was a poignant occasion.[12]

The war had an increasing impact on life at home. Women took over work previously done by men: Madge Martin took over the sweetshop while her brother
'Bim' Martin was in the army and Jane Tribbeck ran the dairy at Wassell Hall while
her son James was serving in the Middle East. In 1916 conscription replaced voluntary enlistment. 'Last day for recruiting' wrote George Titheridge in December
1915. A year later he recorded 'Airplain [sic] wrecked near Hoe Farm.'[13] His diary
contains frequent references to the fact that the war continues: '83rd Day of the
War' (25th October 1914), and 'the Flu Epidemic Raging. Still War' (25th October
1918).

51. Ernest Targett teacher, killed in action Ypres 30th September 1917.
Photo Jack Hoar

By January 1917 food prices were responding to scarcity and rising rapidly. 'Everything is such a price,' he wrote, 'Sugar 6d per pound, Bread 1/8 per gallon, Pork 1/4 to 1/6 per pound, Beef 1/6 – 2/- per pound, Potatoes 10d – 1/- per gallon'. In December 1917, 'Wild rabbits 2/- each; tame 4/- – 5/-', whilst in April 1918 he noted 'A Doe Rabbit Sold at Fareham Market for 27/-. Never Known such a price'. Rationing became inevitable: 'Sugar tickets issued' (September 1917), 'Meat and Butter Ration Came in force' (April 1918) .

The civilian population was affected in other ways too. By 1916 there were police regulations about black out. At the church Evensong was moved to 3 pm during the winter months and at the school arrangements were made for 'darkening the windows'[14]. The Education Committee wrote to the school managers about the collection of chestnuts 'for military purposes'. By 1918 children were needed to help with the hay harvest and fruit picking and there were three weeks holiday in June, whilst in September pupils were released one afternoon each week at the request of the Education Committee to pick blackberries.[15] The Parish Council distributed seed potatoes provided by the county War Agricultural Committee. William Myers arranged for them to be carted to Bishop's Waltham station but there were complaints about their small size![16] The Council purchased a potato sprayer which could be borrowed and later used for lime-washing cow sheds.[17]

In December 1917 the Vicar, John Henry Hodgson, left to become Rector of Dogmersfield. His successor, Edward Francis Shepley Ramsbotham, educated at Charterhouse and Balliol College, Oxford was inducted in February 1918. A man in his mid thirties, he left the parish temporarily in June 1918 to become a chaplain to the Forces and did not return until March 1919.[18] Meanwhile the war ended. 'Peace Proclaimed. War Stopped', wrote George Titheridge. The day after war ended, on 12th November 1918, there was a service in church at 7pm taken by the Revd Edgar Mack, a priest who lived at Donigers and helped in the Vicar's absence, at which the names of the fallen were read. Thereafter Armistice Day was observed on 11th November, at first by a service in the evening.[19] The Memorial Cross containing 35 names of the fallen was erected and dedicated at a service held on Sunday 6th November 1921 at which the Primitive Methodist minister, the Revd Alfred Clarke read a lesson, the Salvation Army band took part and seats were reserved for ex-servicemen. On the following Saturday 11th November, Armistice Day, the British Legion marched from the recreation ground accompanied by the Bishop's Waltham band to the Memorial Cross where Mrs Portal laid the British Legion wreath. Thereafter until 1939 Armistice Day was celebrated yearly at the eleventh hour of the eleventh day of the eleventh month.[20]

Not since the Black Death in the fourteenth century had there been nationwide loss of life on the scale experienced in the first World War. Cholera epidemics in the nineteenth century had brought more devastating death tolls but not to every town and village simultaneously. In the early 1920s every community — schools, colleges, trade unions, business houses, branches of the services – erected their memorials to the dead in 'the war to end all wars'. It is impossible to imagine the impact of the fearful death toll in every parish: Swanmore 35 names on the war memorial, Bishop's Waltham 52, Droxford 14, Shedfield 42 – over 140 dead in only four adjacent rural parishes, almost all men and most under 30. At Swanmore about one third of all those who had volunteered did not return. Many were buried in anonymous graves in France. Others were disabled, some permanently and some mentally scarred by the memories of the trenches or Gallipoli. Every

52. Newly built Memorial Cross, c.1922.

village had its war widows and war orphans, some engaged to be married during the war who would always remain single.

There are 35 names of those who died in the First World War on the Swanmore war memorial. All but one are men. Violet Horner who served in the Queen Mary Army Auxiliary Corps is the only woman. She died in July 1918 at the age of 20 and is buried in Swanmore church yard. Of the men the great majority, no less than 22, served on the western front and are buried in cemeteries in France or Belgium: Lieutenant Archie Ainslie 23, Private Frank Brooke 37, Private Walter Emery 18, Rifleman Alfred Godwin 36, Lance Corporal George Godwin 36, Private Geoffrey Hodgson 23, Lieutenant Howard Hewitt, Lieutenant Arthur Maclean, Second Lieutenant Edgar Mack 22, Sergeant Alfred Murrant 27, Major Raymond Poland, Gunner Edward Pink 22, Private James Pink 22, Gunner Ernest Reeves 25, Private Frederick Shepherd 22, Sergeant Andrew Blanch 35, Lance Corporal Walter Shepherd, Corporal Ernest Targett 31, Lance Sergeant James Trivett 21, Sergeant Frank Terry, Private Alfred Wearne 27, Sapper Richard White 21.

Six served in the navy and died at sea: Able Seaman Sidney Barnes 19, Able Seaman Reginald Flowers, Shipwright Joseph Kennett, Gunner Walter Mears 29, Stoker Harry Reeves 37, Leading Seaman William Woods 32. Corporal James E. Warren 24, is buried in Jerusalem. Four were buried in St Barnabas' churchyard – Colonel Edmund Watson in 1915, Private Cecil Hingott in July 1918, Gunner

George Apps 21, in October 1918 and Thomas Whiting in 1919. They probably died from wounds received earlier in the war. The name of Arthur Thomas Southwell is not on the war memorial but his grave is on the right of the path going into St Barnabas'. He died in 1928 aged 39, ' After ten years of suffering caused by the Great War.'

In addition to Arthur Maclean three of Swanmore's clergy lost sons. Private Geoffrey Hodgson, son of the Vicar, served in Princess Patricia's Canadian Light Infantry and died in France on 14th October 1915 at the age of 23 whilst 2nd Lieutenant Edgar Mack , son of the Revd Edgar and Margaret Mack of Donigers had been killed less than a month earlier on 27th September 1915 aged 22. The name of Walter Barrington Medlicott, son of Walter and Emily Medlicott , born at Swanmore Vicarage in 1872, is not on the war memorial though he is commemorated like Geoffrey Hodgson by a plaque in the church. Although he served throughout the war he died in captivity in Cilicia in September 1920.

Two families each lost three sons. Rifleman Alfred Godwin was killed in May 1915 aged 24, Lance Corporal George Godwin in February 1917 and Harry Godwin about whom details are not known. The Gunner family who now lived at Ridgemede, Bishop's Waltham but had earlier been prominent in Swanmore also lost three sons; Sub-Lieutenant Edward Gunner on *HMS Bulwark*, in November 1914, Captain Benjamin Gunner, First Northumberland Fusiliers, in October 1915 aged 23 and Captain John Gunner, Hampshire Carabiners, in August 1918 at the age of 34. They are commemorated in a stained glass window in the south aisle of St Barnabas. Village life between the wars was lived in a state of prolonged mourning[21]

In a fit of triumphalism all too typical of the post-Versailles years, German war relics were distributed round the country. Swanmore in common with other villages, was offered and accepted what were described as 'war trophies'. The German rifles and steel helmets offered by the war office were 'accepted with thanks' by the Parish Council but oddly, 'It was left to the managers of the school to decide where they should be placed'![22] At Corhampton a German trench mortar was duly installed in front of the mill where it stood until removed for re-use as scrap metal at the beginning of the Second World War.[23]

By the mid 1930s the personalities who had dominated village life since the 1890s had left the scene. They were not replaced: never again would squire, parson and schoolmaster stand at the apex of a village hierarchy, recognised and respected by all, and providing leadership to community, village and church. Medlicott, Myers and Martin were not however the only leading figures who departed. Jack Hoar remembered clearly hearing the news of the death on 30th April 1914 of Walter Daubeny, his father's employer and the owner of Hill Place.[24] The house had belonged to the Goodlad-Daubeny family for over a century. There was no heir. In late July the furniture was sold at a three day sale at the house.[25] In May 1916 the

53. Swanmore House 1939.

54. Swanmore House, inner hall looking north east, 1939
Photo Sale particulars Knight, Frank and Rutley

55. Swanmore House, North Drive 1935
Photo Catalogue of Sale Pink & Arnold

estate of 1059 acres, including Jervis Court Farm, Jervis Lodge, five farms, a score of cottages and small-holdings, as well as woodland and fishing rights, was sold at auction at the Oddfellows' Hall in Bishop's Waltham.[26] Thereafter Hill Place had no long-standing occupant though during the 1930s Major Harold Inglis was a leading figure in the parish.

After the war Swanmore Park was never again the venue for many of the activities of the village's social calendar as it had been between 1880 and 1914. No longer were Harvest Homes for the village, choir suppers at Christmas or school treats held there. William Myers reached the age of 65 in 1919 but continued to take an active part in village life for another decade, resigning from being church-warden, member of the ruri-decanal conference and chairman of the Parish Council on account of declining health and increasing deafness in 1930. He was presented with a framed extract from the Minutes recording his long chairman-ship of the council and the Bishop of the newly created diocese of Portsmouth came to Evensong to make a presentation to him on Palm Sunday 1930.[27]

When William Myers died in December 1933, at the age of 79, leaving £191,000, (at least £4 million in present day terms), there was no heir since nei-ther his brother nor his sisters had married. He had, it seems, intended the estate to pass to his wife's nephew, Peter Francis Prideaux-Brune.[28] He died however at the age of 23 in April 1932 and is buried as is his Prideaux-Brune grandmother, with other members of the Myers family in Swanmore churchyard. [see Table G9] Frances Myers moved to Catisfield taking with her Laura Goodchild, her erst-while maid as house keeper and one of the footmen as her butler. Curiously she is not buried in Swanmore churchyard though there appears to have been a plot reserved for her.

The death of Squire Myers and the subsequent sale of the estate was a shock to the village. No longer was there a father figure and universal provider to whom to refer every need. In January 1935 the PCC noted that a new arrangement would be necessary to provide altar flowers for the church. For as long as anyone could remember they had been sent down from Swanmore House each week.[29] Sheila Gadsby who came to live in Swanmore in the 1930s recalled to the author her impression of a dependent village, which had to learn to stand on its own feet after the death of its longstanding father figure.

William Myers' will is dated October 1933 just two months before he died. In April 1935 the Swanmore Park estate of about 1357 acres was sold by auction, at the George Hotel, Winchester, divided into 42 lots[30]. The house and 90 acres of the surrounding park were bought by South of England Real Estate in which William Myers' wife Frances and brother, Canon Charles Myers, who were the chief bene-ficiaries of his will, had a controlling interest. It was sold almost at once to Arthur James Espley. The owner of a chain of chemists' shops in Lancashire, Espley had sold out to Timothy White and Taylor and had become its managing director. He demolished the servants wing which connected the kitchen and laundry as being out of keeping with modern conditions. He did not however live for long at Swanmore House and in November 1939 sold the property. The new owner seems to have leased the house back and it was used by Timothy White and Taylor as a warehouse when their Southsea headquarters was bombed. After the war they bought it. It was however sold again in 1949 and 1951. This time the catalogue of sale suggests that it might be suitable for conversion to a school, nursing home or hotel. Alternatively it could be divided into flats or houses. The buyer chose the latter. Swanmore House was made into eight self-contained freehold houses each with its own assigned garden and garage.[31]

The exterior of the house is more or less intact and became a Grade 2 listed building in 1966. Most of the interior of the original house was destroyed includ-ing one of its most distinguished features, the three storey galleried central hall, which is now an open courtyard. The walled garden survives though the north facing glasshouses collapsed and were cleared in the 1960s. Boiler houses, mush-room sheds and potting shed are still standing though put to new uses.

The losses of the inter-war years were not just the squire and the big estates but the personalities who had impressed themselves on village life. Edwin Molyneux, estate manager at Swanmore Park, widely known as a distinguished gardener, churchwarden since 1899, Overseer of the Poor, Parish Councillor and school manager, died suddenly in 1922. Charles Martin long serving schoolmaster died in 1925, and Walter Medlicott, Vicar for 37 years, in 1926 at the age of 84.[32] The Gladstones had been at Hampton Hill since 1896 and had rapidly become pillars of church and village. Murray in particular was a well known character. He died in 1928 at the age 80 whilst his sisters Catharine and Florence died in 1921 and 1935 respectively.[33]

The Parish Council continued its activities. Although women were from the beginning eligible for membership no woman was elected to the Swanmore Parish Council until 1925 and then in inauspicious circumstances. Norah Powys became a member only because the candidate above her in the poll stood down. Her career as a councillor was brief and stormy. At her second meeting in July 1925 she proposed the appointment of a health visitor to take part in the medical inspections at the village school. The chairman ruled the resolution out of order as the Parish Council had no power in the matter. Norah Powys nevertheless addressed the Council. When the chairman ruled that she could not proceed she left the meeting. Before the Council met again she had resigned and the candidate who had stood down was duly elected to replace her. It was not until April 1937 that another woman, Mrs A.M. Watson, became a member of the Council.[34]

Wheatley's Housing Act of 1921 envisaged a substantial house building pro-gramme by local authorities to provide council houses for all who needed them. Even today these post First World War houses are readily identifiable in many vil-lages. They were however viewed with suspicion in the countryside where opin-ions were conservative. Receiving a letter from the RDC in 1919, the Parish Council replied that members did not think any housing of this sort was needed. When the RDC pressed the point they resolved: 'With regard to the housing of the working classes ... to write to owners of unlet houses to know if they would be prepared to let them.'[35] No further record appears in the Parish Council Minutes. Eight council houses were however built on the north side of Chapel Road in the centre of the village. They were incidentally the last houses in Swanmore to have wells provided. The post-war move to provide allotments and small holdings for those returning from the war was also reflected at Swanmore. Sites was obtained in Vicarage Lane and Cot Street, but few allotments were ever taken up and the scheme soon lapsed.[36]

These years saw the arrival in the village of the amenities which had been taken for granted in the towns for many years. Mains water, gas, electricity, street light-ing, telephone, tarmaced roads, refuse collection and bus services – were all, avail-able in most of the village before the Second World War.

The Gosport Water Company renewed its attempt to persuade the Parish Council to install water mains in 1919. Villagers were still hesitant on grounds of cost which would be threefold: installation of the supply, the annual water rate and a ten year guarantee to the Water Company in case insufficient households sub-scribed. It was not until 1922 that a scheme was drawn up, costs determined and a village canvas held to ascertain support.[37] This time 82% of the 216 houses on the proposed route were in favour and it was decided to proceed. Work started in May 1923 and was finished by August.[38] At last lower Swanmore would no longer be dependent on wells and pumps. A drought would never again oblige people to draw from the river at Mislingford as had happened in the hot, dry summer of 1911 when families had drawn tanks on wheels to the river, making two journeys on wash day. The water butt against the wall of cottages to catch the rain water fell into disuse too. Mains water was extended to Spring Lane in the mid-20s.[39] With the advent of piped water there was less need for ponds: the two in Vicarage lane were filled despite protests in the late 1920s.[40]

Ten years later in the early 1930s it was the turn of oil lamps and the open range to give way before gas and electricity for lighting and cooking if not yet for heat-ing. The West Hampshire Electricity Company wrote to the Parish Council in 1929 indicating the area to which it proposed to extend its supply.[41] Three years later there was further correspondence about the route across the parish to be fol-lowed by the overhead supply lines then being erected.[42] When the company sug-gested in 1933 the lighting of the telephone box outside the post office it was turned down on account of cost.[43]

Meanwhile the Bishop's Waltham Gas Company had been taken over by the Gosport and District Gas Company which pointed out that the result would be cheaper gas.[44] It was laying mains via Wickham, Shedfield and Waltham Chase, a move welcomed by the Parish Council. By 1933 the Swanmore Ratepayers Association was asking the Parish Council to consider the installation of gas street lighting. The Gas Company installed three lights at the top of New road without charge as an incentive and according to George Titheridge , 'The lamp [was] light-ed for the first time at the crossroads', on 25th March 1933. There was however concern about the state in which the Gas company had left New road after laying the mains.[45]

The change from open ranges to gas and electricity together with the increas-ing use of tins created a new problem – refuse disposal – a service not yet provided by the local authority on the rates. The possibility of getting 'tins, bottles and simi-lar refuse' collected and disposed of was first raised in April 1937.[46] In 1938 a con-tractor offered to undertake a monthly refuse collection at a charge of £20. The Parish Council agreed and volunteers proceeded to gather subscriptions but by March 1939 the scheme was in the red and more subscribers were needed to restore solvency.[47] In October 1939 the Droxford RDC announced its intention of launching its own General Scavenging scheme. There was indignation: the parish-es had not been consulted and it would cost the product of a 4d rate. Swanmore's own scheme was working well and was much cheaper![48] Two years later however the parish's self- help scheme broke down. Subscriptions were not being paid and the contractor was told that he would have to collect the money himself. He demurred and collections of refuse ceased. The Parish Council now suggested to the RDC that it should set up a scheme but that it should not cost more than the product of a 2d rate. The need was amply demonstrated in the coming months when there were complaints that tins, iron and other rubbish were being deposited in ponds, ditches and on private property.[49] Not until March 1946 was a monthly refuse collection begun, run by the RDC, which was however now appealing for possible dumping sites.

The first telephone exchange was opened in Britain in 1879 but the telephone too was largely a town facility until well into the twentieth century. In 1920 the Parish Council agreed to the financial guarantee to the Post Office to install a telephone in the Post Office.[50] This meant that it was not available when the Post Office was closed, on Tuesday afternoons, Sundays or evenings! Not until 1928 was a public call box erected outside the Post Office.[51] Since calls had to go through the exchange there were still delays when the post office was closed.[52] Telephone numbers of commercial premises appear in Kelly's Directory in 1927 – Mid-Hants Stores Bishop's Waltham 3 and Harry Watson, Jervis Court Farm, Bishop's Waltham 21.

Fire fighting is a further service which we take for granted but not until the Fire Brigades Act of 1938 was maintenance of a fire brigade a local authority responsibility. The need had been dramatically demonstrated in 1891. At 9pm on an April evening a fire broke out at the premises of Obed Hammond in Vicarage lane. Lord Northesk who lived eight miles away at Longwood, Owlesbury saw the blaze at Swanmore. He kept private fire fighting equipment and at 11pm he and his fire-fighting team arrived to tackle the blaze but too late to save much from the fire.[53]

Between the wars the parish improved fire fighting provision. In 1928 the Parish Council agreed to join Durley, Curdridge, Shedfield and Upham and subscribed £117 to the new self- propelled Bishop's Waltham motor fire engine purchased in 1930 to replace a manual engine bought in 1899.[54] A canvas of the village was held to elicit donations towards the parish's quota.[55] One of the first major fires to be attended by the new engine was at Jervis Court farm in June 1933 when four steam wagons, four petrol lorries and other vehicles and buildings were destroyed.[56] Until the Fire Brigades Act of 1938 the parish contributed £12 per year to the upkeep of the fire engine.[57] In 1933 the Parish Council was pleased to note the purchase of a 'motor ambulance' for local use kept at Bishop's Waltham.[58]

The unemployment which was such a marked feature of the early 30s in town and country alike did not pass Swanmore by. Early in 1933 the Parish Council, determined 'to do something to enable the local unemployed men to occupy their spare time', suggested that they should be provided with allotments free and should receive a loan for seed and tools. They called a special meeting of the Council at which it was resolved to hold a public meeting a week later.[59] When

later in the year the Bishop's Waltham Area Employment Association was formed
the Parish Council supported the venture and 'recommended all local unemployed to attend the Centre'.[60]

A further sign of the times was the neglect of the village's time honoured footpaths. In the wake of the Rights of Way Act 1932 Frederick Arnold and Frank
Whitaker personally walked every footpath and right of way in the parish, con-
sulting older inhabitants on 'doubtful points' with a view to ensuring that traditional rights were not lost through disuse. Arnold noted his regret that 'the use of
these [footpaths] seemed to be passing as the public took to more use of motor
vehicles.[61]

Though the village was still a largely self-contained community, access to the outside world became steadily easier as transport improved between the wars. Before
1914 a visit to Southampton or Portsmouth was an occasion, requiring a walk,
cycle or carriage ride to trains at Bishop's Waltham, Droxford or Wickham. Until
regular bus services began boys going to Price's Grammar School at Fareham
would cycle to Bishop's Waltham, leave their bicycles at a shop, catch the train to
Fareham, changing to the Portsmouth line at Botley and then walk from the station to the school in Park lane. In the summer boys would bribe the porter at
Fareham with strawberries, to mark their ticket with a later time of arrival than
was the case so that they could miss assembly and instead enjoy an illicit smoke
before first lesson![62] The 1920s were a golden age for the railways. People travelled
more than they had ever done before and there was a precarious equilibrium
between new methods of transport by motor car, motor bus or charabanc and the
old transport by rail. By the 1930s the spread of private cars was already threatening the railways. The Bishop's Waltham branch line closed for passenger traffic in
1933 though the Meon valley line survived until 1955.[63]

Horse and carriage could be hired from several of the village inns but the main
Job Master's business was run from Albert Horner's premises at the top of New
Road. He advertised in the Parish Magazine ' Open and closed carriages. Pony
and trap for hire. Children's hunters'. He had two horses, and in the coach house
adjoining his stables was the Victoria, an open carriage with folding hood used
mostly for weddings. For more workaday purposes there were the Landau, a
closed carriage, and the Wagonette, an open carriage, capable of taking four passenger facing each other and a fifth beside the driver. Carriages would be hired to
meet trains or used for outings, for example to Lee-on-Solent. During the First
World War Gertie Horner drove soldiers, returning from leave, through the pitch
dark lanes to catch the mid-night train from Botley, sometimes falling asleep on
her way home and relying on the horse to find its own way back to Swanmore. In
the mid-1920s the horses were sold and William Horner invested in his first car, a
second-hand Studebaker, soon to be joined by a Buick, also second hand[64]. In 1939
Albert Horner advertised himself as 'Motor Engineer'.[65]

Bus services came to Swanmore in the early 1920s and gradually replaced horse and carriage from the roads as surely as, twenty years later, tractors were to replace horses in farm and field. The first buses, solid tyred and of quaint appearance, were owned by Tutt's and ran from Gosport to Bishop's Waltham, via Swanmore. Their appearance was such a novelty that children were released from school to watch them pass through the village. The novelty was not however confined to children. When old Mrs Stone reappeared, after several hours during which relatives and the police had searched for her in vain, she was asked where she had been, she replied 'I've been out on one of they 'ere rickety backs to Fareham and back'.

The 'Anzac', so called because its proprietor Mr Gamblin had fought with the Australia and New Zealand Army Corps (ANZAC) at Gallipoli, ran from Fareham to Bishop's Waltham, via Shirrell Heath. When he sold out to Mr Butcher the firm was not allowed to retain the name and it became Shirrell Buses. There was however keen competition to run bus services and at first no regulation. The Hants and Dorset already ran from Petersfield to Southampton but set out to compete with Hutt's. Loyalty was strong and when the Hants and Dorset bus arrived, passengers at the stop would refuse to enter, waiting instead for Hutt's. There was considerable indignation when in due course Hutt's sold out to the Hants and Dorset.

Buses were of various types. Early Southdown buses were charabancs which you entered at separate seats along the side. The conductor made his way precariously along the running board to collect fares. By the early 1920s there were twice daily coaches running from Gosport to London, picking up passengers at *The Hunters Inn*. The Droxford road once again became a coaching road as it had been eighty years earlier, before the advent of the railways!

The main roads had been tarmaced by 1914 but not minor roads. In 1924 George Titheridge reported 'Graveled The Road Passed our Cottage' [Hampton Hill]. In almost the last entry in his diary in May 1936 he recorded 'Finished the Roads through Swanmore'. From now on the distinction between unsurfaced green lanes and tarmaced roads would be clear.

The Hadow Report of 1928 recommended a major change in the structure of state education. It proposed that at the age of 11 pupils should enter a new phase of education to be called secondary and that this should take place in separate schools which would take pupils to the school leaving age which then stood at 14 but should as soon as possible be raised to 15. The so-called all-age school catering for pupils from 5 to 14 should be phased out as soon as possible. By 1939 almost half of all pupils in England over the age of 11 were in separate secondary schools. In the country progress was much slower than in the towns. The part of Hampshire of which Swanmore formed part was one of the last in the country to educate its children in all-age schools. By the time Swanmore Secondary Modern School opened in 1961 less than 4% of all pupils in England over the age of 11 were in all-age schools.[66]

56. Ernest Frank Whitaker, headmaster 1913–1942
Photo Joan Whitaker

57. (*centre*) A class at Swanmore school
November 1920
58. (*bottom*) Swanmore school Standards
6 & 7, October 1921

From the early 1930s the inadequacies of all-age schools were increasingly recognised. In 1935 His Majesty's Inspectors (HMI) noted in their report on Swanmore School that 'conditions are as favourable as can be expected in an un-reorganised school'.[67] and went on to comment on the absence of any Practical Instruction for older boys, '. . . from time to time an intensive course in Domestic subjects is held for the older girls but the boys have neither Gardening nor Handicrafts'. In addition to the class for girls at Bishop's Waltham Institute to which they walked or cycled on Monday afternoons, there was a Dairy Class in the Parish room attended in 1935 by 8 boys and 4 girls.[68] Drill – it could scarcely be described as Physical Training – took place, when the weather was suitable, in the playground.[69]

For a very few there was an alternative at the age of eleven. Those who passed the County Common Entrance and obtained scholarships or special places (which were means-tested), went to grammar schools, Price's Grammar School at Fareham for boys, Winchester County High School for girls or Barton Peveril Grammar School at Eastleigh for both boys and girls. The number qualifying was however small, two in 1929, one in 1930 and one in 1931, for example.[70] A few children never went to the village school at all, but to independent schools; the son of Courtney Wilson, vicar from 1922 to 1935 for example was at Charterhouse in the 1920s.

The village school was crowded. Numbers which were 163 in 1929 reached 181 in 1931. There were four teachers, Frank and Alice Whitaker, Mollie Twine and Ellen Blunden, whose classes averaged 40 and spanned two or more age groups and were still called standards. Conditions were improved when the large class-room was partitioned in 1929[71]. Pressure on space however grew worse. In 1938 HMI considered the school unacceptably full and the managers resolved to take no more pupils from outside the parish into the Infant School which would in due course reduce pressure higher up.[72] In 1933 the playground was at last surfaced but the state of the cess pits remained a perennial problem for the managers. Electric light was installed in both the infant school and the main school in 1935.[73]

The major crisis of these years was however the state of the roof which was regarded as unsafe. The cost of repairing it was estimated at £120 but the county architect thought it would be £200-£230, a figure which put its repair well beyond the resources of the managers.[74] An appeal to the church or the village was unlikely to yield such a sum and the diocese offered only £10. Frederick Arnold the representative of the Parish Council on the board of managers resigned in April 1936 since he was no longer prepared to accept liability for injuries which might result from the defective condition of the roof. He also referred to the apathy of the church authorities to the financial situation.[75]

Perhaps it was his resignation which led at last to decisive action. Faced with the prospect of having to hand the school over to the LEA and thus lose the church connection the managers appealed to the Myers family. Even though William

Myers had died over two years before and the family no longer owned Swanmore House or lived in the village it was to the Myers family that the managers looked for salvation. In May 1936 a deputation went to Salisbury to meet Canon Charles Myers, brother of the late squire. They came away with a promise of £150 on condition that the managers would do their best to ensure that the school remained a Church of England school in the future.[76] Frederick Arnold withdrew his resignation at the next meeting of the Parish Council and the crisis was over.[77]

The pattern of school holidays was determined in part by the needs of a farming community. Until 1943 the school year began in April. In 1921 there was a fortnight's holiday for strawberry picking from 13th to 24th June and as a result the summer holiday ran from 15th August to 9th September.[78] The fruit picking holiday was abandoned later and not resumed until the 1940s. There were occasional holidays for special events: the Winchester Musical Festival, the Aldershot Tattoo, the marriage of Prince Henry to Lady Alice Scott and 'the Funeral of King George V, the Beloved'. Empire Day was marked by a patriotic address delivered to the children by some leading local figure and on Armistice Day, they attended the Ceremony of Silence and Remembrance at the Memorial Cross.[79]

Epidemics cut attendance drastically. In January 1922 it was flu, in April 1930 measles. In July 1932 attendance dropped to half through a simultaneous visitation of mumps, chicken pox and scarlet fever. The doctor would issue a certificate enabling these weeks to be omitted from the calculation of average attendance which would otherwise affect adversely the Board of Education grant. Provision of school milk began in October 1936.[80]

Discipline was not easy to maintain in a school, some of whose pupils came from deprived rural backgrounds, where classes were large and facilities for older children in particular were inadequate. In 1937 after dealing with a difficult disciplinary case the managers decided that 'The character of Waltham Chase children generally should be pointed out to the LEA.[81] Offences recorded in the Log Book included bullying, 'dirty behaviour in the lunch time', stealing – apples, plums, flowers and chocolates. Punishment was usually the cane, on one or both hands, and for more serious offences, 'on the posterior'.[82]

The managers, six in number, came from the upper crust of Swanmore society and were accorded due respect by staff and pupils alike: all stood when a manager entered a classroom. Until his withdrawal from village affairs on account of age and infirmity, they met at Swanmore House, the home of William Myers. He was last present at a meeting in October 1931. In 1920 the managers included in addition to Myers, the Vicar, ex officio chairman, Edwin Molyneux, Admiral Sir Edward Bradford, the Revd Edgar Mack and Miss Gillson.[83]

In 1938 HMI recorded that Swanmore School was 'still in an unreorganised area and still lacks suitable provision for practical instruction for boys of senior age'. 'Girls' they reported 'receive instruction in domestic subjects at a centre in the neighbouring country town' (Bishop's Waltham). They were critical of the quality of the reading and of 'pupils' ability to talk about the context of the lessons'. 'Practical exercises' they thought 'should be key features of lessons in history, geography and general science.'[84] Few people can have imagined that it would be another quarter of a century before all Swanmore pupils would have access to a local secondary school.

The Infant School remained a separate school meeting in the building next to the church, now part of the Paterson Centre, until January 1946 when it was amalgamated with the junior school across the road.[85] Mabel Wootton, appointed in 1915 was still its head assisted by Madge Martin who taught the five year olds and is remembered for her stern unsmiling demeanour and the black ankle length dress with lace at the neck which she wore. She had joined the staff at the age of 18 in 1895. Now over 60 and with over 40 years service in one school she was as much a village institution as her father had been before her. Martins had taught at the school for over 60 years.

The single room in the Infant School was divided by a curtain. It was heated by a tortoise stove which stood against the wall and was used in the winter to heat the milk for the Horlicks served at morning break. Windows were well above the level at which outside distractions might have been visible. The playground was surrounded by railings and gravelled so that children frequently had to be treated for cut knees. There was a huge yew tree by the door and amenities included smelly earth closets at the side of the building used with the utmost reluctance by sensitive children. Vera Tribbeck recalls marching round the playground with Union Jack flags on Empire Day, 29th May.

Learning was basic in content and traditional in style – spelling, reading, arithmetic and scripture, all involved rote learning. Slates were still in use though gradually being superseded by exercise books. Monitors collected the exercise books, cleaned the blackboard and when instructed to do so closed or opened the windows.[86]

10

Village life between the wars

THE HARVEY FAMILY MOVED FROM PORTSMOUTH IN 1912 TO A thatched cottage at Hill Pound, next to *The Rising Sun*. The rent was 1/9 pence (8p) per week and had they been more affluent they could have bought it for £35. It was not large enough for a family of nine and two years later they moved next door to a double tenement whose rent was 3 shillings (15p) per week. 'Dink' Harvey, a boy aged five in 1912, grew up in the village and spent over 60 years of his working life as a farm labourer at Hill Grove Farm.[1]

Like many villagers of those years he retained to the end of his life clear recollections of the smells and sounds of the countryside. In the days before mechanised hedge and ditch maintenance, foliage and undergrowth luxuriated and tree tops often met across narrow lanes giving the enclosed appearance characteristic of the picture post card scenes of those years. Honeysuckle and red and white dog rose were as typical of June days as were bluebells, primroses, wild daffodils and cowslips of early spring. The smell of freshly baked bread mingled with the scent of stable manure and pipe tobacco. The sound of the blacksmith's hammer rang out alongside the church clock, whilst birdsong, including that of the nightingale, was far louder and more insistent than it is today when the bird population is only a fraction of what it was before the use of chemical pesticides. And lest the scene seems too idyllic many remember the squeals of pigs slaughtered once a week by one of the village butchers. Muffin men and pedlars would shout their wares. The mid-day postman approaching Hill Farm on his way from Droxford to Swanmore would sound his whistle to remind workers in the fields that it was lunchtime.[2]

By the late 1930s the established village hierarchy of earlier years had gone and the new occupants of the big houses did not stay as long nor have the same impact on village life. The village was in any case by now less self contained and less isolated. Swanmore House was only briefly occupied by its new owner Captain Arthur James Espley. The chairman of the Parish Council from 1934 until 1941 and also a

Justice of the Peace was Major Harold Inglis of Hill Place who held the DSO and MC, won in what was referred to then as the Great War. He resigned from the Parish Council when he left Swanmore to rejoin the army in 1941. At Swanmore Cottage lived Judge Bernard Lailey, King's Counsel and also a Justice of the Peace. A third JP who also held the DSO was Major Maurice Portal of Hollywell House. When Florence Gladstone died in 1935 Hampton Hill House was bought by Sir Charles Rose. Two extra- parochial clergy lived in the village throughout the inter-war years – the Revd Basil Phelps who lived at Myrtle Cottage was an organising secretary for the Missions to Seamen and the Revd Edgar Mack who helped to restart Corhampton Golf Club after the first World War lived at Donigers.[3]

Swanmore was a village of small farms and market gardens – no less than 15 are listed in *Kelly's Directory* for 1935. Most of the farms were mixed arable and pasture, keeping a few cows, pigs and poultry and employing up to half a dozen labourers in addition to the family. At milking time you were liable to meet a herd of cows on their way from field to farm or from farm to field. Some specialised in cows, poultry or market gardening. Only two farms exceeded 150 acres in extent: Swanmore Park Farm run by Leonard Draper and Hill Grove Farm run by Edwin Watson. Harry Watson farmed at Jervis Court Farm and William Parrington at Forest Farm. Two people described themselves as 'cow keepers' – Bertha Brown at Cottles and Agnes Knight of Forest Farm road. Fred Marsh described himself as 'dairyman' and H. Messam as a dairy farmer. There were two poultry keepers and a poultry breeder at Forest lodge. There were market gardeners at Hill Pound (Ernest Downs) and Spring Lane (Alfred Edney) whilst Joshua Lewis was a nurseryman.[4]

The main builder in the village was William Horner of North Dene, responsible in the early 1920s for building the council houses as well as two semi-detached houses and two bungalows, all on the north side of Chapel Road whose appearance was thus transformed.[5] William's brother Albert Horner was a motor engineer. William Parsons in New Road was not only a builder but undertaker, wheelwright and maker of wheelbarrows and ladders. F. Freeman was the blacksmith whose business included shoeing horses as well as fitting metal hoops to the wheels of farm carts.

A country craft which by 1920 was obsolescent was that of well sinker, undertaken in Swanmore by James 'Dump' Millard, whose name still appears in *Kelly's Directory* in 1927. It was a dangerous and difficult job. The sides of the well might collapse or the air become sparse or contaminated with gas. As a safety measure the well sinker would work with a candle in a jam jar. A windlass was used to remove buckets of soil as the well became deeper whilst the top section would be bricked to a depth of 10-20 feet or until solid rock was reached. In Swanmore most wells were 12-16 feet deep though some, including that at the School House, were much deeper.

Those brought up in Swanmore before the Second World War recall the multiplicity of shops in the village, about seventeen in all. Some were multi-purpose stores, others sold a restricted range of specialist items, no longer available in Swanmore at the end of the century, whilst others were scarcely shops at all; just a shed or lean-to from which an enterprising villager would supply a gap in the market and supplement a meagre income. Needless to say customers were served personally, items were weighed individually and nothing was pre-packed. Sugar was weighed out into blue bags, cheese and butter were cut from large pats on the counter, biscuits were served loose from a tin and sweets were stored in tall jars with glass stoppers. Cold ham was sliced from a side of ham. There were no refrigerators and on a hot summer day maggots hatched quickly on exposed meat.

William (Jack) and Edward Linter were brothers who represented the ultimate in diversification. William who lived at Hill Cottage advertised in the *Parish Magazine* as 'Cycle Agent and Repairer, Hairdresser and Tobacconist' whilst Edward was 'Bootmaker and Cycle Agent.' When Hubert Martin died in 1955, Jack took over the shop at the corner of Chapel Road and New Road, selling sweets, crisps and lemonade. In the garden was a Nissen hut where he kept second hand clothes, prams and beds whilst next door he sold bicycles, shoes and paraffin and ran a shoe repair service.

Opposite *The Bricklayers Arms* was a clothing store; almost next door was a bungalow with a wooden shed, in one half or which was a newsagent and sweet shop and in the other the village barber. In the centre of the village was the Mid Hants store which included the Post Office and at the back a bakery. It was one of the few premises in Swanmore to have its own telephone line in the 1930s – the number was Bishop's Waltham 3! Percy Tubbs was a baker in Forest Farm road. In Vicarage Lane was a shed where ironmongery was sold. The village boasted three butchers, – Harry Tibbles, specialised in pork sausages whilst Ernest Kerton was the butcher in Chapel road. Harry Tibbles' mother was a midwife who could be called out day or night to assist at a home birth (the norm in those days) or to lay out a corpse.

Elsie's fish and chip shop was run from a black timber shed in the garden of Hill House at the top of New Road. Service was slow as each order was individually cooked over a primus stove until Elsie modernised and bought a paraffin cooker. If 'Dump' Millard represented the past then Leslie Kirkham, wireless dealer in Forest Farm road represented the future. In Chapel road was a second shop selling wireless equipment and accumulators. There were further shops in New road and Forest road. By the 1930s the village boasted two petrol stations , one in New road and one where Meon gardens now stands. Both survived until the 1980s but both were then closed.

At Hill Pound was a sweet shop built in 1873 on land bought from *The Rising Sun*. In 1921 James Tribbeck and his eldest sister Mary moved here from Wassall Hall, went into partnership, set up a bakery and built a new bake house. They were joined in the business by their sisters Edith and Alice and together ran it for 40 years: Mary and Alice died in the 1950s and James and Edith retired in 1961. In the 1920s James met Beatrice Turner an Essex girl who worked at Hill Place for Admiral Mc Clintock. They married in 1930 and built a bungalow in the garden of the bakery. It was named *Kasvin* after the town in Persia (now Iran) where James Tribbeck served during the First World War and it is where at the beginning of the twenty first century his daughter Vera still lives.

The shop became a general store serving Hill Pound and selling groceries, haberdashery and lemonade as well as vinegar from the barrel. Flour came from Botley mills and the bread was cooked in an oven fired by bundles of wood called bunts which were kept in a huge stack in the garden. James Tribbeck would be up early each morning to prepare the dough and bake the bread and lardy cakes, for which he was well known, before setting out on his delivery round in the village in the early years by horse and cart, later in his Ford Model T. The bread oven was always hot and at Christmas might be used for the cakes of his customers who did not have a large enough oven. A goose was once wheeled down the road from *The New Inn* to be cooked at the bakery.

Despite the large number of shops there appears to have been scope for a proliferation of door-to-door salesmen, some of whom called daily or weekly, others once or twice a year or like the coalman on request. Some were welcome as part of the village scene, others were resented for the competition they constituted to village shopkeepers. 'Yorky' the pedlar from Bishop's Waltham carried a basket of haberdashery in one hand, wore strings of bootlaces round his neck and over his shoulder hung a sack in which he collected rags. Also from Bishop's Waltham came Noah Dixon, a short smiling figure with a pointed white beard and white apron, whose grinding machine, used to sharpen scissors and shears, was a source of fascination to crowds of children intrigued by the sparks which flew off in all directions. Hezekiah Griggs came from Soberton selling clothes pegs, baskets and cane chairs whilst Gipsy James sold lace and told fortunes.

There were two milk deliveries: Frederick Marsh's for upper Swanmore, Clarke's for lower Swanmore. Milk was carried in churns on a horse-drawn cart and dispensed from a metal dip directly into a jug left on the doorstep: 'fresh farm milk and very creamy'. Bread was delivered by Chase's of Wickham in competition with local suppliers. From Wickham came too the weekly door to door deliveries of ironmongery from Warwick and Hemming. Hire purchase was in its infancy but tallymen from Landport and Dupont called in the village as did insurance agents. William Milligan was an insurance agent living in Chapel road.

Public houses were at the centre of the social life of the village in the years between the two wars when wireless (*sic*) and cinema were in their infancy and television was as yet undreamt of outside science fiction. Until 1920 Swanmore boasted five public houses. The oldest were *The Bricklayers Arms* and *The Rising Sun*, both of which are named in the Trade Directories of the nineteenth century.

The Black Boy which closed in 1920 was so named because its first landlord in the 1860s, David Hillyer was also a chimney sweep (and so was its last).[6] It was situated on the north side of Chapel road and is now a private house. George Titheridge records 'The Last Meeting of the Slate at The Black Boy' on 6th December 1920. In addition to *The Bricklayers Arms*, and *The Rising Sun* were *The New Inn* in the centre of the village and *The Hunters Inn* on the road from Droxford to Wickham, not far from *The Rising Sun*. Competition was keen. In 1927 *The Bricklayers Arms* described itself as 'The Bricklayers Arms Hotel: board and residence; parties catered for, luncheons and teas provided'. Not to be outdone *The Hunters Inn* advertised ' Beautifully situated, large tea rooms, parties catered for at short notice, bowling green, tennis court and garage'.[7]

The New Inn whose licensee for most of the inter-war years was Walter John Downer, has changed little externally over the years, but inside it is scarcely recognisable as the pub known and loved by the villagers of those years. Saloon bar, public bar and tap room each had its own ambience and clientele. When ladies patronised *The New Inn* they were to be found in the saloon bar. The public bar with sawdust on its brick floor, wooden benches, open fire and spitoon and thick with pipe smoke, was the meeting place of regular customers, many of them older men, each with his own seat and with a preference for dominoes. The tap room was where youths and casual customers would congregate, their pint accompanied by pub games. darts, ringboard and shove ha'penny were popular, the latter played on a slate with small coins with a hole in the middle. In winter the slate had to be dried in front of the fire before play could commence. It was here too that sing songs, clog dancing and mouth organ recitals took place. In between the saloon bar and the public bar was a passage where off-licence customers could bring their jugs to be filled with draught beer drawn from wooden barrels fitted with brass taps.

In front of *The New Inn* was a triangular field which extended as far as the Flint Cottage, land now occupied by houses. Here once or twice a year came Hadlams Fair, its roundabout towed to the site by a steam engine. Life for the family at *The New Inn* was not unlike that of other villagers. Earth closet toilet, wash house with a copper boiler to heat the water for the tin bath, lay across the back garden. 'We had a bath once a week whether we needed it or not!' records Gwen Woods who lived there as a girl in the 1920s. House and pub were lit by oil lamps. You would go to bed by candle light or carrying a tumble-bottom oil lamp, so called because it was shaped to resist overturning. It had to be filled with oil and its wicks trimmed regularly. Cooking was carried out on a coal-fired open range and water was heated over a paraffin primus stove.

The old *Bricklayers Arms* was a tile-clad building close to the main road. Demolition began in January 1920 and its successor, opened on 23rd August 1920.[8] It was built behind the original building though the stables, built at the turn of the century, can still be seen to the left of the new building.[9] The original cellar was not it appears filled until a vehicle left in front of the building plunged into the cellar.[10] Its licensee in 1927 was Ernest Garnett, by 1935 Alfred Kirby had taken over.

The Rising Sun, kept in the 1930s by Alfred Primmer, was the only place in Swanmore where wine and spirits could be bought. These were commodities which in any case were beyond the means or social pretensions of most people in the village. Those in need of a medicinal dose of brandy would go to the door of the Vicarage in the time of the Revd Courtney Wilson (Vicar 1922–1935) and beg a drop of cooking brandy.

The Hunters Inn was run from 1904 to the late 1920s by John Newnham and his wife Fanny (nee Tribbeck) who persuaded the brewery to buy extra land and established bowls and tennis clubs. It was the only pub in the village which provided residential accommodation. Outside was the sign of the Cyclists' Touring Club whose members stayed there on their weekend outings. Concert parties touring neighbouring villages and workmen building the British Legion Hall in the 1920s were among other guests who stayed at *The Hunters Inn*. During the First World War the landlord was obliged to keep a Register of Aliens which later served as a Visitors' book. It was during the First World War too that licensing laws restricting opening hours were introduced. At first the hours were fixed by the licensing authority; in the case of Swanmore this was Winchester. Soberton came under the harsher licensing regime of Portsmouth so when the Soberton pubs closed their customers would make for *The Hunters Inn* already well oiled. There was a good deal of drunkenness until national licensing hours were introduced later in the war.

Children made their own entertainment. Tops, hoops, marbles, hop-scotch, kite flying, would follow each other as the craze of the month by some mysterious empathy whilst conkers reappeared every autumn. During school holidays many children would spend contented days on Droxford Downs, reached either from Droxford road beyond Swanmore Park Farm or from Mayhill lane. They would take sandwiches and a bottle of water, pick wild flowers or play hide and seek. In the autumn they were often sent to pick blackberries for jam or to glean ears of corn left behind after the reaper and horse rake had finished their work. Enterprising children who had collected a sizeable bundle of corn would have it threshed and take it to the mill to be ground into flour. The outer husks or bran were fed to the rabbits whilst the flour was turned into home-made bread, to supplement the family budget.

Poverty was an ever present reality. Fred White was the Relieving Officer under the Poor Law which was unaltered until 1929. In case of hardship he had to assess the value of possessions such as a piano before he authorised poor relief of 10 shillings (50p) per week. A family which remained unable to make ends meet would be accommodated in the Droxford workhouse.

11

The Second World War
and after

FOR THOSE WHO WERE CHILDREN DURING THE SECOND WORLD WAR the memory is still a vivid one. Many can recall the exact circumstances in which they heard the lugubrious tones of Neville Chamberlain announcing, at 11.15 am on Sunday 3rd September 1939, that a state of war existed between Great Britain and Germany. June Clarkson, then aged six, remembers her father listening to the broadcast: 'He stood, switched the wireless off and turned to go out into the road . . . [which] . . . was full of other men, standing in groups and talking in subdued voices. To a child, on a morning when the road was bathed in gentle September sunshine, it felt strange and wrong.' Vera Tribbeck, also then aged six, remembers her father and mother listening to the fateful broadcast and 'conveying to us that something awful was going to happen'. Kath Reed, a young mother living in Broad lane, was 'overwhelmed with fear at what was going to happen. I was dumbstruck'.

The war had already cast its shadow before it. Gas masks, now to be carried everywhere, had been issued in September 1938, before Munich brought a year's reprieve. Conscription began in the Summer of 1939 and many of Swanmore's young men had already joined up. The outbreak of war had two immediate consequences, both the result of the expectation of enemy bombing: black out and evacuation. Black out meant the obligation to conceal even a chink of light and was enforced rigidly from the first by air raid wardens, police and fire watchers. A breach of the regulations could lead to a court appearance. In bigger and older houses long disused shutters could be pressed into service. Most people bought black out material and made their own curtains. Some masked their windows with gauze to prevent flying splinters of glass.

Evacuation of children from the cities took place on Friday 1st September, in anticipation of the outbreak of war, which occurred two days later. The Autumn term began at Swanmore school as usual on Monday 28th August.[1] On Thursday notice was received that Grove road Infant school, Gosport was to be evacuated to

Swanmore and that teachers would be needed to help the Billeting officer, so there would be no school 'tomorrow'.[2] Bob and Kath Reed were allocated Nina, a girl of eight and her five year old brother. In addition a cousin brought her mother in anticipation of immediate raids on London. A small family of two adults and a two year old child was transformed overnight into a household of four adults and three children. They, like so many others in the crisis of war, coped. The cousin left when it became clear that London was not at once to be devastated and the homesick five year old returned to Gosport. Nina, like many other Gosport evacuees remained longer, in her case for two years.

School did not resume until Monday 11th September and then only for outdoor activities.[3] When lessons began on 21st September Swanmore pupils and the older evacuees worked in the mornings while Grove road infants used the school in the afternoon.[4] It was not until February 1940 that afternoon school began again for Swanmore children, with two classes at school and two at the British Legion hall, a venue later changed to the Methodist school room.[5]

The evacuees brought a new and exciting dimension to the lives of Swanmore children. They were street-wise (particularly the boys), climbed telegraph poles, formed gangs and made dens, rode two on a bicycle, queued at the newly-opened fish and chip shop and did not go to bed until they chose. In the months of double summer time it did not get dark until well after 11pm. 'I remember those months as being nothing but glorious, with the freedom to run wild with exciting new friends', wrote June Clarkson. The evacuees and others played in the now disused brickworks, entered from the recreation ground. Here they could clamber over derelict machinery, swim or sail precariously in the water-filled pits. The first evacuation did not last long. When the expected Blitzkrieg failed to materialise the evacuees began to drift back home. Many were homesick and parents missed their children whilst those upon whom they were billeted found the boisterous town children hard to cope with in addition to their own offspring.

The air raid warning siren sounding the sinister alert and the welcome all-clear became part of the routine of life. Swanmore did not have its own siren but was dependent for warning of an impending raid on the siren on the roof of the council offices in Bishop's Waltham. If the wind were in the right direction the Droxford siren above the police headquarters in Droxford could also be heard. Both were installed by Ron Crook then working for the West Hampshire Electricity company. There were no street lights and car headlamps were masked with metal shields. In October 1938 the Parish Council was asked to appoint Air Raid Wardens and in January 1942 Salvage Wardens to encourage the collection of anything which could be recycled to help the war effort.[6] The pavilion in the Recreation ground was used to store waste paper and small salvage before it was taken to a central dump.[7] The village took part in a number of special efforts – Warship week in 1942 and Wings for Victory week in 1943, for example. At a more mundane level the Parish Council paid 1d for the tail of each rat destroyed.[8] The brickyard in New road was used by a small factory making wooden wings for Horsa troop carrying gliders and employed women of the village. Others worked at a factory in Wickham making nuts and bolts for aircraft.[9]

In the summer of 1940 with invasion likely the Local Defence Volunteers, soon renamed the Home Guard, was formed and Swanmore had its own platoon of Dad's Army. It formed part of 30th Battalion of the Hampshire regiment. The headquarters was in the upper storey of a building, now demolished, near the Parish room reached by an external staircase. Meetings and briefings were held here but facilities were limited and there were also meetings in the Parish room and the British Legion hut in New road whilst drill took place in the school playground.

The first commanding officer was Lt. Fred Rudd succeeded in 1941 by Lt William Green who lived at Hill Top, upper Swanmore. Sgt Major Jack Mills who was drill instructor had served in the Hampshire regiment in Dublin during the Troubles in 1922 whilst Corporal Henry Gadsby, a stockbroker and former First World War Captain was musketry instructor and offered a five shilling piece as an incentive to recruits who became competent to his satisfaction. Ron Crook remembers a nerve-racking evening when a regular army sergeant was sent to teach the platoon how to prime live Mills grenades in the British Legion hut and later how to throw them to maximum effect. Exercises were held in the local countryside in conjunction with other Meon valley platoons. Rifle practice took place on the firing range at Dean farm, Bishop's Waltham and competitive shooting at Chilcomb near Winchester.

The platoon developed a strong sense of camaraderie holding convivial off-duty evenings at *The Rising Sun* whose landlord, Henry Willing moved from London and took over the pub in 1940, and was a member of the Home Guard. When the unit had a night exercise or went to camp Violet Willing would provide a hamper whose contents went well beyond what rationing allowed.

In 1946 William Green honoured a promise made back in 1943 to take members of his platoon to London. Travelling by car they took in a football match at Brentford, a restaurant meal and a visit to the London Palladium where Flanagan and Allen were on the bill.[10]

Most families had an air raid shelter of some sort. A few erected a Morrison shelter in the house or an Anderson shelter in the garden, others took refuge under a substantial wooden table or the stairs whilst yet others had a cellar which could be made snug for night time use. Some dug a hole in the garden and built their own shelter sometimes shared with a neighbour, from concrete or in the case of the Tribbecks of aircraft packing cases. Some flooded or smelt musty through lack of ventilation.

The phoney war came to an abrupt end with the invasion of Norway in the

Spring of 1940. France fell, German troops neared the Channel ports, invasion seemed imminent and the south coast was in the front line. School resumed during the Whitsun holiday on instructions disseminated by wireless so that swift evacuation could if necessary be organised.[11] By July air raid warnings were occurring daily and school attendance was badly affected.[12] The summer holidays were curtailed and school began again on 19th August.[13] The Battle of Britain was in full swing. Planes could be seen circling and diving overhead. One evening a blazing German plane, its Iron Cross clearly visible, passed over the roof tops and came to rest in a field at Dundridge where police and Air Raid Wardens swiftly cordoned off the area. Debris was scattered widely and the mangled hedge and chalky white scar were visible for months.

On 6th September 1940 the school Log book entry reads, 'After a very disturbed night few children present. Air Raid warning at 9.30. As there is an unexploded bomb in the vicinity the school will be closed on the All Clear being sounded. It should be safe to open the school on Monday.' On Monday the bomb was still unexploded and the 29 children who came to school were sent home.[14] The bomb was not in fact removed until 28th September but school seems to have resumed in the meantime. The owner of Hill Place, Harold Inglis charged 6d. to view the crater made by the bomb, donating the proceeds to the Red Cross.[15]

From 1940 to 1946 holidays were organised round the farming year to meet the need for casual labour. School closed for Good Friday and Easter Monday but the two week holiday was postponed until late April and early May to coincide with potato planting.[16] In mid-September school closed for a further two weeks for potato picking. In 1941, but not again, there was a three week holiday from 20th June to 11th July for soft fruit picking and hay harvest.[17] War years saw an enlargement of state provision of welfare anticipating the arrival of a full blown welfare state in the post-war years. All schools were for example obliged to provide lunch. At Swanmore the first school lunch was served on 3rd July 1944. Food was brought from the Portchester Cookery Centre and served in the British Legion Hall.[18]

The early war years were marked by some of the most severe winters of the century. In January 1940 school attendance dropped to a third on account of heavy snow.[19] Two years later conditions were even more severe. Between 21st and 23rd January 1942 the number attending fluctuated between 10 and 22 children.[20]

Swanmore was not directly affected by the bombing which devastated Southampton and Portsmouth in the winter of 1940-41. It was however close enough to hear the incessant droning of planes and observe the light of the countless fires set off by incendiary bombs. An attempt was made to disorientate the Luftwaffe. A fluorescent red decoy light, parked at *The Bricklayers Arms* during the day, was sited at night in upper Swanmore, one of several devices deployed in various places in the Meon valley. Once more refugees from the bombing came to the village. Audrey Richards whose father became landlord of *The Rising Sun* in 1940 recalls that the cellar was fitted out with bunk beds to accommodate those who came each night to escape from incessant night bombing in Portsmouth and Southampton. Others slept in the village hall and used the washing facilities of local houses before returning to work in the cities by day.

Rationing began on 1st January 1940. Ration books were issued for six months at a time at the Food Office in the Institute at Bishop's Waltham. Life was austere. Nobody went hungry but ingenuity was needed to provide a varied and adequate diet particularly for children and men working on the land. Those whose husbands were in the forces would collect a weekly allowance of about £5 from the Post Office. Even if they could be afforded many items were not available or in short supply. Utility furniture and crockery appeared in the shops. Many people made their own and their children's clothes and repaired their own shoes using metal protectors on the heels. Clothes, shoes, books and toys were all alike passed down in the family from older to younger.

Many people in Swanmore were self-sufficient. 'Dig for Victory' was the government slogan put into practice by countless households. Potatoes, carrots and onions stored in sacks would last until next year's crop was ready whilst home grown beans could be salted down. Sprouts, cabbage and broccoli grown in the garden would last until the spring. June Clarkson's mother aimed to make 100 lbs of jam each year – raspberry, strawberry, blackcurrant, plum, damson, and of course blackberry – needing she reckoned 2lbs a week to satisfy the insatiable appetite of her family of five children. Plums, apples and rhubarb were bottled in Kilner jars, sealed in the gas boiler.

Most people produced their own eggs which could be preserved in jars for use when hens were not laying. Many kept a pig, slaughtered it in the autumn and shared it with neighbours. Others supplemented the meat ration with rabbit, sometimes bought from one of the poachers in the village who would return from the fields and woods with rabbits slung over their handlebars. Some people kept a goat though goat meat was not to everybody's taste. More robust palates would tackle rook or hedgehog. The latter was wrapped in clay and cooked over an open fire; when it was ready the skin and prickles would fall away leaving the succulent flesh. Snoek, spam, whale meat and dried egg were further additions to wartime diet, each accompanied by government recipes for making tasty meals whilst disguising such unappetising ingredients. Anything off ration was scarce and if you saw a queue you joined it, sometimes with unexpected results.

Evacuees were not the only wartime visitors. Members of the Womens' Land Army came to help with the potato harvest. American soldiers stationed locally, some of them the first black people seen in Swanmore, came to dances in the village hall. German prisoners of war, some in camp at Romsey, were brought by lorry to work on local farms. Because the transport was so often late, Wilf and

Carrie Bone eventually rehabilitated a shepherd's van bought in a sale and accommodated their POWs, Alfonse and Horst, during the week.

After a respite of some three years on the home front any complacency was shattered in the summer of 1944 by a new threat. At almost exactly the same time as the allies invaded France the Germans launched their rocket propelled flying bombs the V1 and shortly afterwards the V2. Southampton and Portsmouth were within range and so Swanmore was once again in the front line. Air raid shelters in garden or house were called back into use. The rockets had an unmistakable drone, like the sound of an approaching motor-bike. There was then a tense, ominous silence as the rocket cut out followed by a reverberating thud as it hit the ground and buildings and exploded producing a column of smoke and dust. The best remembered rocket in Swanmore fell on a pig farm in Curdridge lane scattering dismembered pigs' corpses over a wide area.

As the D Day Museum in Portsmouth testifies south Hampshire played a crucial part in the preparation for the Normandy landing in June 1944. Throughout the war convoys of troops and vehicles came through the village and children would wave and cheer and were sometimes rewarded by badges distributed by the soldiers. In the run-up to D Day troops were everywhere, parked in lanes and lay-byes and camped in Bere Forest. One convoy of French Canadians camped in the village for weeks before D Day, erecting their tents outside the Mid-Hants stores (now Masons), in gardens by *The Bricklayers Arms* and on the wide verges at the end of Hampton Hill and Lower Chase road, in Spring lane and Mislingford road. They left after a week for Bere Forest and embarkation for Normandy.

In the run-up to D day the Swanmore Home Guard platoon was set to guard Droxford station on the Meon valley railway line. On patrol one morning Sergeant Ron Crook encountered two distinguished figures whose features seemed familiar – one with a pointed beard and the other taller and wearing a foreign uniform. They turned out to be General Smuts and General De Gaulle out for a stroll. In return for a smart salute Sgt Crook received a greeting from General Smuts though General De Gaulle remained impassive. On Tuesday 2nd June 1944 a train carrying the War Cabinet including Winston Churchill arrived at Droxford station on the Meon Valley line. It stayed there in the run up to D Day, leaving on Sunday 5th June. The following day the D Day invasion of Europe began.[21]

If many parishioners recollect their sense of foreboding on 3rd September 1939, they also remember the uninhibited rejoicing of VE Day (Victory in Europe day) 8th May 1945. The bonfire on the forecourt of *The Rising Sun* was particularly memorable. In their exuberance young men of the village in particular commandeered everything in sight to create the biggest fire anybody could remember. There were fears for the thatched cottage next door. An old hand barrow, long disused was dragged from *The Hunters Inn* and burnt. The perpetrators, two servicemen about to depart for the war in the Far East were identified, arrested and charged at Droxford Magistrates' Court with burning council property.[22]

Thirteen names of the men (no women) who died in the services in the Second World War, were added to the village war memorial, far fewer than in the First World War (see pages 107–108) Just over half served at sea. Four were in the Royal Navy: Ernest Farr aged 38 was Chief Stoker on *HMS Royal Oak*, torpedoed in October 1939; Harry Gomer aged 39 was on *HMS Hood* sunk in May 1941 and Cecil George aged 41 and Sidney Light aged 24 went down in *HMS Barham* in November 1941. Two were in the Merchant navy, Anthony Carpenter drowned in March 1942 and George Law aged 29 in March 1943, whilst Frederick Pothecary served in the Royal Marines but died in a prisoner of war camp in Crete.

Six of those who died were in the army: Eric Dainty aged 24 was killed at El Alamein in 1941, Hubert Ford aged 25 at Casino in Italy in 1943, and Robert Vincent aged 24 in France, fighting near Bayeux in July 1944. The remaining three are buried at Swanmore, dying probably from war wounds: Douglas Roberts aged 30, who had served in the Royal Army Ordnance Corps, in 1942; Harry Wood aged 24 in the Royal Artillery, in 1943 and Wilfred Linter aged 36 in the Royal Engineers in March 1946.[23]

By 1943 victory seemed in sight and attention was turned to post-war reconstruction. The Parish Council was asked to suggest sites for 16 houses to be erected under the Post War Housing Scheme.[24] They were more cooperative than their predecessors after the First World War and suggested three possible locations: the north side of Mislingford road at Hill Pound, opposite Hampton Hill house and on the Swanmore-Bishop's Waltham boundary opposite Moorlands road. What became Donigers Close was eventually chosen as the site for eight houses for 'agricultural labourers' built in 1948.[25] To the Parish Council fell the task of allocating eight houses to the 26 families who had applied to the Hampshire War Agricultural committee.[26] To the Council too was given the job of distributing gifts of food from the Dominions; on one occasion 62 pounds of raisins![27]

Street lighting was restored before the war ended. The three gas lights erected in 1933 and originally lit free of charge by the gas company could once again be illuminated but the gas company announced that the Parish Council would have to pay for the gas.[28] A public meeting was held and it was decided instead that the village should be lit by electricity and the first lights were switched on on 7th September 1946.[29] Meanwhile 'kerbing', hitherto a characteristic of town and suburban roads, was carried out in Chapel road, New road and Bishop's Waltham road between 1948 and 1950.[30]

The final step in providing the village with the amenities taken for granted in the towns was the provision of mains sewerage. A scheme came before the District Council in 1946. It would be expensive. By 1947 plans were laid for Bishop's Waltham and Waltham Chase to be connected but on account of cost, £120 per house, Swanmore was not yet included and had to wait until the 1960s before connection to mains sewerage.[31]

The Parish Council was active. Its first minute book covers almost 60 years (1894-1953), the second 18 years and third ten. Minutes were kept in long hand of varying degrees of legibility and read out at the beginning of each meeting – six or more foolscap pages. Only in 1980 were typed sheets pasted into the Minute book and copies circulated to members.[32] Meetings were held in the Reading Room until 1980 when the Council moved to the Village Hall. It met quarterly with frequent additional meetings however when business was brisk. For a few years meetings were held every two months and from 1960 the present pattern of eleven meetings a year – monthly apart from August – was adopted.

In the later years of the Second World War and immediate post-war era the parish had its youngest vicar of the twentieth century. Edward Wakefield's brief incumbency, 1943-1946, saw a new vibrancy in church life. The Vicar was under 30 and had a young family. He related naturally to young people and blew many of the cobwebs away. The parish magazine was modernised, with a new format, simpler cover design and up-to-date type face. There was now more room for village news rather than just church news. A Youth Club was started, the Sunday school was renamed the Children's (later Young People's) church. There was closer co-operation with the Methodist church than at any previous period. When the Revd James Lindsay, Methodist minister from 1939-1945, took part in the St Barnabas' Harvest Festival in 1943 he became the first free church minister to preach in the church. Joint services marked the end of the war in May 1945 and the official celebrations of victory in June 1946. The year war ended was also the centenary of the opening of St Barnabas, marked by special services during the year.[33]

Edward Wakefield was the third vicar whose departure was accelerated by the size and dilapidated condition of the Victorian vicarage. The diocese refused to allow the division of the house, which was wholly unsuitable for a vicar with a small family, limited means and no servants. Edward Wakefield resigned in 1946 announcing that 'he had regretfully come to the conclusion that he could no longer carry the heavy financial burden of the large Victorian vicarage. Also its size and inconvenience was a great strain on Mrs Wakefield and the Dilapidations Board had refused to allow it to be made into two houses'. The PCC agreed that 'the Vicarage was much too big and inconvenient for present day incomes and staff difficulties'[34] The diocese at last agreed to divide the house. After long negotiations division was completed in 1948 with the west wing separated from the vicarage and named the Glebe.

The new vicar, the Revd Albert McCaig was an Ulster protestant, a graduate of Trinity college Dublin. His period as vicar saw the introduction of two services which have become much loved parts of the traditional Christmas at St Barnabas' as elsewhere in the Church of England. The first Service of Nine Lessons and Carols, modelled on the service introduced at King's College, Cambridge by the Dean, Eric Milner-White, after the First World War, was held at St Barnabas in

1948. The first Midnight communion on Christmas Eve took place in 1952 with 43 communicants.[35] Albert Mc Caig had a stroke and died suddenly on 23rd May 1960 after returning from a meeting of the Parish Council at which he had been reelected Chairman.

Ernest Whitaker, who became headmaster of the village school on the eve of the first war, retired in the middle of the second. 'My duties as Headmaster ceased today', he wrote in the school Log on 31st January 1942. He was succeeded by Margaret Belbin, the last head of the all-age school, the only woman and still in her 20s.[36] She was head for over twenty years and would like to have become head of the secondary school when it opened in 1961. The post went instead to John Gimblett from Bishop's Waltham and Margaret Belbin retired in 1963 and died soon afterwards. Margaret Belbin was a Congregationalist. The new Vicar Albert McCaig had serious reservations about a non-Anglican head. When, after much soul-searching, Miss Belbin decided to be confirmed into the Church of England, the Vicar was in no way mollified and relations between them continued to be tetchy.[37]

June Clarkson was a pupil in the war years. She recalls a crowded playground shared by pupils of all ages and both sexes. The boys up to the age of 14 and after 1947 of 15, appeared to younger pupils 'enormous' and intimidating and they felt obliged to make themselves scarce. Discipline in the school was not easy. Ellen Crofton's loud voice and natural authority could quell tough farm lads who were only waiting to leave school while Frank Whitaker wielded the cane to good effect. Ellen Crofton was a teacher at Swanmore school from 1938. Elected to the Parish Council in 1958 she was Chairman from 1960 to 1969 and was a prime mover in the development of Spring Vale. Crofton Way is named after her.[38]

HMI who visited the school in June 1947 reported that the infant playground was 'unsurfaced and dangerous' and that desks in the infant school should be replaced by tables and chairs. This latter change took place in December 1948. In the junior school 'the offices [sic] should be converted to the water carriage system.' The earth closets had for many years been regarded by those who had to use the as 'a nightmare' and by HMI who didn't as 'needing replacement'. At last action was taken. In December 1958 a sale, concert and dance was held in aid of 'The School Office Fund', advertisement for which must have been a matter of some delicacy and perhaps ribald humour, though the euphemism 'office' no doubt helped! It was in any case successful and the school Log reported on 12th September 1949 'The water carriage now ready for use'.

The curriculum was utilitarian with an emphasis on basic skills and factual knowledge. English included grammar, spelling, dictation and punctuation and mathematics was exclusively arithmetic. History covered key events from Julius Caesar to the Boer War and pupils were encouraged to write their own account of events. Geography meant a knowledge of rivers, mountains and capital cities of the world. Physical education was limited by the lack of facilities: there were no changing rooms or showers. Physical Training, as it was usually called, took place in the playground, wearing outdoor clothes and shoes. What would now be described as PSHE (Personal, Social and Health Education) was limited to hygiene with only guarded references to sex. There was no science, no modern language teaching and no technology beyond sewing for girls and handicrafts for boys. Music consisted largely of class singing of folk songs: as yet musical performance was confined to the few whose parents arranged instrumental lessons.

By the late 50s when the post-war baby boom reached their teens the school was unacceptably full. In 1947 there were 150 pupils on roll. In 1959-60 there were 266 children in seven classes with seven teachers plus the head, an average of 38 pupils per class. Class 7, pupils of 14 and 15 contained 46 pupils and class 6 no less than 48 pupils.[39] Pupils reached Class 5 at the age of about eleven and might then be entered for the grammar schools entry test held in two parts: part one in December or January consisted of an Intelligence test, designed to assess pupils so called Intelligence Quotient (IQ) and part two, held a few weeks later for those who had been successful in part one, consisted of English and arithmetic. The number passing from Swanmore was small: between 1948 and 1963 an average of only 1.6 boys and 2 girls per year[40].

Margaret Belbin however made the most of the opportunities of a school with the handicap of poor facilities and her pupils look back on her work with gratitude and affection. Her first innovation was to group pupils by age instead of by ability. In future it would be for teachers to group pupils so that they were learning appropriately.[41] She placed a new emphasis on assembly: four classes were squeezed into two adjoining classrooms with the head conducting proceedings from the open doorway between the two. *Songs of Praise* was introduced and weekly hymn practices were held. Margaret Belbin was herself no mean musician. She trained a choir and entered it in the annual Hampshire Schools Music Festival held in the Guildhall at Winchester.[42]

For the first time the school had a secretary and the staff a staff room. The purchase of the field at the rear of the school was negotiated and as a result there was a substantial increase in football and cricket for boys and netball and shinto (mini-hockey) for girls.[43] The horizons of pupils were expanded: the aspiration of many pupils leaving at 14 and after 1947 at 15 had been limited to becoming farm hands or entering village crafts for boys and entering domestic service or becoming shop assistants for girls. Girls were now urged to enter the Gregg school in Southampton to qualify in commercial subjects or to become nurses. Boys too received careers advice and began to apply for apprenticeships at Hamble or to become draughtsmen. 'She was tireless in her efforts to widen our horizons' wrote June Clarkson who with Vera Tribbeck entered Winchester High School for Girls from Swanmore in the 1940s.

12

Growth and Transformation
since 1960

IN THE YEARS SINCE 1960 SWANMORE HAS GROWN MORE RAPIDLY than at any time in its history. Between the censuses of 1961 and 1981 the population increased by 53 per cent (1678 to 2561) and about three times as fast in the 1970s as the 1960s. (see Table F) The number of houses rose from 549 in 1961 to 832 in 1981 and 1026 in 2001, an increase of 86% in 40 years.[1] In these decades the commuter villager arrived, living in Swanmore but working, shopping and often spending leisure time in Fareham, Southampton, Portsmouth or Winchester. The commuter villager might work for IBM at Hursley or Portsmouth or for the navy in Gosport or might teach or run a business in Winchester or Fareham. He and she were however unlikely to work in Swanmore. The arrival of mains sewerage in the village in the mid-60s was the final stage in bridging the gap between the amenities of town and country. Town living was becoming steadily less attractive and life in the country more desirable. The spread of car ownership, often multiple, created traffic jams in the towns and meant that the inadequacy of public transport in the country mattered less. This is the background against which 40 years of growth and transformation has to be viewed.

These years saw a minor adjustment to the boundaries of the civil parish originally fixed in 1894. Waltham Chase, an area where there had been a good deal of new building was divided between no less than four parishes – Shedfield, Curdridge, Bishop's Waltham and Swanmore. It wished to become a separate parish; instead it was agreed that it should become part of Shedfield with consequent adjustments to the boundaries of the other three parishes, a change which came into effect on 1st April 1967.[2]

The Hampshire volume of the well-known *Buildings of England* series published in the 1960s, describes Swanmore as 'mostly Victorian cottages thickly scattered in small plots, with a few dwellings of what had been an older hamlet on the northern fringes'.[3] This may have been the impression of a casual visitor to the centre of the village but it was not true of the village as a whole, even in the 1960s. By the

1980s development round the fringe of the village left a Victorian and Edwardian
core surrounded by small, modern housing estates on the periphery. Over a quarter of all houses in Swanmore had been built in the previous ten years and over
half had been built since 1950.[4]

Building began modestly with the first phase of Spring Vale, bungalows for
older people, built between 1952 and 1954.[5] Moorland road was built in 1955.[6]
Growth accelerated in the 1970s : Spring Vale phase 2 with 85 houses and bungalows in 1972, Orchardlea on land previously occupied by a house of that name in
1973, and Glendale on a site previously occupied by Glen Cottage in the early
1970s.[7] Crofton Way was the name chosen for the road on the site of the brickyard
(see chapter 8) built in 1974-76. Badgers Copse off Spring Lane followed in 1979.
Not all projected new building took place: for example a planning application for
building on 11 acres in Lower Chase road was rejected in 1971.[8]

One development in the early 1980s caused more controversy than all the others – Donigers Dell, at the corner of Hampton Hill and Swanmore road. The land
on which it was built had been regarded erroneously as village property since it
had been undeveloped for so long. Early in the century it had belonged to Murray
Gladstone, the owner of Hampton Hill House. It had been the scene of village
fetes and garden parties. It was planted with wild daffodils cowslips, primroses,
bluebells and wild garlic. In the spring in particular it was a paradise of colour,
sound and scent. When it was sold both the Parish Council and the Winchester
District Council opposed planning permission for housing which was however
granted by the Department of the Environment. A tree preservation order was
applied for but before it could be served the Dell was bulldozed overnight. Trees
were uprooted and bulbs and plants scattered so that it looked like a wartime
bomb crater. The village was profoundly shocked. The Donigers Dell episode
graphically illustrated fears that the village environment was changing and not for
the better. The Dell subsequently became the site of a development of 12 exclusive, five bedroom houses .[9]

There was also a good deal of in-filling, refurbishing and rebuilding of older
properties round the village. Apart from Spring Vale all the developments were of
larger houses, with three, four or five bedrooms, and often double garages, well
beyond the means of the first-time buyer. Not surprisingly as a result the age-
group missing from the village was the twenties. Most houses were well out of
reach of newly married residents who wanted to stay in the village where they
had been born and brought up. This contributed to the feeling that, not only was
the village growing too fast, but it was becoming gentrified. Those who had spent
a life-time in the village began in the 70s to feel defensive towards change and
hostile towards the newcomers. Two comments reported in the *Village Appraisal*
published in 1983 illustrated the incipient resentment: 'a large influx of middle
class snobs unsuited to rural life', 'immigration from other parts of the country by
people who cannot understand how we managed before they came'.[10]

Even new facilities were seen by some as threatening the character of the village. The British Legion hut, the Pavilion in the Recreation ground and the village school might be run down, lack modern facilities or even be downright ugly but they had proved adequate for generations of users and carried treasured associations of people and events of the past. They were however inevitably replaced and the village tidied up. In the early 80s the unsightly filling station in Church road was dismantled and replaced by Meon Gardens, sheltered accommodation for older people, whilst a wall was built and car park with tarmac surface, constructed outside the Post Office and Masons Stores.

The corrugated iron British Legion hall built after the First World war was reaching the end of its useful life and went into liquidation in 1956. It was bought for £250 and the Swanmore Village Hall committee was set up after a Parish Meeting in March 1957.[11] Some wanted to renovate the existing building, others to replace it on the same site, yet others to build on a larger site where there was less likelihood of complaints about loud music and rowdy dances. Its siting close to adjoining houses was a regular cause of complaint. In May 1965 the Parish Council received a petition from 18 residents 'protesting at the noise, drunkenness and fighting which takes place during and after dances in the village hall' whilst in March 1976 the excessive noise was referred by desperate neighbours to the Ombudsman![12]

The decision to build a village hall on a new site was made by a majority of 18 to 10 at a parish meeting held in December 1970. The search was on for a site. The Charity Commissioners would not allow building on the Recreation ground

59. The Village Hall opened 1980. Photo Kate Watkins 2001

whilst the District Council rejected an application made in 1976 to build on the existing site.[13] Eventually Swanmore Educational Charity agreed to lease a site opposite the new secondary school in New Road. It nonetheless took ten years before grants were secured, funds raised and the building erected, in part by volunteer labour. Building began in November 1978 but still there were delays and costs escalated. The first phase of the Hall was opened by the Vicar, Ron Paterson and David Green, then Mayor of Winchester, in May 1980.[14]

The Pavilion in the Recreation ground had been erected in 1903 and was repeatedly vandalised in the 1960s. Few projects can have occupied so much of the Parish Council's time as the proposal to dismantle it and build a new one. Volunteer labour was enlisted for the preparation of the foundations, plumbing, carpentry and electrical work in order to reduce costs. It was formally opened on 28th August 1972 with a six-a-side football competition.[15]

A third new building was the Scout headquarters built by volunteer labour on a site next to the village hall, also made available by the Educational Charity and opened in 1982

The British Legion hall and the old Pavilion were not the only landmarks to disappear in these years. Broad Pond, originally lying across the boundary separating Bishop's Waltham from Droxford, had a place in village folklore. Here boys, now old men, remembered lazy days before the First World War, spent fishing for minnows in its depths. Now it was full of rubbish and, even if it were cleared, it was doubtful whether there would be sufficient water supply to enable it to be a viable pond once more. It was decided to fill it in and the contractors agreed to use the spoil when the sewers were constructed bringing mains drainage to Swanmore in 1966.[16] In the late 1980s, in a fit of nostalgia, it was rehabilitated but water was little more than a trickle and it was no more than a token pond.

The village wells in Spring Lane and Lower Chase road had been closed in 1928 and 1935 on the advice of the Medical Officer of Health and were now unusable because they were polluted.[17] When they were filled in the 1960s only a memory remained with a house in Lower Chase road named Wellside recalling the site.[18] By 1962 the village allotments at Gravel hill had only two tenants and when they became vacant there were no new applicants.[19] The other village allotments disappeared when the secondary school was built on the site.

The churchyard was almost full and from 1954 there was a sporadic search for additional provision. A proposal for a joint burial ground with Bishop's Waltham whose churchyard was also reaching capacity was considered but rejected.[20] The relationship between the two adjoining villages had always been one of guarded suspicion. The first proposal was a site behind the Vicarage in Vicarage lane but this was not acceptable because of the narrow approach road and difficult access.[21] It was not until 1979 that a three acre site at Hoe road was developed jointly by the parish councils of Bishop's Waltham and Swanmore with Swanmore meeting one third of the capital and running costs and the Parish Council being represented on the management committee.[22]

There were no regrets when, in the early 1960s, work began to install mains sewerage in the village. The cost of installation, £150,000, was borne by the County Council as far as the boundary of premises. Linking houses to the system was the responsibility of the householder. The expense however was largely offset since the cost of emptying cess-pits no longer had to be met. The work took several months and involved a good deal of inconvenience and disruption while ground was excavated and main sewer installed. Tyres punctured by sharp flints were a frequent cause of complaint. By 1982 ten per cent of houses, in outlying parts of the parish, were still not on mains drainage.[23]

The newcomers joined in village activities, run by church or school, as well as organisations like the Women's Institute. The Sports and Social Club was started largely as a result of their initiative. Ground near the Vicarage was secured for tennis courts which opened in 1978. It continued to rankle that there was a waiting list for membership and that many came from outside the village.

The Twinning Association which established links with Maneglise in Brittany in 1980 was also an initiative by newcomers.[24] Swanmore has no branch library, though the County library provided a collection of books, kept in the church school and regularly changed. (In 1931 the number of books available had been increased to 150!)[25] It was replaced by the mobile library service which began on 17th January 1963.[26] Now that so few people had open fires and garden fires were frowned on for environmental reasons, the fortnightly refuse collection was inadequate and replaced with a weekly one in 1965. Wheely bins came in 1985 and separate collections of paper, plastic and metal in the mid-1990s with recycling bins provided from October 2000.

If some facilities improved, others deteriorated. Transport was now dominated by the motor car and public transport declined in frequency and efficiency. The Meon Valley railway closed for passenger trains in 1955 and the nearest railhead was now at Botley four miles away.[27] Roads were no longer felt to be safe for children to cycle. By the 1980s only half the households in the village had a bicycle. Children no longer cycled to school; they were either bussed in and out or increasingly delivered to school and collected by parents in private cars creating Swanmore's daily traffic jam in New road. By the early 1980s 43% of families had two or more cars, whilst 20%, mostly the elderly, had no car.[28] It was these who were most affected by the decline of public transport. Frequency and variety of service deteriorated though the 1990s saw some improvement resulting from deregulation and the consequent provision of smaller, more versatile vehicles and a greater variery of routes. Paradoxically though the number of cars increased both the village petrol stations closed in the 1980s.

The number of shops in the village has also declined unable to compete with super stores at Hedge End and Fareham where prices are often lower and choice larger. The general store and newsagent opposite the recreation ground closed in the mid-1980s, followed soon afterwards by the delicatessen opposite Meon Gardens and farm shops at Hill Pound and Hill Farm as well as a short lived book shop below Leacock House. The five shops which remain are all in the centre of the village : no longer are there shops at Hill Pound, Forest Road or lower down New road. The village has a small but flourishing supermarket and newsagent in Mason's Stores which took over from the Mid-Hants stores in 1980. The Post Office previously accommodated in the store has since 1973 been a separate establishment next door. Robert Stewart's butcher's shop was built in 1973 and draws customers from well beyond the village. Peggy Abbot's Hair Design establishment occupies the shop opened by Bernard Martin in 1910 and since Peggy's death in 2000 is run by her daughter Jennie. The village still boasts four pubs though these too draw custom from beyond the village.

The educational opportunities of Swanmore children through schools in the village changed dramatically for the better between 1960 and 1980. Although there had been plans for a secondary school to serve the area since the 1930s, it was not until the late 1950s that a site at Swanmore was acquired by the County Council. Initially it was intended to build a middle school for pupils aged 9 to 13, adjacent to the primary school and land was purchased.[29] Land intended for the abortive middle school provides the centre of the village with an uninterrupted view of fields stretching into the distance.

For the proposed Secondary Modern school initially for pupils 11 to 15, land belonging to the educational charity in New Road, previously occupied by allotments, was bought, and the Charity compensated with land owned by the County Council on the opposite side of New Road and now occupied by the Village Hall and Scout headquarters. Delays however seemed endless. Though John Gimblett, headmaster of the all-age school in Bishop's Waltham was appointed headmaster in November 1958, the new school did not open until April 1961 and even then was not complete. John Gimblett's first entry in the Log Book reads 'Yard unfinished, stage unfinished, woodwork room unfinished, paths unfinished, library unfinished. Workmen in abundance.'[30]

Of the first 286 pupils who entered the secondary school, 95 came from Swanmore Church of England School, which now became a primary school. Others came from Bishop's Waltham and Droxford. Until then the only children from Swanmore who received separate secondary education, apart from the few educated privately, were those, usually between two and five a year, who passed the Eleven Plus and went to grammar schools in Fareham, Winchester or Eastleigh. However good a school it might be, Swanmore Church of England School could not compare in facilities with a purpose-built secondary school.

In the secondary school horizons broadened. Although the school leaving age was not raised to 16 until 1973 pupils began to stay on voluntarily to take the General Certificate of Education (GCE) or Union of Education Institutes (UEI) examinations and from 1965 the new Certificate of Secondary Education (CSE). (GCE & CSE were replaced in 1988 with a single examination the General Certificate of Secondary Education) There was an ambitious programme of school expeditions. At Easter, Whitsun and summer holidays in 1964 a total of 140 pupils visited the North York Moors, Scotland, Holland, the Irish Republic and Guernsey. Out-of-school activities flourished. A Young Farmers' Club had 50 members and there was a Camera Club and Old Pupils' Youth Club. Games were more varied than had been possible at the all-age school: rugby, netball, hockey and athletics were added to football and cricket. At the first Speech Day the guest was the Rt Hon. George Thomas, MP for Cardiff West, a friend of John Gimblett and later Speaker of the House of Commons before entering the House of Lords as Lord Tonypandy.[31] The secondary school expanded rapidly: by the Autumn term 1963 numbers had risen to 376 and temporary classrooms were needed. The increase in numbers has continued and in September 2000 there were almost 1200 pupils on roll.

Meanwhile selection at eleven continued at first by means of written attainment tests but from 1968 using only verbal reasoning tests. In 1973 Hampshire schools were reorganised and Swanmore Secondary Modern School became comprehensive. From now on all but the few who went to independent schools usually in Portsmouth or Southampton, were educated in the village to the age of 16. Initially pupils could then choose between Sixth Form Colleges at Fareham, Eastleigh or Winchester. From 1980 the local authority would only pay for travel to the designated college, Barton Peveril at Eastleigh. (Price's Sixth Form College, Fareham closed in 1984 and became part of the new Fareham Tertiary College.)

In its last days the all-age school was uncomfortably crowded and obliged to operate at a variety of sites round the village including the Methodist church hall and the Reading Room belonging to the church, as well as the British Legion Hall where lunch was served. The old Infants' School was sold to the church in 1965.

There were plans to rebuild almost the entire school and this was achieved in three phases over ten years. The managers had opted for voluntary aided status under the Education Act of 1944 and were therefore responsible initially for 50% later for 20% and later still for 15% of the cost of a capital building programme. It was the result of the drive and determination of the Vicar, the Revd Ron Paterson, helped by Robert Phillimore and Elizabeth Law that such an ambitious programme was launched and successfully completed. The total cost of the rebuilding was about £93,000, of which the parish raised, through a variety of events spread over the years, over £7,000, about £70,000 in present day terms. (Phase 1 £19,151, Phase 2 £31,551 and Phase 3 £42,589)[32] The Friends of Swanmore Primary School was formed in 1968 and served as a focus for fund raising by parents. (It was disbanded in 1974 and refounded in 1980).

The first phase of the new building was inaugurated by Albert Horner, the oldest living former pupil in 1963: he had entered the school as a three year old in 1883. Just over a year later the school celebrated its centenary with the opening of Phase 1 of the new building by John Phillips, Bishop of Portsmouth.[33] Phase 2 comprising three junior classrooms and administrative offices was begun in March 1968 and completed in June 1969 marked by another visit from the Bishop. The third phase, the most ambitious of all, included a new Assembly hall, kitchen and link with the existing building. On 19th June 1973 Bishop John Phillips came yet again to mark the completion of this major project, a remarkable achievement for a small village. The day concluded with a strawberry tea for everybody.[34]

Not even the church, most enduring of institutions, was immune to change in the second half of the century. As church attendance declined there was a danger that the Church of England, despite being the established church of the country, might concentrate its ministry on the committed few rather than on the whole community. The wider ministry to the whole village was exemplified in Swanmore by Ron Paterson who was Vicar for over half of the last 40 years of the twentieth century (1962-1985) It was also characterised by the introduction of a parish magazine delivered free to all houses in the village. This was already in train when Ron Paterson's short lived predecessor, John Leslie Bell, left suddenly in February 1962.

Ron Paterson was unusual in a number of ways. He was the first Vicar of Swanmore whose ordination was a second vocation: he had already served for 26 years in the Royal Navy before entering the priesthood at the age of 44. Apart from a brief curacy, Swanmore was his sole parish: he was the first Vicar since 1907 to retire from Swanmore, after 23 years as Vicar. He was probably also the first since Walter Medlicott who enjoyed unreservedly living in the large Victorian Vicarage, with his wife and four young children, appreciating its tennis court, vegetable garden and spacious lawns as well as its wine cellar. He never distinguished between church-goers and others; all had an equal call on his time and care. He served on the Parish Council for almost twenty years and was its Vice-Chairman in 1969-70. He helped to re-start the Scouts, the Cricket Club and the Youth Club. He will be remembered also as the Vicar whose first and second wife died ten years apart in the same hospital while he was at Swanmore. In the same period he lost his younger son Andrew aged 25 who was then the youngest recipient of a heart transplant, with which he had lived for three years.[35]

Old Swanmorians reunions were a feature of Ron Paterson's years as Vicar. They arose out of a series of articles in the parish magazine by Jack Hoar.[36] Although he had lived for many years at Ongar in Essex, he had enormous affection for the village in which he had grown up in the first twenty years of the century. He was born in a house opposite the church in January 1903 and his father was carpenter to Major Daubeny at Hill Place. After Major Daubeny's death the

60. The Revd Gordon Ronald Paterson, MBE in 1962,
Vicar 1962–1985.

Hoar family moved to Hill Place as caretakers.[37] Reunions were originally intended for those who had attended the village school before 1920 and took place every two years from 1964 onwards, attended in 1970 for example by over 120 Old Swanmorians and their spouses. At the second in 1966 the Revd E.F.S. Ramsbotham, Vicar at the end of the First world war returned to preach whilst at the 1968 reunion the Bishop of Portsmouth was the preacher.[38]

61. Swanmore Vicarage built 1985.
Photo Kate Watkins

Ron Paterson retired in 1985 at the age of 69. The parish recognised that a successor might be deterred from accepting the living by the large Victorian Vicarage. A site was obtained and a new Vicarage was built behind the church, ready for occupation by the new Vicar, Michael Welch, who arrived from Portsmouth in November 1985. Ron Paterson retired to Bishop's Waltham but parishioners, particularly non-church goers, still wished him to conduct weddings, funerals and baptisms.

In the mid-60s Betty Watson was the first woman to become a churchwarden at St Barnabas'. Thereafter it became the custom whenever possible to elect one woman and one man.[39] Not until 1969 could women become Readers in the Church of England and not until 1994 were the first women ordained to the priesthood. In 1995 Christine Winslade was licensed as a Reader to St Barnabas'. A year earlier Pat Fletcher a member of the St Barnabas' congregation was ordained to the permanent diaconate though she did not serve in the parish. Marion Mort a Reader in the parish of Shedfield became Swanmore's first curate since the early years of the twentieth century when she was ordained as a non-stipendiary minister (NSM) to the diaconate in 1997 and the priesthood in 1998. In 2001 she was made an Honorary Canon of Portsmouth Cathedral.

In 1995 during the ministry of Michael Welch the church celebrated the 150th anniversary of its consecration and the creation of the parish.[40] The year before celebrations were held to mark the creation of the civil parish in 1894 and centenary of the Parish Council.

The appearance of the centre of the village changed in these years. The rebuilding of the school, completed in 1974, replaced a well-loved Victorian landmark with a functional, flat-roofed and undistinguished structure. In response to village opinion and the agitation of the Victorian Society part of the original facade on Church road was retained but with enlarged windows. The wall and tarmac car park in front of the Post Office made for a tidy appearance but destroyed the rural ambience. The biggest change however was the building of the new church centre adjoining the west end of St Barnabas.

Villagers do not accept change readily and the building of the Paterson Centre stirred up more controversy than any other single innovation. There was a pressing need for new ancillary premises for church use. The parish room and parish house had been built in 1900 and the Reading room was added in 1922. Both dilapidated and inadequate, they were in any case in the wrong place – some distance from the church and across an increasingly busy road. The old Infant school had been bought by the church in 1965 but chiefly for the land attached to it which became

62. The Paterson Centre opened 1992.
Photo Kate Watkins 2001

part of the grave-yard. The building itself was leased to the Red Cross and although still belonging to the church was usually referred to as the Red Cross Centre.[41]

The need was clear to the church, but not to the village. Devising a solution presented a host of problems. A new parish centre adjacent to the church would be costly and involve disturbing graves. The new Village Hall had recently opened and there was doubt whether another meeting place was needed. The first scheme was a modest one unveiled in 1984. It was proposed to erect a building adjacent to the church to supplement rather than replace the Parish room. It was to be named the Paterson Centre, to commemorate the ministry of Ron Paterson who was on the point of retiring, and on that account to assist fund raising. A more ambitious plan however was approved by the Parochial Church Council in January 1986, early in the ministry of the new vicar, Michael Welch. It was for a substantially larger centre joined to the old Infant school, which would be refurbished. The new Centre would replace entirely the Parish room and Reading room, which would be sold and thus help to meet the greatly increased cost of this ambitious scheme.

In the village there was vociferous and determined opposition to the proposal.[42] Though run down, the Parish rooms were viewed by some as part of the parish heritage. Far more serious however was the disturbance and exhumation of bodies buried under the planned Centre. A petition opposing the Centre attracted 550 signatures and the Parish Council called a public meeting for 18th August 1986 which was attended by 150 people. It was claimed that only 14 graves would be disturbed of which 11 were over 50 years old whilst just over 5% of the churchyard would be affected.[43] Opposition continued and as a result of the scale and obduracy of the opposition a Consistory Court could not give permission and an Order in Council was necessary, involving further delay. It was finally granted in August 1989.[44] Exhumation took place in June and July 1990 and the remains of 80 people, far more than had originally been anticipated, were reburied in 27 coffins in a collective grave. A service of reburial was held early in the morning on 10th July 1990.

The Parish room, the Reading room and the Parish house were sold and the foundations of the Paterson Centre were begun in November 1991. The Centre was first used for the Harvest Supper in October 1992 and formally opened by Timothy Bavin, Bishop of Portsmouth in January 1993. Meanwhile costs had escalated, not least because of the unexpected expense of exhumation. Though the building cost about £140,000 the whole scheme amounted to £250,000 and the Centre opened with a debt of £65,000. That it was paid off in under four years was due largely to the efforts of Ron Paterson, who was responsible for raising about £37,000. Two thirds of this sum came from a series of sponsored walk-pilgrimages which he organised and led in 1994 and 1995. A service of thanksgiving for the completion of the scheme was held in January 1997 during the vacancy following the retirement of Michael Welch. The Paterson Centre has proved to be a major village amenity, providing meeting places at the centre of the village for a variety of church, deanery, village and community events. It is scarcely ever out of use and in 2001 was extended by the addition of a staircase and room in the roof-space. Hostility has not however entirely disappeared.

The population of Swanmore according to the Census of 1991 was 2677. Teenagers (10-19) represented 17% of the total and their parents, for the most part in their forties, represented a further 20 %. The smallest proportion below retiring age was people in their twenties (just under 10 % of the population) and children under 10 (11%). These figures graphically illustrate the make up of the village: it is not a place for first time buyers but for those settled into professional life and able to afford larger houses and relatively high cost of living. (The highest numbers of people of specific ages were 43 (62 people), 46 (61), 44 (80), 12 (58), 17 (56), 45 (54). At the other end the village contained only 18 people ages 28, 16 aged 26 and 12 aged 29.)[45]

Housing developments in the 1990s were mostly small scale in-filling rather than large estates, with one exception: over 50 houses were built off Spring lane in Medlicott way, Martin close, Rowan close and Russet close. These were three and four bedroom houses with two or three reception rooms and single or double garage. At Bucketts Farm Close off Vicarage lane seven large houses with five bed-rooms and double garages were built. In Dodds lane and off Lower Chase road there were further small scale developments of large houses. The Vicarage was no longer isolated as it had been when it was first built in 1985. The largest new hous-es were however those built some way from the village centre in Hollywell road, on the way to Mislingford. Westfield Drive is a small exclusive estate of eight sub-stantial executive residences with four reception rooms, five bedrooms and triple garages, certainly the largest modern houses built in the village.

Finally the Bere Forest Housing Association was active aiming to provide small-er two and three bedroom houses for the first time buyer. Fullegar Cottages are six semi-detached houses without garages at the top of Vicarage lane, the develop-ment named after May Fullegar who served on the Parish Council for 35 years and was its chairman from 1995 to 1999. The other Bere Forest housing develop-ment is Larkspur Close built on part of the Cortursel site off Crofton Way.

In the last decade of the twentieth century two concerns dominated the meet-ings of the Parish Council: the pressing need for additional recreational space and the determination to maintain the character of the village and to resist encroach-ment on adjoining villages.

From 1984 onwards there were various suggestions for additional open spaces to relieve the pressure on the recreation ground in New road: the old allotment site in Gravel Hill was proposed but it was too far from the village centre; glebe land north of the old vicarage could be suitable but access was difficult; land below the Scout headquarters in New road would be convenient if it were drained but it

turned out not to be available. Finally in 1986 the field south of the secondary
school was sold by Hampshire County Council to the Parish Council and the first
new recreation area since 1855 consisting of six and a half acres was opened known
rather unimaginatively as New road playing field and the Pylon field.[46]
Recreational opportunities were further enhanced by the provision of a nine hole
golf course in Bishopswood road.

In keeping with the spirit of the times the last years of the twentieth century
saw an increasing awareness of conservation. Broad Pond was restored but with
disappointing results: there is no longer sufficient water to sustain a live pond and
the accompanying plant life, insects and fish. When Peter Marsh acquired land at
the top of Lower Chase road and close to the new Vicarage for houses he gave two
pieces of land to the parish as conservation areas, known respectively as Marsh's
Meadow and Green's Wood. The latter is particularly interesting since it contains a
bank marking the original boundary between Droxford and Bishop's Waltham,
moved in 1846 when Swanmore became a separate ecclesiastical parish.[47]

Tables

A. Landmarks in Swanmore history

 826 Charter of King Egbert sets out the boundaries of the parish of Droxford which includes Swanmore
1205 First recorded use of the name Suanemere
1551 Manor rental of Droxford includes Swanmore
1661 First recorded burial in the Quaker burial ground off Hampton Hill
1801 First national census of population: Droxford 1199
1831 Population of Droxford 1620
1833 School built on the subsequent site of the War Memorial
1836 Bishop of Winchester, Charles Sumner, licenses the school room for worship.
1841 Census of population: tithings of Hill & Swanmore 674
1842 Tithe award for the parish of Droxford provides details of land use and land owners
1844 11th June, St Barnabas' day, stonelaying of church
1845 11th December, consecration of St Barnabas' by the bishop of Winchester
1846 Swanmore made a consolidated chapelry and ecclesiastical district by Order in Council
1847 The Revd E.B.Creek licensed as minister
1849 The first Parsonage built at Jervis Court
1855 Enclosure of Waltham Chase: laying out of roads in lower Swanmore, land allocated for recreation ground, allotments and to endow the school
1863 Chancel added to the church
     Primitive Methodist chapel built
     Bishop's Waltham branch railway line opened
1864 The National School built on land opposite the church
1871 Death of the Revd E.B.Creek; Revd Walter Medlicott becomes Vicar
1872 Men's Reading Room established
     Second Vicarage built in Vicarage lane
1876 Charles Martin becomes Master of the National school
     South aisle and vestry added to the church
1877 Charles Myers buys Swanmore Park estate from Bettesworth Pitt Shearer
1877 Tower with peal of bells added to the church
1878 Rebuilding of Swanmore House begun; architect Alfred Waterhouse
1879 On the death of Charles Myers Swanmore Park is inherited by William Myers

1880   William Myers becomes Churchwarden

1882   June, first parish magazine published

1884   Infant school built on land adjoining the church (now part of the Paterson Centre)

1894   Parish Councils Act; Swanmore becomes a civil parish and the Parish Council is formed

1895   Recreation ground and parish allotments become the responsibility of the Parish Council

1896   Resident policeman stationed at Swanmore with police house on the corner of Vicarage lane

1899   New Reading room and adjacent house built by the Vicar

1901   Electric light installed at Swanmore House
Telegraph wires erected to the Post Office

1903   Meon valley railway line opened; Parish Council asks unsuccesfully for a halt at Mislingford

1907   Retirement of the Revd Walter Medlicott after 37 years as Vicar

1911   Hot, dry summer; village wells dry up

1912   Provision of piped water rejected by parish on account of cost

1913   Retirement of Charles Martin headmaster of the school, after 37 years

1916   Hill Place estate sold

1920   Public telephone installed at the Post Office
Council houses built in Chapel road
The Bricklayers Arms rebuilt

1922   British Legion hut built in New road
Parish room added to the Reading Room and opened by Revd Walter Medlicott
Lower Swanmore connected to mains water

1927   Ponds in Vicarage lane filled in

1930   William Myers resigns from Parish Council after 36 years as chairman and ceases to be Churchwarden after 50 years

1931   Gas mains laid

1932   Overhead electricity cables erected through the parish
Public well in Lower Chase road polluted and to be closed

1933   Three gas lights erected at cross roads by the church as an experiment
Death of William Myers

1935   Swanmore Park estate sold
Bishop's Waltham branch railway line closed to passenger trains

1946   Electric street lighting installed after public meeting
Monthly refuse collections begin

1948   Houses for 'agricultural labourers' built at Donigers Close

1950   First roadside curbs in Bishop's Waltham road, upper part of New road and Chapel road

1952   Spring Vale phase 1 built

1955   Meon valley railway closed
Cortursel factory opened on the site of the brickyard in New road

1957   Village hall committee formed and buys British Legion hall in New road

1958   Resident policeman withdrawn from the village
1961   Spring lane well filled in
       Swanmore Secondary Modern school opens; village school becomes a primary
       school
1962   New Parish magazine is distributed free to very house in the village
1963   Rebuilding of the primary school begins
       Installation of mains sewerage begins
       Old peoples' bungalows built at Spring Vale
1965   Broad pond filled in
1974   Swanmore secondary school becomes a comprehensive school
       Rebuilding of the primary school complete
1979   Opening of the new pavilion in the recreation ground
1980   Opening of phase 1 of the Village hall
1983   Publication of Village Appraisal *Swanmore, a Hampshire Village*
1985   Third Vicarage built behind the church
       Retirement of the Revd Ron Paterson
1992   Opening of the Paterson Centre
1994   Centenary of the Parish Council
1995   150th Anniversary of the consecration of St Banabas'
2001   Village Design statement published

B Vicars of Swanmore

Years as Vicar	Name	Born	Died	Ordained Priest
1843–47	Henry Hotham BA	1814	1900	1844
1847–71	Edward Basnett Creek MA ★	1816	1871	1844
1871–1907	Walter Edward Medlicott MA	1842	1926	1867
1907–18	John Henry Hodgson MA	1856	c1940	1879
1918–21	Edward Francis Shepley Ramsbotham MA	1882	1974	1908
1921–35	Courtney Harold Wilson MA	1879	c1948	1903
1935–43	Alan Herbert Brown MA	1901	c1950	1925
1943–46	Edward Stephen Wakefield BSc	1913	1974	1939
1947–60	Albert Edward McCaig MA★	1901	1960	1925
1960–62	John Leslie Bell	1926	1966	1950
1962–85	Gordon Ronald Paterson, MBE	1916		1960
1985–96	Michael Robin Welch, MBE BSc	1933		1960
1997–	Peter Hugh Kelly+	1946		1985

★ Died in office

+ Priest-in-charge

c Approximate date since until recently no central records were kept

Compiled with the help of the Church of England Record Centre.

C. Superintendent Ministers of the Droxford Methodist Circuit

The Droxford Circuit formed part of the Primitive Methodist Church until the latter joined with the Wesleyan and United Methodist churches in 1932 to form the Methodist Church. The Droxford Circuit came into existence in 1885 though until 1892 it was referred to as the Hambledon Branch (of the Winchester Circuit). It is unusual in consisting entirely of ex-Primitive Methodist churches and none from other Methodist traditions. In 1920 there were ten churches in the Circuit: Droxford, Hambledon, Swanmore, Shirrell Heath, Warnford, Meonstoke, Waltham Chase, Bishop's Waltham, West Meon and Curdridge, with a total membership of 159. By 1939 the membership had grown to 316. Warnford had closed but in 1932 a chapel at Soberton had come in from the former Winchester United Methodist Circuit. By 1999 chapels at Droxford, Meonstoke and West Meon had closed and Soberton was now described as a class rather than a society (church). In 1975 Bishop's Waltham joined the Congregational church in the Methodist building to form the Bishop's Waltham United Free Chuch. In the year 2000 the Droxford Circuit was renamed the Meon Valley Circuit.

Years in the Circuit	Name	Born	Died	Entered the ministry
1885–87	John S.Buckley+	1858	1927	1880
1887	Alfred Sutcliffe	1865	1943	1887
1887–89	William Wilcock	1864	1937	1887
1889–91	George H.Birch	1861	1942	1887
1891–92	William Fidoe	1862	1939	1887
1892–94	William Watts	1825	1907	1851
1894–97	Edward Stephens	1838	1900	1860
1897–1900	Thomas Lloyd Page	1871	1959	1893
1900–03	Walter Barnsley	1873	1958	1896
1903–05	Nathaniel Watts	1839	1914	1860
1905–08	Frederick H.Clark	1878	1953	1901
1908–11	John Leach	1850	1912	1872
1911–14	John S.Buckley	1858`	1927	1880
1914–17	Edgar J.Hull	1878	1937	1902
1917–20	Herbert F.Stretch★	Not known		
1920–21	George A.Howard	1886	1980	1913
1921–24	Alfred Clarke	1868	1946	1895
1924–30	Percy W.Hassam	1889	1965	1918
1930–32	Daniel Dunn	1873	1942	1903
1932–39	James M.Ridge	1873	1947	1903
1939–45	James Lindsay	1885	1963	1912
1945–49	William H.Collins	1888	1974	1913
1947–50	E.Donald Mason $	1914	1984	1964
1949–53	Herbert W.Marsh	1884	1958	1913
1953–58	John H.J.Barker B.Sc	1903	1976	1927

Years in the Circuit	Name	Born	Died	Entered the ministry
1958–64	Frank Ockenden	1906	c. 1997	1931
1964–71	Harold A.Anfield	1924		1948
1971–78	David Catterson	1922	2000	1958
1978–85	Donald D.Barratt	1919		1948
1985–86	No resident minister#			
1986–91	Jack Jenkins	1925		1980
1991–2001	Robert J.Kitching M.A, B.A	1944		1974
2001–	Andrew P.Baguley	1944		1992

+   Served twice in the Circuit, 1885–87 & 1911–14
*   Not a minister of the Primitive Methodist Church
$ Became Lay Pastor in 1937 and entered the ministry 1964
#   The Chairman of the Southampton District, the Revd Laurence A.Ashman, BD (who died in 1987) acted as Superintendent Minister.

This list was compiled with the help of the Revd Bob Kitching Superintendent Minister of the Droxford Circuit 1991–2001.

D Heads of Swanmore Church of England School

The school has had a number of names in its history. From 1864 to 1902 it was usually called the National School, from 1902-61 it was the Church of England Mixed School and from 1961 the Church of England Primary School. The infant department was run as a separate school from 1898 to 1943.

[1841]	William Terry ?	Census 1841 'Schoolmaster'
[1850s–1861?]	Elizabeth Singleton	Census 1861 Kelly 1855,59
[1863]	Miss Willsdon	
1863–64	Mr Hellings	
1864–65	Miss L.Jones	
1865–67	Sarah Coombs	
1867–68	Miss Northeast	
1868–69	Sophia Toller	
1869–71	Anna M.Smith	
1871–76	Walter James Joseph Knight	
1876–1913	Charles Martin	
1913–42	Ernest Francis Whitaker	
1942–63	Margaret M.Belbin	
1964–1981	John Stephen Kirton	
1982–91	David Picton-Jones	
1991–	Lesley Hutchings	

Source SNS & SCE except where indicated otherwise

E Chairmen of Swanmore Parish Council

1894–1930	William Henry Myers
1930–31	Ernest Francis Whitaker
1931–32	George Sherington
1932–34	Frederick John Arnold
1934–41	Major Harold John Inglis★
1941–43	Revd Alan Herbert Brown#
1943–47	William John Green
1947–49	Colonel R.E.Sanders
1949–50	Frank Smith
1950–54	Sheila Gadsby
1954–55	William Milligan
1955–58	Sheila Gadsby
1958–59	William Milligan
1959–60	Revd Albert E.McCaig+
1960–69	Ellen Dorothy Crofton
1969–79	John David Green
1979–85	H.G.Peter Nicholas
1985–87	Michael J.Westwell
1987–88	Roy Cuthbertson
1988–92	F. Norman Clay
1992–95	William J.G. Smith
1995–99	May Fullegar
1999–	Michael J.Westwell

★   resigned on account of absence on war service
\#   left the parish October 1943
+   died in office May 1960

F Population 1841–2001

	Population	Houses		
1841	674		134	
1851	681★	White 1859	c.150	Hill c 60, Swanmore c.90
				White 1859
1861	746		154	
1871	884	PO 1875	173	
1881	813		170	Add houses in B.W.
1891	855	Kelly 1895	166	Add Houses in B.W.
1901	931		215	
1911	1139		280	
1921	1085		279	
1931	1218		337	
1941	No census			
1951	1429		432	
1961	1678		549	
1971	1893	New boundary	620	
1981	2493		832	
1991	2561		946	
2001	[2912]+		1026	

It is not easy to arrive at accurate or consistent figures for the population or number of houses in Swanmore during the 19th century. Until 1894 the census returns were based on the civil parish of Droxford which included the tithings of Hill, Swanmore, Droxford, Shidfield and earlier Steeple Court, a detached piece of the parish near Botley. Swanmore, the ecclesiastical parish formed in 1846, contained most but not quite all of the tithings of Hill and Swanmore together with a small part of the parish of Bishop's Waltham. The census enumerator was not always consistent in what he included in the two tithings.

To arrive at an accurate figure for the ecclesiastical parish of Swanmore it is necessary to exclude houses and their occupiers in the two tithings who were not in the ecclesiastical parish and to include part of the civil parish of Bishop's Waltham which was included in the ecclesiastical parish of Swanmore. This can be illustrated from the census of 1881.

Tithing of Swanmore	481	
Less those not in the ecclesiastical parish	34	
		447
Tithing of Hill	289	
Less those not in the ecclesiastical parish	43	
		246
Total in the two tithings and who were in the ecclesiastical parish of Swanmore	693	
Add those in the civil parish of Bishop's Waltham who were in the ecclesiastical parish of Swanmore	120	
Total in the ecclesiastical parish of Swanmore		813

In the 20th century there are two problems. First, the civil parish created in 1894 did not have exactly the same boundaries as the ecclesiastical parish created in 1846 so figures are not entirely consistent. Second, Swanmore lost a few houses and people to Shedfield when boundaries were adjusted in 1967. The figures above however convey a reasonably accurate picture of the growth of the parish.

★   White's Directory 1859 gives 584 in Droxford civil parish and 97 in Bishop's Waltham civil parish.

+   Estimate based on Electoral roll (over 18) 2184 plus 33% for those under 18.

Source Census returns, Trade Directories and Electoral roll.

G. Families

These family reconstructions are based on a variety of sources including St Barbabas' Registers of Baptisms, Marriages and Burials, Census returns 1841–1891, Swanmore Parish Magazine, wills in the Gunner papers in HCRO and tombstones in the church-yard. The family trees are intended to clarify the relationships between people mentioned in the text. Complete family trees are not possible in the space available.

The ages which appear in the Census returns are not reliable: in some cases ages are given to the nearest five years, some people's ages change by more or less than ten years from census to census. Some people may have wished to appear younger than they were! The census took place in March or April so translating census ages into year of birth cannot be undertaken accurately unless there is further evidence of date of birth.

1. BETTESWORTH–SHEARER

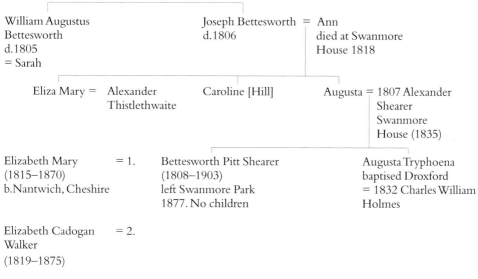

William Augustus Bettesworth d.1805 = Sarah

Joseph Bettesworth d.1806 = Ann died at Swanmore House 1818

Eliza Mary = Alexander Thistlethwaite

Caroline [Hill]

Augusta = 1807 Alexander Shearer Swanmore House (1835)

Elizabeth Mary (1815–1870) b.Nantwich, Cheshire = 1. Bettesworth Pitt Shearer (1808–1903) left Swanmore Park 1877. No children

Augusta Tryphoena baptised Droxford = 1832 Charles William Holmes

Elizabeth Cadogan Walker (1819–1875) = 2.

Sources Hope 1999, Gunner papers Box 248,249,308

2. DOLLAR

Peter Dollar, Bricklayer
Directory 1792

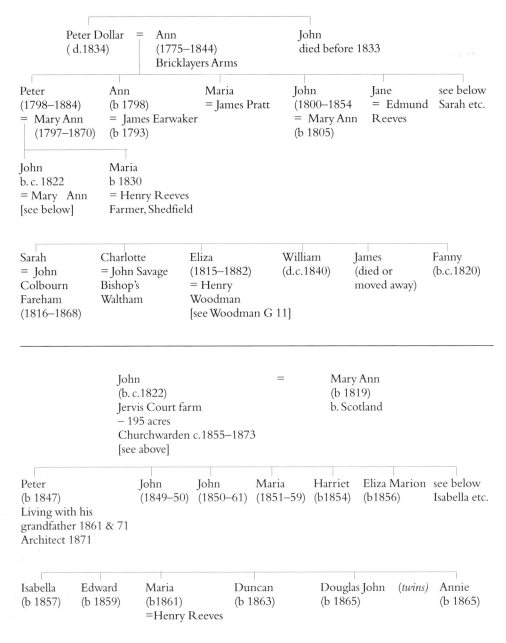

Peter Dollar = Ann   John
(d.1834)   (1775–1844)   died before 1833
                  Bricklayers Arms

Peter   Ann   Maria   John   Jane   see below
(1798–1884)   (b 1798)   = James Pratt   (1800–1854   = Edmund   Sarah etc.
= Mary Ann   = James Earwaker   = Mary Ann   Reeves
(1797–1870)   (b 1793)   (b 1805)

John   Maria
b. c. 1822   b 1830
= Mary   Ann   = Henry Reeves
[see below]   Farmer, Shedfield

Sarah   Charlotte   Eliza   William   James   Fanny
= John   = John Savage   (1815–1882)   (d.c.1840)   (died or   (b.c.1820)
Colbourn   Bishop's   = Henry   moved away)
Fareham   Waltham   Woodman
(1816–1868)   [see Woodman G 11]

John   =   Mary Ann
(b. c.1822)   (b 1819)
Jervis Court farm   b. Scotland
– 195 acres
Churchwarden c.1855–1873
[see above]

Peter   John   John   Maria   Harriet   Eliza Marion   see below
(b 1847)   (1849–50)   (1850–61)   (1851–59)   (b1854)   (b1856)   Isabella etc.
Living with his
grandfather 1861 & 71
Architect 1871

Isabella   Edward   Maria   Duncan   Douglas John   (twins) Annie
(b 1857)   (b 1859)   (b1861)   (b 1863)   (b 1865)   (b 1865)
                             =Henry Reeves

1. *There are two wills which help to identify the children of Peter (died 1834) and Ann Dollar(died 1844). They are not however entirely compatible. In Peter Dollar's will dated 1827 with a codicil in 1833 he refers to 'my six daughters' – Ann Earwaker, Maria married to James Pratt, Sarah Colbourn, Charlotte Savage, Eliza Dollar and Fanny Dollar, and to ' my four sons' – Peter, John, William and James. Though the order of the daughters and sons separately is no doubt chronological it is not possible to determine the order of all the children. Peter's son John died in 1854. He left a legacy to 'Maria Pratt' and names 'my brothers and sisters' – Peter, Ann, Jane married to Edmund Reeves, Sarah married to John Colbourn of Fareham, Charlotte married to John Savage of Bishop's Waltham, Eliza married to Henry Woodman 'inmate of the Hampshire County lunatic asylum', Francis widow of Charles Apps (is this the Fanny of Peter Dollar's will?) Two of the boys – William and James are not mentioned, nor are they listed in the Census of 1841 or 1851 so had presumably died before 1841.*

2. *In 1841 Ann Dollar (65) is described as 'victualler' and lives at The Bricklayers Arms. She has Fanny (20) her youngest daughter and George Dollar (15) living with her. I have not been able to identify George – he was probably a relation but not a son.*

3. *Harriet, Eliza and Isabella the children of John and Mary Ann Dollar do not appear in the Census of 1871, nor are they in the Burial Register so perhaps they were away from home at the time of the Census.*

4. *'Young' Peter lived with his grand-parents (Census 1861) and with his grandfather Peter (Census 1871) after his grandmother's death. He is described as 'Architect' in 1871. When he submitted designs for the projected tower of the church in 1875 he did so from a London address.*

5. *John Dollar later of Jervis Court Farm is aged 15 in 1841 (when ages could be indicated to the nearest five years) but 29 in 1851, 39 in 1861 and 50 in 1871.*

6. *'Old' Peter Dollar left Swanmore to live in Bishop's Waltham after 1875 – when he appears in Kelly's Directory – and before 1881, since he does not appear in the 1881 Census. His house was left to his son in law Henry Reeves in return for an annuity. He died in December 1884 though curiously the date on the headstone in Swanmore churchyard is December 1880. John Dollar left Jervis Court Farm in 1876 to live at Lichfield Grange, Micheldever.*

7. *Other members of the Dollar family appear in the Census of 1841 and the Tithe award of 1842. Lydia (51) who was a grocer at Hill Pound, has a daughter, Charlotte (30) living with her. Mary Dollar (17) is a living- in servant in the household of Leonard and Sophia Lidbetter.*

Sources include Gunner papers Boxes 304 & 309

3. GLADSTONE

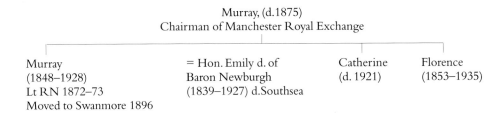

Murray, (d.1875)
Chairman of Manchester Royal Exchange

Murray	= Hon. Emily d. of	Catherine	Florence
(1848–1928)	Baron Newburgh	(d. 1921)	(1853–1935)
Lt RN 1872–73	(1839–1927) d.Southsea		
Moved to Swanmore 1896			

4. GOODLAD – DAUBENY

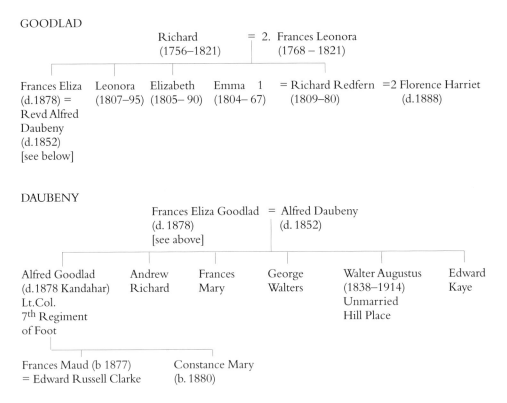

GOODLAD

Richard   = 2. Frances Leonora
(1756–1821)   (1768 – 1821)

Frances Eliza	Leonora	Elizabeth	Emma 1	= Richard Redfern	=2 Florence Harriet
(d.1878) =	(1807–95)	(1805– 90)	(1804– 67)	(1809–80)	(d.1888)
Revd Alfred					
Daubeny					
(d.1852)					
[see below]					

DAUBENY

Frances Eliza Goodlad   = Alfred Daubeny
(d. 1878)   (d. 1852)
[see above]

Alfred Goodlad	Andrew	Frances	George	Walter Augustus	Edward
(d.1878 Kandahar)	Richard	Mary	Walters	(1838–1914)	Kaye
Lt.Col.				Unmarried	
7th Regiment				Hill Place	
of Foot					

Frances Maud (b 1877)   Constance Mary
= Edward Russell Clarke   (b. 1880)

Sources: I am indebted to Arthur & Pat Apsimon for information about the Goodlad-Daubeny family. Also Gunner papers Box 82

5. GUNNER

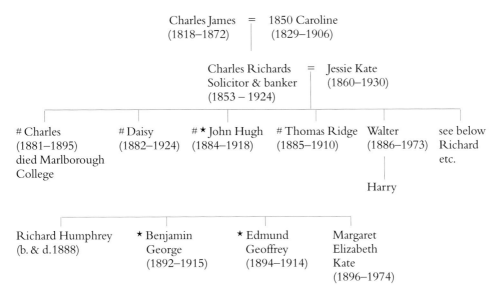

Charles James = 1850 Caroline
(1818–1872)   (1829–1906)

Charles Richards = Jessie Kate
Solicitor & banker   (1860–1930)
(1853 – 1924)

Charles   # Daisy   # ★ John Hugh   # Thomas Ridge   Walter   see below
(1881–1895)   (1882–1924)   (1884–1918)   (1885–1910)   (1886–1973)   Richard
died Marlborough   etc.
College

Harry

Richard Humphrey   ★ Benjamin   ★ Edmund   Margaret
(b. & d.1888)   George   Geoffrey   Elizabeth
                      (1892–1915)   (1894–1914)   Kate
                                                          (1896–1974)

\# Born in Bishop's Waltham
★ Killed in the First World War

Sources include conversations with Harry Gunner. There are three stained glass windows in the south aisle of Swanmore church given in memory of five of the sons of Charles and Jessie Gunner. Charles their eldest son died at Marlborough College and the window is given by masters and school fellows at Remenham Place, Henley. Four sons served in the army or navy. Three died in the first World War. Thomas was a Lieutenant in the Northumberland Fusiliers and died of typhoid in India in 1910.

6. HORN[E]

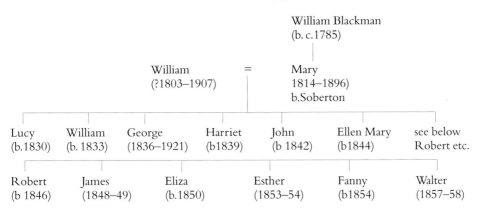

William Blackman
(b. c.1785)

William   =   Mary
(?1803–1907)   1814–1896)
                        b.Soberton

Lucy   William   George   Harriet   John   Ellen Mary   see below
(b.1830)   (b.1833)   (1836–1921)   (b1839)   (b 1842)   (b1844)   Robert etc.

Robert   James   Eliza   Esther   Fanny   Walter
(b 1846)   (1848–49)   (b.1850)   (1853–54)   (b1854)   (1857–58)

7. HORNER

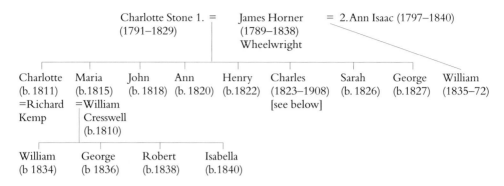

In his will dated 1838 (Gunner papers Box 305) James Horner, wheelwright, names two married children, 'my six younger children by my first wife' and 'one child by my wife Ann.' In the 1841 Census return his four sons Henry, Charles, George and William are listed in the household of Maria (their elder sister) and her husband William Cresswell. The remaining three John, Ann and Sarah do not appear in the Census.

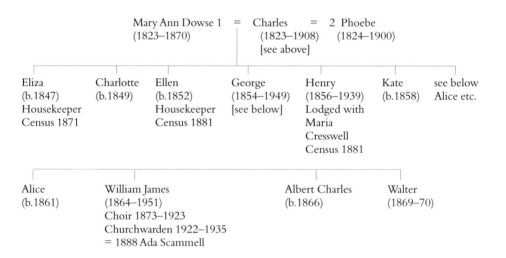

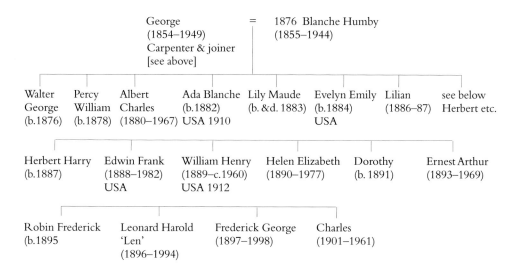

George (1854–1949) = 1876 Blanche Humby (1855–1944)
Carpenter & joiner [see above]

Walter George (b.1876) — Percy William (b.1878) — Albert Charles (1880–1967) — Ada Blanche (b.1882) USA 1910 — Lily Maude (b. &d. 1883) — Evelyn Emily (b.1884) USA — Lilian (1886–87) — see below Herbert etc.

Herbert Harry (b.1887) — Edwin Frank (1888–1982) USA — William Henry (1889–c.1960) USA 1912 — Helen Elizabeth (1890–1977) — Dorothy (b. 1891) — Ernest Arthur (1893–1969)

Robin Frederick (b.1895 — Leonard Harold 'Len' (1896–1994) — Frederick George (1897–1998) — Charles (1901–1961)

Sources includes conversations with Len Horner. and Kath Reed. Charles Horner's will is in Gunner papers Box 248 and Phoebe Horner's in Box 305. List of George and Blanche Horner's children in Bible entry lent by Kath Reed.

8. MARTIN

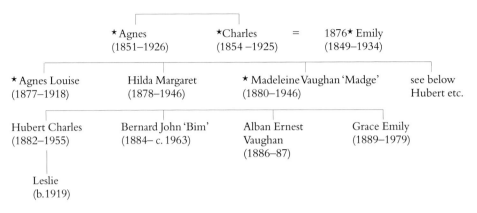

* Agnes
(1851–1926)

Charles   =   1876 Emily
(1854 –1925)   (1849–1934)

* Agnes Louise   Hilda Margaret   * Madeleine Vaughan 'Madge'   see below
(1877–1918)   (1878–1946)   (1880–1946)   Hubert etc.

Hubert Charles   Bernard John 'Bim'   Alban Ernest   Grace Emily
(1882–1955)   (1884– c. 1963)   Vaughan   (1889–1979)
                                                    (1886–87)

Leslie
(b.1919)

★ On the staff of Swanmore school

9. MYERS – PRIDEAUX-BRUNE

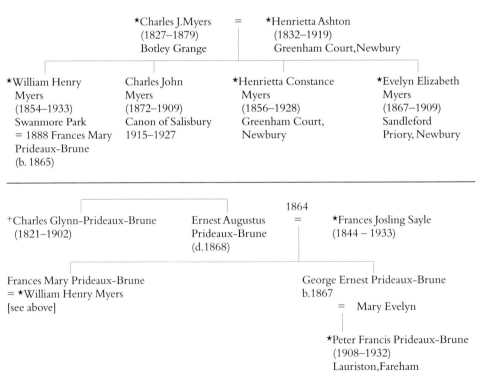

*Charles J.Myers   =   *Henrietta Ashton
(1827–1879)   (1832–1919)
Botley Grange   Greenham Court,Newbury

*William Henry   Charles John   *Henrietta Constance   *Evelyn Elizabeth
Myers   Myers   Myers   Myers
(1854–1933)   (1872–1909)   (1856–1928)   (1867–1909)
Swanmore Park   Canon of Salisbury   Greenham Court,   Sandleford
= 1888 Frances Mary   1915–1927   Newbury   Priory, Newbury
Prideaux-Brune
(b. 1865)

+Charles Glynn-Prideaux-Brune   Ernest Augustus   1864   *Frances Josling Sayle
(1821–1902)   Prideaux-Brune   =   (1844 – 1933)
                                       (d.1868)

Frances Mary Prideaux-Brune   George Ernest Prideaux-Brune
= *William Henry Myers   b.1867
[see above]   =   Mary Evelyn

                                                              *Peter Francis Prideaux-Brune
                                                              (1908–1932)
                                                              Lauriston,Fareham

+ Gave away Frances Mary at her wedding to W.H.Myers 1888
★ Buried in Swanmore churchyard

Source: Prideaux: a West Country Clan R.M.Prideaux Phillimore 1989 p.107

10. SUMNER – MEDLICOTT

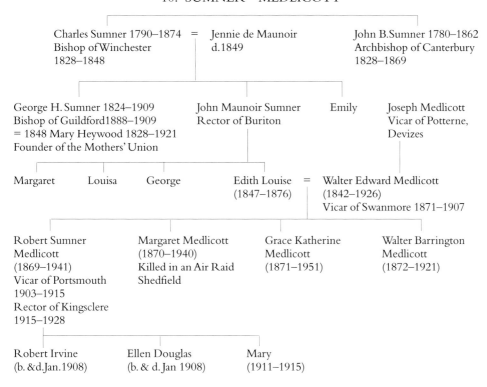

Charles Sumner 1790–1874 = Jennie de Maunoir   John B.Sumner 1780–1862
Bishop of Winchester   d.1849   Archbishop of Canterbury
1828–1848   1828–1869

George H. Sumner 1824–1909   John Maunoir Sumner   Emily   Joseph Medlicott
Bishop of Guildford 1888–1909   Rector of Buriton   Vicar of Potterne,
= 1848 Mary Heywood 1828–1921   Devizes
Founder of the Mothers' Union

Margaret   Louisa   George   Edith Louise   =   Walter Edward Medlicott
                                (1847–1876)   (1842–1926)
                                                     Vicar of Swanmore 1871–1907

Robert Sumner   Margaret Medlicott   Grace Katherine   Walter Barrington
Medlicott   (1870–1940)   Medlicott   Medlicott
(1869–1941)   Killed in an Air Raid   (1871–1951)   (1872–1921)
Vicar of Portsmouth Shedfield
1903–1915
Rector of Kingsclere
1915–1928

Robert Irvine   Ellen Douglas   Mary
(b. &d.Jan.1908)   (b. & d. Jan 1908)   (1911–1915)

11. WOODMAN

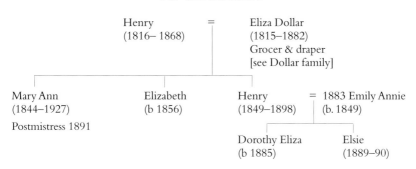

Henry   =   Eliza Dollar
(1816– 1868)   (1815–1882)
                         Grocer & draper
                         [see Dollar family]

Mary Ann   Elizabeth   Henry   = 1883 Emily Annie
(1844–1927)   (b 1856)   (1849–1898)   (b. 1849)

Postmistress 1891

                                       Dorothy Eliza   Elsie
                                       (b 1885)   (1889–90)

*Mary Ann, Elizabeth and Henry were all born at Bishop's Waltham. The Woodman family came to
Swanmore between 1851 and 1855. Eliza was the daughter of Peter and Ann Dollar and marrried to
Henry Woodman who spent many years of his life in the Hampshire County Lunatic Asylum (later
Knowle Hospital) where he died. Eliza is described in Kelly 1855 as 'grocer'. Their son Henry
appears to have become sub-postmaster between 1871 and 1875 and to have shared the job with his
sister until his death in 1898. Mary Ann carried on the post office until her death in 1927 when the
Mid-Hants Stores took on the shop and post office.*

Abbreviations

HCRO	Hampshire County Record Office
Log	Log book of Swanmore Church of England School 1929–1964
OHP	Oral History Project 1995
PCC	Minutes of Swanmore Parochial Church Council 1920–
PCM	Swanmore Parish Council Minutes 1894–
PMM	Swanmore Parish Meeting Minutes 1894–1989 (now lost)
RDC	Minutes of the Droxford Rural District Council
Registers	Registers of baptisms, marriages and funerals at St Barnabas' church 1846–
SCE	Swanmore Church of England School Minutes of Committee of Management 1903–
SNS	Swanmore National School Minutes of Committee of Management 1863–1903
SPM	Swanmore Parish Magazine 1882–
VA	Village Appraisal 1983

Sources

UNPUBLISHED

Unpublished sources include documents which may once have been printed privately but which are not available in libraries. Most of them are to be found in the Hampshire County Record office in Winchester. In the list below the name Swanmore has normally been omitted as a title word.

Bridge Revd Stephen, MA *The Righteous in Death* printed by G.Morrish, Camberwell, London 1871 'A sermon preached at the church of St Barnabas, Swanmore on Sunday March 26th 1871 and occasioned by the death of the Rev E.B.Creek MA, Vicar of Swanmore', copy in HCRO.

Census returns 1841-1891 (on microfilm in HCRO)

Churchwardens account books 1841-91 HCRO

Circuit Newsletter June 1910 (issued by the Droxford Primitive Methodist Circuit, copy in HCRO)

Confirmation registers, St Barnabas HCRO

Cygnet – Swanmore Secondary school magazine 1963-

Enclosure Award 1855 (map and award HCRO Q23/2/38/1)

Enlargement of Swanmore church – printed letter and list of subscribers, undated, probably 1860

Evans Pamela C. Brick making in rural communities 1850-1930 (a study of the brickworks of Swanmore, Hampshire 1995 unpublished dissertation for the Open University)

Faculty for enlarging the parish church of Swanmore, June 1876 HCRO 80M996/9

Gadsby Sheila, Letter to Mr Milliagan 2nd September 1954 containing history of the Quaker Burial ground) HCRO 55M80/PZ98

Gunner papers HCRO 44M73

Hill Place estate, Hampshire. Catalogue of sale by Richard Austin & Wyatt 17th May 1916

Hoar F.J.H. Swanmore 1908-1918, 1969 (articles in Swanmore Parish Magazine, later collected; typescript in HCRO 80M/96/8)

Hope G.D. 1999 AD 1550- AD1850 in the Tithing of Swanmore in the Manor of Droxford in the Hundred of Bishop's Waltham in the County of Hampshire (Research commissioned by Mrs Brenda Austin)

Old Swanmorians reunions (lists, correspondence etc HCRO 80M96/20)

Oral History Project 1995 Contributors include Lucy and Kenneth Chant, Dorrie Fry, Bill Parsons, Bob Reed, Evelyn Tier, Vera Tribbeck, Gwen Wood, Mabel Wood.

Ordnance survey map Hampshire first edition 1810 HCRO 137M96/2

Ordnance survey map Hampshire 6 inch edition 1910

Parish Council Minutes 1894- (held by the clerk to the Parish Council)

Parish Meeting Minutes 1894- 1989 (read by the author but now missing)

Parish Magazines June 1882- (incomplete set in HCRO 55M80PZ8-PZ85)

Parochial Church Council (PCC) Minutes 1920- (HCRO 55M80A PP1-ff)

Parochial Report Easter 1873 printed by H. Symes, Southampton (copy in HCRO)

Preacher's Book 1897- (service register recording services, attendance at Holy Communion and some sermon titles; later volumes are called Service Register all in HCRO)

Registers of Baptisms, Marriages and Burials 1846 - (HCRO)

School

    Accounts year ending 31st March 1880 (80M96/10)

    'A few words about our school' 1902 (80M96/17)

    Conveyance of school site 14th August 1863

    Log Book 1929-1964 (80M96/6)

    Magazines 1958-1962 (80M96/21-24)

    Managers' Meeting Minute book 1903-51,51-59,59-67 (80M96/2-4)

    Minutes of Committee 1863-1903 (80M96/1)

    Request for subscriptions 1893 (80M96/13)

    Scrapbook re history of the school (80M96/26)

    Subscriptions for building of Infant School 1883-84 (80M96/11)

    'To the parishioners of Swanmore' May 1893

    Well at the School House 1885 (80M96/12)

Sentences of Consecration, St Barnabas church and churchyard, diocese of Winchester 11th December 1845 HCRO 55M80/PB10

Swanmore Park Cricket Club Minute book 1873-1885 (in possession of Swanmore Cricket Club)

Swanmore Park estate, Hampshire, catalogue of sale by auction by Gribble, Booth & Shepherd, 29th April 1935.

Tithe map and award, parish of Droxford 1841 & 1842 (HCRO 21M65/F7/63/1-2)

Titheridge George, manuscript diary

Vestry Book 1864-1904, 1905-1929 HCRO 55M80APV1 &2

Village Appraisal, Swanmore, portrait of a Hampshire Village, 1983 (privately printed copy in HCRO)

PRINTED

Barstow Harold G., Manor Rentals 1551 Droxford etc, Harold Barstow 1996

Bettey J.H,. Church and Parish, Batsford 1987

Bosworth John, Bishop's Waltham Fire Brigade 1891-1991, John Bosworth Publications 1991

Briggs Asa, Victorian Things Batsford 1988

Chadwick W.O., The Victorian Church 2 volumes, A.& C Black 1966 & 70

Coates Richard, Hampshire Place Names, Ensign Publications 1993

Cobbett William, Rural Rides 2 volumes, London 1886

Collins F.B. & Hurst J.C. Meonstoke and Soberton, Winton Publications 1978

Derry T.K & Williams Trevor, A short history of technology Oxford University Press 1960

Directory of Hampshire 1792 (copy in HCRO)

Grundy G.B. The Saxon Land Charters of Hampshire Volume 1 1928 (copy in HCRO)

Harvey H.V. ('Dink') Memories of Swanmore in *Hampshire Magazine* January 1989

Hoar F.J.H. Recollections of Swanmore in *Hampshire Magazine* January 1976

Emery Grace, Some of the history of Shedfield parish, Paul Cave 1991

Hope G.D., 800 Years in Droxford, published privately 1980

Hurst John C., Corhampton and Exton Hampshire published by the author 1980

Kelly Directory of Hampshire and the Isle of Wight published at regular intervals 1848-

Kitching Revd Robert J., No longer poor old Droxford: a history of Methodism in the Meon valley 1840-2000, 2001

London Gazette

Marsh D.C., The changing social structure of England & Wales 1871-1961 Routledge & Kegan Paul 1958

Pevsner N. & Lloyd D., Buildings of England: Hampshire, Penguin 1967

Poole K.P. & Keith-Lucas B. Parish Government 1894-1994, National Association of Local Councils 1994

Rushton Gillian A. 100 Years of Progress 1889-1989, Hampshire County Council 1994

Simon Brian, Education and the social order 1940-1990 Lawrence & Wishart 1991

Stapleton B. & Thomas J.H. eds, The Portsmouth Region, Allan Sutton 1989

Stone R.A., The Meon Valley Railway, Kingfisher Railway Products 1983

Tate W.E., The Parish Chest, Phillimore 3rd edition 1969

Vickers J.A. ed, The Religious Census of Hampshire, Hampshire County Council 1993

Victoria County History of Hampshire volume 3, Institute of Historical Research 1908

Watkins P.R., A history of St Barnabas' Church, Swanmore, published privately 1995 (copy in HCRO)

West John, Village Records, Phillimore 1982

Notes

Chapter 1   The Ancient Parish of Droxford   Pages 5-15

1. Coates
2. Grundy pp.73-79
3. Grundy pp.79-81
4. Stapleton & Thomas p.48
5. Coates
6. Coates p.159, Hope p.9
7. Gordon Hope in conversation with the author
8. Hope 1980 p.9
9. Stapleton & Thomas p.89
10. Barstow
11. Barstow, Hope 1980
12. Barstow p.9
13. West pp.30-31 Hope 1980 p.19
14. Tate pp.138 ff Hope 1980 p.23
15. Gadsby & Hampshire Telegraph 19 November 1970 HCRO 55M80PZ98
16. Hope 1980 pp.40-41 Emery pp18-21
17. Hope 1980 p.32
18. Hope 1980 p.35. For Droxford Union Emery pp27-28, Collins & Hurst pp 99-101
19. Hope 1980 p.35
20. Cobbett Vol.2 pp. 265-266
21. Ib
22. Trade Directory 1792
23. Stapleton & Thomas p.91, Hope 1980 p.42, Census Droxford 1801, 1871

Chapter 2   Mid-Victorian Village   Pages 16-29

1. For revival of church life see Bettey c.8. Shidfield is the older and original spelling of present day Shedfield; Coates, Emery pp.5, 29-30.
2. Register of the Diocese of Winchester 1824-1844 HCRO
3. Subscription list HCRO 55M80A PW1
4. Subscription list for erection of church & parsonage HCRO 55M80PW2
5. Benjamin Ferrey account to Revd J.A.G.Colpoys 13th August 1845 HCRO 55M80PW27
6. Agreement & contract for building Swanmore church & account from Charles Pink to Revd J.A.G. Colpoys 1845 HCRO 55M80PW28-29
7. Sentences of consecration of St Barnabas church and churchyard. HCRO 55M80PB10
8. Patronage of Swanmore and Shedfield was transferred to the Portsmouth Diocesan Board of Patronage in 1938. London Gazette March 18th 1938.
9. Application to Church Building Commissioners signed J.A.G.Colpoys & William Brock Rector of Bishop's Waltham. HCRO & London Gazette April 21st 1846.

10. Ordnance Survey map 1810 & Hope 1980.
11. Chadwick vol.2 p.306
12. West pp.145-146. For a local example see Collins & Hurst pp.108-113.
13. See Table G2
14. Hope 1982 p.14
15. West pp.137-138, Tate pp.270-272, Enclosure award 1855.
16. Droxford Enclosure 1855 HCRO
17. Foregoing paragraphs based on analysis of Parish Registers and Census returns.

Chapter 3   The Village School 1864-1914   Pages 30-41

1. Diocesan Directories; for Shedfield schools Emery 1991 pp32-41
2. Kelly 1855, Census 1861
3. Conveyance of school site 14th August 1863. Land owned by Eli Singleton and sold for £50 HCRO. SCE lists main building developments 1864-1913 inside front cover
4. SNS inside front cover
5. SNS opposite entry for 1st April 1864
6. SNS 5th February 1863
7. SNS 25th April 1864
8. Census 1871
9. ' A few words about our school' 1902 includes his reminiscence of the school he found when he arrived in the parish in 1871.
10. SNS 5th April 1872
11. SNS 15th February 1872
12. Parochial Report 1873; see also accounts for 1866 & 1868-1869 in SNS.
13. SNS 10th & 24th April 1875.
14. Swanmore school – fee list – later typescript HCRO
15. Parish Report 1873 and Accounts 31st March 1880.
16. 'To the parishioners of Swanmore' May 1893 signed W.E.Medlicott on behalf of the managers.
17. SNS 21st December 1875
18. SNS 1st April 1890
19. SNS 1st September 1891 & 16th April 1898.
20. SNS 1895
21. SPM February 1884
22. 'A few words about our school' 1902
23. SPM August 1881
24. SNS August 1883
25. SNS August 1883 & September 1897
26. Receipt from George Apps July 1885 HCRO.
27. Purchase of land from B.T.Hewitt HCRO; SNS 1894 & G.T. 28th May 1894.
28. SNS 1894
29. Parochial Report 1873
30. SNS 1876 contains prize list & programme of 'songs and recitations by the children'.
31. SPM September 1883
32. Census 1891
33. Ib
34. SPM August 1897, November 1898
35. 'A few words about our school' 1902
36. SNS 1st September 1903- the last meeting of the managers of the National school.
37. SCE 26th October 1907
38. Hoar p.9
39. SCE 23rd April 1904
40. L.Horner in conversation with the author & Hoar p.9.

41. Hoar p.9
42. L. Horner in conversation with the author.
43. SNS 21st November 1892 & SCE April 1908.
44. SCE 6th October 1915
45. Hoar p.9
46. Obituary notice of Jack Hoar in SPM January 1994.

Chapter 4   Houses and People   Pages 42-54

1. Hope 1999 pp9 &20 and Gunner Box 249 HCRO
2. Compare Ordnance Survey map first edition 1810, which shows the road past Swanmore House, with Tithe map 1842.
3. Vestry Book 1864-1904 p.88, December 1903
4. Abstract of title of Swanmore House by kind permission of Barry Stokes.
5. Census 1881
6. SPM September 1888, Titheridge 21st August 1888.
7. 'Hampshire and Isle of Wight Leaders': C.A. Manning-Press 1903
8. Country Life Vol.5 1899 pp. 208-212
9. Catalogue of Sale 1935
10. Titheridge 28th November 1902. Barrie Stokes informs me that a note on one of the beams in the roof written by a workman commemorates the event.
11. Bibliography of British Gardens R.Desmond 1984.
12. Titheridge 19th July 1881 also 25rd July 1883, 23rd July 1884 and 14th July 1886. In 1885 the Flower Show was held in Bishop's Waltham, Titheridge 17th July 1885.
13. SPM October 1888, Titheridge 13th September 1888
14. Kay Crawshaw in conversation with the author.
15. Census 1891
16. Swanmore Park Cricket Club Minutes; SPM summer months 1882-1884 and Hampshire Chronicle eg 24th April 1881.
17. Pevsner & Lloyd p.617.
18. Memorial tablet in Droxford church.
19. Hoar pp 5 & 19, Gunner papers Box 82 and will of W.A.Daubeny HCRO.
20. Catalogue of Sale 1916.
21. Watkins 1995 p.10
22. Letter from J.A.G.Colpoys to the Ecclesiastical Commissioners HCRO
23. White's Directory 1859 p.580, Benefactions to the living of Swanmore. The act of parliament of 1868 allowing the use of the title vicar to incumbents not described as rector is pasted in front cover of the Vestry book 1864-1904.
24. Census 1851
25. Burial Register, also Bridge.
26. Titheridge August 1872.
27. Trade Directories, Gunner papers Box 82.
28. Census 1881
29. Hampshire Directory 1792
30. Pevsner & Lloyd p.295. Information supplied by Lord Clarendon in a letter to the Revd Michael Welch 12th April 1995.
31. Trade Directories.
32. Country Life 18th February 1999 pp.76-78.
33. Trade Directories.
34. Titheridge February 1872, 14th June 1883
35. Titheridge 2nd August 1886.
36. Probate
37. Hoar pp 12,19.

38. Titheridge 11th & 15th May 1935.
39. SPM June 1970. Hampshire Magazine Vol. 82 No.12, Vol.84 No.3 Vol. 93 No. 2

Chapter 5 Church and Village 1871-1914 Pages 55-66

1. For church attendance on 30th March 1851 see Vickers p.143.
2. 'Enlargement of Swanmore Church', photograph in Watkins 1995 p.14
3. HCRO55M80AP45
4. Vestry Book 1864-1904, 1880.
5. Hampshire Chronicle 18th December 1870 quoted in SPM January 1971.
6. Information supplied by David Lloyd
7. 'Memorial to the late Miss Leonora Goodlad of Hill Place, Swanmore', HCRO
8. Vestry Book 1864-1904, April 1882
9. Vickers pp140, 143. 'Benefactions to the living of Swanmore' signed W.E.M. no date. Letter to the Ecclesiastical Commissioners dated 9th December 1879 & London Gazette December 19th 1879.
10. Vestry Book 1874 & Churchwardens' Accounts 1871-1933.
11. Vestry Book May 1879.
12. Churchwardens' Accounts.
13. SPM September 1882.
14. SPM December 1883. For Shedfield reading room opened 1868 and the Chase reading room 1899 see Emery p.18
15. These paragraphs are largely based on Parochial Report Easter 1873. This was a one-off; no later reports were produced. For Shedfield cottage hospital see Emery pp.42-47
16. Chadwick Vol.2 pp. 426-427.
17. SPM August 1897 – perhaps in February 2012?
18. Details of sermon subjects from The Preacher's Book.
19. Chadwick Vol.2 pp. 192-193.
20. SPM March 1887
21. SPM February 1898
22. SPM March, April & September 1883
23. SPM September 1900
24. SPM September 1900, September 1911
25. SPM February 1905
26. SPM September 1906
27. Harvey
28. SPM February 1883
29. SPM January 1892
30. SPM August 1896
31. Titheridge 16th May 1922.
32. SPM March 1912 & Titheridge 9th February 1912.
33. SPM May 1911
34. Hoar p.8
35. Examples drawn from The Preacher's Book.
36. Titheridge 29th March 1900.
37. Confirmation register
38. Hoar p.10
39. Hoar p.10, also Titheridge eg 'Hambledon Races. A Glorious Day', 2nd May 1913.
40. Hoar F.J.H. 1976.
41. SPM March, May 1907, November 1909, February 1913.
42. SPM June 1910, November 1911, February 1912.

Chapter 6   The Parish Council and Pre-war Village Life 1891-1914   Pages 67-91

1. Census 1891, Marsh c.1&2
2. Trade Directories & Census
3. For example Primitive Methodist Handbook of Services July – September 1910
4. Trade Directories & PCM 11th November 1902.
5. Derry & Williams p.390
6. Kelly 1899
7. RDC 25th February 1896
8. Primitive Methodist Circuit Handbook of Services July – September 1910
9. Hoar p.18
10. Poole & Keith-Lucas; Rushton; SPM December 1894. A public meeting was held in the school room at Swanmore on 3rd March at which it was agreed to petition the county council to grant an enquiry into making Swanmore a civil parish. This was held at the courthouse in Droxford on 30th May. The commission reported in favour and an order of the county council was issued on 11th August 1894 to come into force on Michaelmas day 1894 – Vestry book pp66-67, HCC order HCRO 55M80A P21.
11. PMM 4th December 1894, SPM January 1895
12. SPM February 1895
13. PCM 31st December 1894
14. PCM 15th April 1904
15. PMM 1901, 1902, 1905, 1913, PCM 20th April 1895. 'Mr H. Woodman Hung Himself Swan.' Titheridge 22nd December 1898.
16. PMM April 1895, PCM 20th July 1895.
17. PCM 25th June 1900, 23rd October 1922, 12th March 1923.
18. PCM 8th January 1895
19. PCM 13th January 1900
20. PCM 20th April 1903
21. Titheridge 31st October 1906
22. RDC 1st June 1897
23. PCM 20th January 1904
24. PCM 3rd August 1910
25. Titheridge 9th November 1910, 8th February 1911, 28th March 1912, 14th August 1912, 14th December 1912 & 16th June 1913.
26. PCM 21st January 1905, 29th July 1905.
27. Rules for the Recreation Ground, Swanmore, 1891 HCRO 55M80APK2
28. PCM 12th October 1897
29. PCM 23rd October 1907, 27th July 1908
30. PCM 1st September 1903.
31. PCM 18th January 1899, 23rd October 1905, 27th January 1910.
32. PCM 21st November 1903
33. PCM 27th July 1908, 10th March 1909
34. PCM 18th May 1910, 3rd August 1910, 22nd October 1910.
35. PCM 14th November 1910.
36. PCM 22nd January 1912
37. PCM 25th July 1921
38. SPM September 1980
39. Hoar pp.15-16
40. Hoar pp.6-7
41. Hoar p.5, Titheridge 5th June 1899; now called Lime Cottage.
42. Len Horner in conversation with the author.
43. Harvey
44. Titheridge 9th January, 5th October 1896.
45. Hoar pp.12-14

46. Hoar pp. 17-20.
47. Len Horner in conversation with the author.
48. Censuses 1841-1891
49. Hoar p.19 & Gwen Wood
50. Section on the Horner family based on Len Horner in conversations with the author, Registers of Baptisms, Marriages and Burials at St Barnabas, Census returns 1841-1891, Horner family tree lent by Kath Reed, Gunner papers Box 305, SPM July 1994. George & Blanche Horner's children are listed in a Bible which was presented to them by the Revd Walter & Mrs Medlicott on the occasion of their marriage – photocopy provided by Kath Reed. See also Table G7.

Chapter 7 *The Primitive Methodists* Pages 92-98

1. This chapter is based on research undertaken by the Revd Bob Kitching for his book, No longer poor old Droxford. Some records of the Droxford Circuit are in HCRO 58M75 but most of these refer to the period after 1900.
2. Vickers p.144
3. Vickers p.141
4. Titheridge 17th & 21st August 1903.
5. Droxford Circuit Newsletter June 1910
6. Droxford Circuit Plan July-September 1910
7. Kitching appendix1 provides a fascinating analysis of the occupations of fathers of children baptised in the Droxford Circuit between 1885 and 1962.
8. PMM 4th March 1907
9. Hampshire Chronicle 3rd June 1910 & Droxford Circuit Plan July – September 1910
10. Droxford Circuit Quarterly Meeting Minutes March 1917

Chapter 8 *Brickyards and brickmaking* Pages 99-102

1. This chapter is based on research undertaken in 1995 by Pamela C. Evans for an Open University course and entitled Brickmaking in rural communities: a study of the brickworks of Swanmore, Hampshire. I have also used the reminiscences of Bob Reed and references in Trade Directories and Census returns.
2. Tithe map 1842 Census 1841, 1861
3. Titheridge 28th February 1885
4. Titheridge 4th May 1886
5. Titheridge 1st May 1894
6. Deeds of Rose Cottage belonging to Ian & Alison Coulter
7. Titheridge 9th August 1927 ' Mr Read (sic) found Dead in His office at Brickyard'.
8. Kelly 1911 p.601, 1935 p.522 & 1939 p.544
9. Harvey

Chapter 9 *Institutions and Amenities 1914-1939* Pages 103-120

1. Hoar p.16
2. SPM January 1915
3. Titheridge 26th November 1914
4. Jack Hoar, Arthur Blanch in conversation with the author, and Keith Harrington.
5. Hoar p.16
6. SPM January 1915
7. SPM December 1915
8. Titheridge 13th February & 11th March 1915

9. Titheridge 5th November 1915
10. Hoar pp16-17
11. Titheridge 4th August 1914.
12. Hoar p.17 Titheridge 14th October 1917.
13. Titheridge 12th November 1916.
14. SCE
15. SCE
16. PCM 19th January 1917, 20th March 1918.
17. PCM 19th April 1926
18. SPM. Edward Wakefield's death is reported in SPM May 1974.
19. Service register
20. SPM December 1921
21. Details in foregoing paragraphs of those who were killed in the war taken from research by Keith Harrington.
22. PCM 3rd May 1920
23. Hurst p.60
24. Hoar pp.16&19
25. Titheridge 21st-23rd July 1914
26. Catalogue of Sale
27. PCM 17th March, 28th July, 31st October 1930, St Barnabas' Annual Meeting 1930 in PCC Minutes.
28. Kay Crawshaw who lived at Swanmore House until 1980 in conversation with the author.
29. PCC 30th January 1935
30. Catalogue of Sale
31. Abstract of title of Swanmore House by kind permission of Barry Stokes.
32. PCM 11th April 1922, Titheridge 25th February 1925 & 16th March 1926.
33. Titheridge 3rd September 1921, 8th November 1928 & 11th & 15th May 1935.
34. PCM 15th July, 19th October 1925, 15th April 1937.
35. PCM 22nd April , 28th July , 1st September 1919.
36. Information about the Council houses provided by Arthur Ainslie. Allotments PCM 24th January 1921
37. PCM 25th July1921, 19th June 1922, 12th March, 9th April 1923, 15th July 1925.
38. Titheridge 16th May, 18th August 1923.
39. PCM 15th July 1925, 24th October 1927, 23rd January 1928.
40. PCM 16th March 1925, 18th January 1926, 17th April 1929.
41. PCM 13th March 1929.
42. PCM 21st October 1932.
43. PCM 21st April 1933.
44. PCM 28th July, 31st October 1930
45. PCM 13th March 1934
46. PCM 15th April 1937
47. PCM 24th March 1939, 14th March 1940
48. PCM 17th October 1939,16[th] January, 17th October 1940.
49. PCM 21st October 1941.
50. PCM 27th October 1919,26[th] July, 25th October 1920.
51. PCM 18th April 1928
52. PCM 15th April1937.
53. SPM June 1891, Titheridge 25th April 1891.
54. Bosworth p21ff.
55. Bosworth p.21ff, PCM 29th October 1928,30[th] January 1931.
56. Bosworth p.23, Titheridge 27th June 1933.
57. PCM 29th January 1930,19[th] January 1934, 25th January 1939.
58. PCM 20th October 1933.
59. PCM 20th January, 15th February 1933.
60. PCM 20th October 1933.

61. PCM 30th May 1934.
62. Jack Hoar in conversation with the author.
63. Stone pp.94ff
64. Oral history project for this and subsequent paragraphs.
65. Kelly 1939.
66. Simon p.21. Senior children at Shedfield school were transferred to Hedge End senior school from 1935 – Emery p.40
67. Log 19th March 1936
68. Log 2nd November 1936
69. Log 14th October 1938
70. Log 15th July 1929, 1st September 1930, 15th July 1931 – entries in red ink.
71. Inspection report 1929
72. Log 28th July 1938
73. SCE 4th December 1934
74. SCE 7th August 1935
75. PCM 17th April 1936
76. SCE 29th May 1936
77. PCM 10th July 1936.
78. SCE 15th January 1921.
79. For example Log 11th November 1935.
80. Log 26th October 1936.
81. SCE 13th July 1937.
82. Log 27th April 1937
83. SPM 8th May 1920.
84. Log 28th July 1938
85. Log 7th January 1946.
86. June Clarkson

Chapter 10   Village life between the wars   Pages 121-126

1. Hampshire Magazine January 1989 pp.41-42
2. This chapter is largely based on material from contributions to the Oral history project.
3. Hurst 1980 p.57; Kelly 1927, 1935 & 1939.
4. Kelly 1939
5. Titheridge records the start of the Council houses 28th September 1920.
6. Kelly 1867 p.515.
7. Kelly 1927
8. Titheridge 23rd August 1920.
9. Titheridge 25th April 1900
10. Len Horner in conversation with the author.

Chapter 11   The Second World War and after   Pages 127-136

1. Log 28th August 1939. Material in this chapter from Oral history project and other reminiscences.
2. Log 31st August 1939
3. Log 11th September 1939
4. Log 21st September 1939
5. Log 5th February 1940
6. PCM 13th October 1938, 29th January 1942.
7. PCM 29th January 1942.
8. PCM 18th July 1940
9. Ron Crook

10. Paragraphs on the Home Guard based on information provided by Ron Crook.
11. Log 14th May
12. 12th July 1940.
13. Log 2nd August 1940
14. Log 9th September 1940.
15. Author in conversation with Sheila Gadsby.
16. Log 21st April 1941 and later references.
17. Log 20th June 1941.
18. Log 3rd July 1944.
19. Log 29th –31st January 1940.
20. Log 20th –23rd January 1942.
21. Stone pp.69-70.
22. June Clarkson.
23. Information about those who were killed in the Second World War supplied by Keith Harrington.
24. PCM 14th October 1943.
25. PCM 18th June 1948
26. PCM 20th August 1948, 6th April 1949.
27. PCM 12th February, 22nd April 1947, 28th June 1949.
28. PCM 8th February 1945.
29. PCM 26th September 1946.
30. PCM 19th October, 14th December 1949, 19th February 1951.
31. PCM 19th August 1947.
32. PCM 4th February 1980.
33. Watkins 1995 pp44-47.
34. PCC 24th October 1944.
35. Service Register HCRO.
36. Log 3rd March 1942.
37. The author in conversation with Sheila Gadsby & Kay Crawshaw, also Log 2nd December 1948.
38. Obituary in PCM May & June 1976.
39. School Magazine 1959-1960
40. Figures compiled from Log.
41. Log 7th April 1942.
42. June Clarkson.
43. Log 11th October 1951

Chapter 12   Growth and Transformation since 1960   Pages 137-150

1. Census 1961, 1981, Electoral Register 2000.
2. PCM 6th July 1964, 1st August 1966.
3. Pevsner & Lloyd pp 616-617.
4. VA p.10
5. PCM 1st September 1952
6. PCM 25th May 1955.
7. SPM November 1969
8. PCM 1st February 1971.
9. PCM 2nd February, 7th September, 2nd November 1981, 1st November 1982 & author's recollections. Photograph VA p.26
10. VA p.8, PCM 7th December 1981.
11. PMM 26th November 1956 & 11th March 1957.
12. PCM 23rd May 1965, 1st March 1976.
13. PCM 1st November 1971, January 1977.
14. SPM June 1980.
15. PCM 22nd May 1972.

16. PCM 1st April, 1st July, 19th August, 7th October, 2nd December 1963, 7th April 1964, 1st march 1965, 1st August 1966.
17. PCM 29th October 1928, 12th July 1935.
18. PCM 6th February 1961.
19. PCM 8th January 1962.
20. PCM 6th January 1954, 10th January 1955.
21. PCM 5th March 1956.
22. PCM 5th February 1979, 3rd November 1980.
23. PCM 25th November 1957, 7th October 1963, VA p.14 and recollections of Ron Paterson.
24. PCM 1st October, 5th November 1979.
25. PCM 24th July 1931.
26. PCM 5th February 1962.
27. Stone p.95
28. VA p.17.
29. PCM 6th December 1971, 3rd January 1972.
30. Swanmore Secondary School Log.
31. Cygnet (Swanmore secondary school magazine) 1963-64 HCRO 55M80P2 101
32. SPM October 1977.
33. SPM July 1964.
34. SPM July 1973.
35. SPM June 1985, Hampshire Magazine Vol. 85 No.7 p.21, Watkins 1995 p.57.
36. SPM December 1963, & series in 1966-67, copy in HCRO.
37. Hoar pp.2-3 and obituary SPM January 1994.
38. SPM April 1972, March 1973.
39. See Watkins 1995 Appendix B
40. SPM 1995, particularly November & December 1995 & January 1996.
41. Letter from Marjorie Easterby-Smith to the Vicar 23rd May 1971 & Special Projects report in SPM April 1979.
42. PCM 9th June 1986
43. Report of public meeting 18th August 1986 attached to PCM 1st September 1986.
44. Portsmouth Scheme made by the Church Commissioners annexed to Order in Council dated 2nd August 1989. Papers relating to the building of the Paterson centre HCRO 55M80PW42
45. Census 1991.
46. PCM 5th November 1984, 3rd June, 3rd July, 9th September 1995.
47. SPM October 2000.

A note on pre-decimal coinage and comparative values

The pound was decimalised in 1971. Previously it had been divided into 20 shillings each of which consisted of 12 pence so a pound was 240 pence (abbreviated d. for Latin denarius). A shilling was written 1/- and a penny 1d. One shilling and sixpence was therefore written 1/6.

Units of pre-1971 currency with approximate post-1971 equivalents

Unit	Written	Value post-1971
1 farthing	1/4d	just over 0.1 of a penny
1 halfpenny	1/2d	just over 0.2 of a penny
1 penny	1d	0.4 of a penny
6 pence	6d	2½ pence
1 shilling	1/-	5 pence
2 shillings	2/-	10 pence
Half a crown	2/6	12½ pence

Approximate value of the pound in relation to its value in 1860

1860	1
1914	1
1919	2
1939	1.5
1948	2
1960	3
1970	5
1980	17
1990	32
1999	42

Based on Table of Comparative Values in Philip Ziegler Britain Then and Now Weidenfeld & Nicolson 1999 p.424

Index

Not all personal names appearing in decennial censuses or trade directories are included in this index. The names of those who died in the two World Wars are on pages 107-108 and 133. The index covers the text of the book, but not the tables, sources and notes.